DISORIENTING ENCOUNTERS

Comparative Studies on Muslim Societies
General Editor, Barbara D. Metcalf

1. *Islam and the Political Economy of Meaning*
edited by William R. Roff
2. *Libyan Politics: Tribe and Revolution*
by John Davis
3. *Prophecy Continuous:*
Aspects of Aḥmadī Religious Thought and Its Medieval Background
by Yohanan Friedmann
4. *Sharīʿat and Ambiguity in South Asian Islam*
edited by Katherine P. Ewing
5. *Islam, Politics, and Social Movements*
edited by Edmund Burke, III, and Ira M. Lapidus
6. *Roots of North Indian Shīʿīsm in Iran and Iraq:*
Religion and State in Awadh, 1722–1859
by J. R. I. Cole
7. *Empire and Islam: Punjab and the Making of Pakistan*
by David Gilmartin
8. *Islam & the Russian Empire:*
Reform and Revolution in Central Asia
by Hélène Carrère d'Encausse
9. *Muslim Travellers:*
Pilgrimage, Migration, and the Religious Imagination
edited by Dale F. Eickelman and James Piscatori
10. *The Dervish Lodge:*
Architecture, Art, and Sufism in Ottoman Turkey
edited by Raymond Lifchez
11. *The Seed and the Soil:*
Gender and Cosmology in Turkish Village Society
by Carol Delaney
12. *Displaying the Orient:*
Architecture of Islam at Nineteenth-Century World's Fairs
by Zeynep Celik
13. *Arab Voices:*
The Human Rights Debate in the Middle East
by Kevin Dwyer
14. *Disorienting Encounters:*
Travels of a Moroccan Scholar in France in 1845–1846
The Voyage of Muḥammad aṣ-Ṣaffār
translated and edited by Susan Gilson Miller
15. *The Calligraphic State:*
Textual Domination and History in a Muslim Society
by Brinkley Messick

Disorienting Encounters

TRAVELS OF A MOROCCAN SCHOLAR
IN FRANCE IN 1845–1846

THE VOYAGE OF
MUḤAMMAD AṢ-ṢAFFĀR

TRANSLATED AND EDITED BY
SUSAN GILSON MILLER

University of California Press
Berkeley, Los Angeles, London

University of California Press
Berkeley and Los Angeles, California
University of California Press, Ltd.
London, England

Library of Congress Cataloging-in-Publication Data
Ṣaffār, Muḥammad, 19th cent.
Disorienting encounters: travels of a Moroccan scholar in France in 1845–1846: the voyage of Muḥammad aṣ-Ṣaffār / translated and edited by Susan Gilson Miller.
p. cm. — (Comparative studies on Muslim societies; 14)
Includes bibliographical references and index.
ISBN 978-0-520-07462-0
1. Paris (France)—Description. 2. Paris (France)—Social conditions—19th century. 3. Ṣaffār, Muḥammad, 19th cent.—Journeys—France—Paris. I. Miller, Susan Gilson. II. Title. III. Series.
DC707.S13 1991
9144'360463—dc20 90-26314

Printed in the United States of America

11 10 09 08
9 8 7 6

The paper used in this publication is both acid-free and totally chlorine-free (TCF). It meets the minimum requirements of ANSI/NISO Z39.48-1992 (R 1997) (*Permanence of Paper*). ♾

To my family, who has traveled with me

Ouvrez un guide de voyage; vous y trouverez d'ordinaire un petit lexique, mais ce lexique portera bizarrement sur des choses ennuyeuses et inutiles: la douane, la poste, l'hôtel, le coiffeur, le médecin, les prix. Cependant, qu'est ce que voyager? Rencontrer. Le seul lexique important est celui du rendez-vous.

Open a travel guide: usually you will find a brief lexicon which strangely enough concerns only certain boring and useless things: customs, mail, the hotel, the barber, the doctor, prices. Yet what is traveling? Meetings. The only lexicon that counts is the one which refers to the rendezvous.

ROLAND BARTHES
Empire of Signs

CONTENTS

LIST OF ILLUSTRATIONS

MAP

PLATES

FIGURES

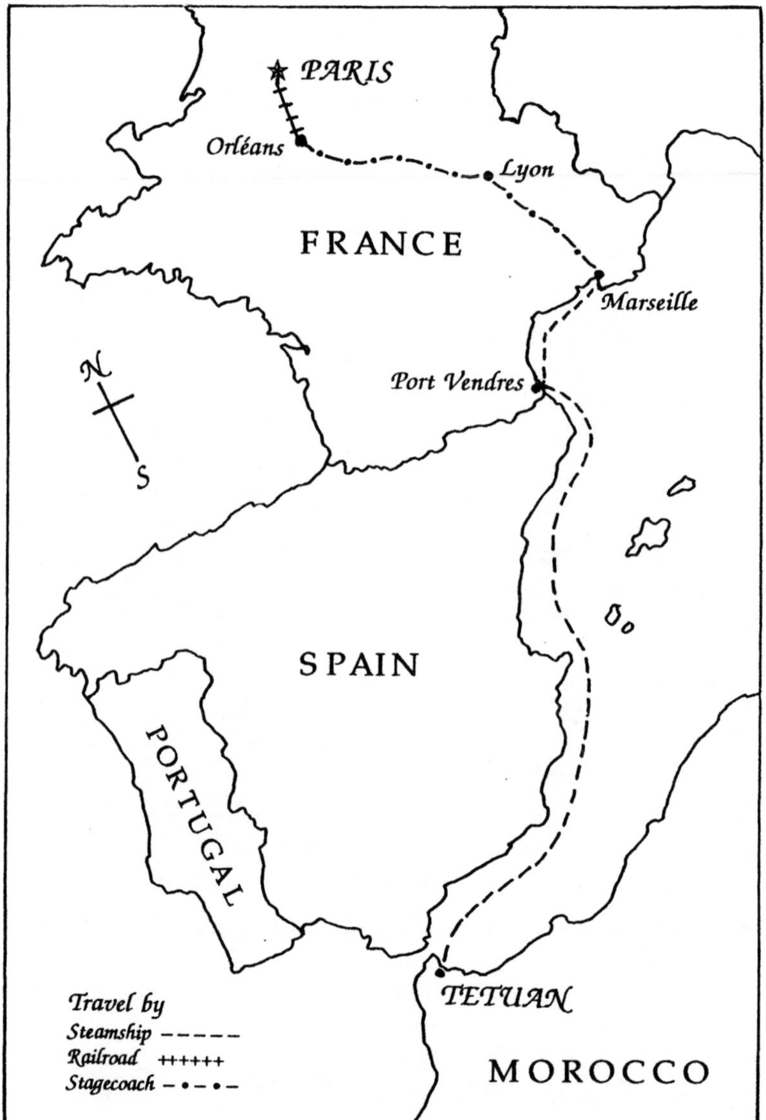

Muḥammad aṣ-Ṣaffār's Journey from Tetuan to Paris in 1845

PREFACE

The Royal Palace archives in Rabat, Morocco, contain the state papers of the reigning ʿAlawite dynasty, the family of the present King Ḥasan II. Included in the collection are documents and manuscripts of an extraordinary variety and richness dating from earliest Islamic times. The mass of material is now in the process of being catalogued,[1] but the most infallible bibliographical guide to it is still the personal knowledge of a few distinguished Moroccan scholars. Among them is Si Muḥammad al-Manūnī, who pointed out to me some years ago the existence of a newly rediscovered nineteenth-century manuscript entitled "The Voyage of the Scholar Sid Muḥammad b. ʿAbd Allāh aṣ-Ṣaffār to France as Secretary to the Ambassador al-Ḥājj ʿAbd al-Qādir Ashʿāsh of Tetuan."[2]

The manuscript was 139 pages in length, each page 21.5 cm long and 17 cm wide, containing twenty-one lines of text, and written in careful Maghribi script. It was not signed, nor was the name of the author mentioned in the opening lines, where authorship is customarily claimed. But internal evidence, the testimony of Moroccan scholars, and a comparison of the handwriting with other documents bearing his signature confirmed that the author was Muḥam-

1. See the series *Fahāris al-khizāna al-malakiya* (Rabat, 1980–), especially vol. 1, *Fihris qism at-tārīkh wa-kutub ar-riḥlāt*, ed. Muḥammad ʿAbd Allāh ʿInān (Rabat, 1980), pp. 427–58. Documents from these archives are published in the series *Al-Wathā'iq: Majmūʿāt wathā'iqiya dawriya tuṣaddiruha mudīriya al-wathā'iq al-malakiya*, ed. ʿAbd al-Wahāb Bin Manṣūr, 7 vols. (Rabat, 1976–89).

2. Included in a "collection," or *majmūʿa*. BGR #113.

mad aṣ-Ṣaffār and the manuscript was indeed an autograph. No other copies have been found, nor has the account ever been edited or published in full, either in Arabic or in any other language.[3]

The subject matter is the report of a journey made by the author to Paris in December 1845 as secretary to the Ambassador ʿAbd al-Qādir ashʿāsh, who was sent by the reigning Moroccan Sultan ʿAbd ar-Raḥmān on a special diplomatic mission. During the journey, aṣ-Ṣaffār took careful notes; when he returned home, he wrote his account, probably at the urging of Ashʿāsh, who was responding to a royal request. Aṣ-Ṣaffār was a professional scribe, and the manuscript is written in a fluid and elegant hand; only toward the end, as he hurried to finish, did he leave signs of his haste in crossed-out words. Evidence of his aesthetic concern are the ornamental chapter headings and paragraphs that begin with large and decorative letters. There are also subject headings in the margins to guide the reader, and in two places the author drew little explanatory sketches which are to be found in the edited text.

The manuscript is divided into six sections, beginning with a prologue and ending with an epilogue. Between are four chapters on different subjects. The formal structure of aṣ-Ṣaffār's travel account, or *riḥla*, reflects the order of "classic" works in this genre, as well as more modern elements. In 1834, the *Takhlīṣ al-ibrasīz fī talkhīṣ Bārīz* of the Egyptian Rifāʿa Rāfiʿ aṭ-Ṭahṭāwī, who spent five years in Paris, was published at Bulaq, Egypt.[4] Both the contents and the arrangement of the *Takhlīṣ* greatly influenced aṣ-Ṣaffār. But

3. A summary and brief sections of aṣ-Ṣaffār's account appear in Muḥammad Dāwud's *Tārīkh Tiṭwān* (*TT*), vol. 3 (Tetuan, 1962), pp. 297–309, 391–92. Excerpts are in Muḥammad al-ʿArabī al-Khaṭṭābī, "Mushāhadāt diblūmāsī maghribī fī Fransā fī ʿahd al-Mawlay ʿAbd ar-Raḥmān b. Hishām," *Daʿwat al-Ḥaqq* 263 (March 1987): 19–29; 264 (April–May 1987): 36–48.

4. The edition used in preparing this study is *Al-aʿmāl al-kāmila li-Rifāʿa Rāfiʿ aṭ-Ṭahṭāwī*, ed. Muḥammad ʿAmāra, part 2: *As-siyāsa . . . wal-waṭaniya . . . wat-tarbiya* (Beirut, 1973), pp. 9–266. A French translation is Anouar Louca, *L'or de Paris: Relation de voyage, 1826–1831* (Paris, 1988).

Muḥammad aṣ-Ṣaffār was no mere imitator. An accomplished man of letters, he embellished his account with original observations, poetry, quotations from the Koran and Hadith (traditions about the Prophet), proverbs, jokes, anecdotes, and other Arabic literary flourishes that mark it as the work of a cultivated scholar. Attempting to identify the sources on which he drew has been one of the most demanding editorial aspects of the project. Muḥammad aṣ-Ṣaffār tells us that finishing the manuscript was an ordeal that occupied him for several months. Translating and unraveling the knots in his text has been a challenge that has taken me more than a few years.

The work was first presented as a doctoral dissertation to the Department of History at the University of Michigan in 1976. Then it rested on my shelf for years, until colleagues urged me to publish it. The present version represents a revision of the original translation, augmented with much additional material and a new introduction.

The Translation

The translation is as literal as possible without sacrificing intelligibility and good sense. The entire text has been translated; the sole omission is on pages 128–35 of the manuscript, in which the expenditures listed in the French National Budget of 1846 are copied into Arabic. The rest is translated following aṣ-Ṣaffār's direct, narrative style, interrupted now and then by the ornamental rhyming prose technique known as *sajʿ*. I have tried to convey the opulent flavor of the rhymed prose, without actually reproducing the rhyme. The same is true of the poetry, often skipped in translations. I have translated all of it, in the belief that the poetry serves as a vehicle for bringing the feeling and opinions of the author into sharper focus.

The system of transliteration used is that of the *International Journal of Middle Eastern Studies*, with the modification that the consonant of the definite article has been assimilated to the "sun-letters" (e.g., "aṣ-Ṣaffār" rather than "al-Ṣaffār") to help the non-Arabic speaker with pronunciation. There are many foreign words in the text, which are transcribed and explained in the notes. Some of these words, particularly those of Spanish origin, were already in use in Morocco; others were new, and were vocalized and pointed in the text by the author, making it easier for his readers to pronounce them. Many French place names appear, and on the whole were easy to identify. They have been rendered as they appear in a standard gazetteer, relying on the *National Geographic Atlas of the World* (1981 ed.) as a guide. Likewise, the names of Moroccan towns and other geographical locations are presented in standard English orthography: thus "Tetuan," rather than "Tetouan" or "Tīṭṭāwīn." Some Arabic terms have already passed into English, like "ulema" and "caliph," and they appear in that form here. Interpolated words have been inserted in square brackets [ ], but only in cases where absolutely essential for clarity; such insertions have been kept to a minimum. Text in parentheses ( ) is found in the original; the parentheses are used in the translation to convey what seems to be an aside of the author.

Acknowledgments

It is a pleasure to recall the many friends and colleagues who have helped me along the way.

Foremost among them are the Moroccan scholars who showed me so much patience, generosity, and good will. I have already mentioned Si Muḥammad al-Manūnī, eminent historian and bibliographer, who not only pointed out the manuscript to me, but directed me to other valuable sources. The then director of the Palace Library, the late Ḥājj Muḥammad Dāwud, author of the monumental *Tārīkh Tiṭwān*, lent me parts of his work then in manuscript form, along with his unsurpassed knowledge of Tetuan history. The Royal Historian, ʿAbd al-Wahāb Bin Manṣūr, has been exceedingly helpful over the years, and his contributions have greatly enriched this study. The Ḥājj Muḥammad at-Tiṭwānī of Salé, now deceased, spent many hours with me discussing Muḥammad aṣ-Ṣaffār and men like him, and served as a model of what it means to be a *faqīh*, a religious scholar. My acquaintance with these learned gentlemen is the foundation on which this project was built.

Research in the Moroccan libraries would not have been possible without the help of Mehdi Dellero, former director of the Tetuan Library, Mohamed Ben Sherifa, director of the Bibliothèque Générale in Rabat, and the director of the Ḥasaniya Library, Muḥammad al-ʿArabī al-Khaṭṭābī. I also wish to thank the descendent of Muḥammad aṣ-Ṣaffār, Si ʿAbd as-Salām aṣ-Ṣaffār of Tetuan, who gave me copies of important family documents, and ʿAbd al-Qādir ar-Razīnī (Erzini) of Tangier, who also lent me material. I am also grateful to the staff of the reading room at the Ministry of Foreign Affairs in Paris for their help in locating the French sources used in this study.

The first stage of this research was carried out under the auspices of a Fulbright-Hays Graduate Fellowship, and a grant from the Center for Middle Eastern Studies at the University of Michigan. Revisions were carried out with help from the National Endowment for the Humanities, and a grant from the Social Science Research Council. This past year of writing has taken place in the congenial surroundings of the Center for Middle Eastern Studies at Harvard University, where I was able to discuss my work with a stimulating group of colleagues. I want to express particular thanks to Roy Mottahedeh, whose knowledge of the medieval sources was freely shared with me. My sessions with the Iranian scholar Ahmad Mahdavi-Damghani, an expert on classical Arabic literature, greatly helped me in understanding the meaning of the verses in the text.

Other friends must also be mentioned. My teachers at Michigan, Richard P. Mitchell and Ernest Abdel-Massih, both of whom regrettably passed away before their time, made an indelible imprint on me, the first shaping my historical sense, the second introducing me to Moroccan Arabic. Kenneth Brown of Manchester University was the first to urge me to work on this topic. In Morocco, Kenneth Sinclair-Loutit extended to me the hospitality of his home and library, and Mbaraka Bint al-ʿArabī Bin Zarwāl advanced my studies of the dialect while providing love and sustenance to my children. The thesis version of this book was typed with patience and care by Sadie C. Miller. Revisions were undertaken with the encouragement of Norman Stillman, Henry Munson, Jr., and Wil Rollman, among others; each represents a standard of scholarship on Morocco worthy of emulation. The book was read in draft by Dale Eickelman and Barbara Metcalf, and the final version benefited from their appraisal. At the UC Press, Lynne Withey deftly guided me on my first voyage in book publishing, Rose Anne White supervised the editing with finesse, and Orin Gensler proved a meticulous and scholarly editor. At the Harvard College Library, my friend Fawzi Abdulrazak generously directed me to sources, and helped me solve several difficulties in the translation. Annelise Martin graciously gave computer advice, Jamil Simon did the photography work, and Robert Smith Shea, former director of the Tangier American Legation Museum, allowed me to reproduce paintings from the Angus Collection. While all of the above contributed to the making of this work, I alone am responsible for the final product. I am grateful to all of you.

S.G.M.
September 1990

ABBREVIATIONS

AAE	Archives du Ministère des Affaires Étrangères, Paris and Nantes (MDM = Mémoires et documents, Maroc; CPM = Correspondance politique, Maroc; ADM = Affaires diverses, Maroc)
ADM	*See* AAE
AM	*Archives marocaines*
AN	Archives Nationales, Paris
APT	Archives du Port de Toulon
BGR	Bibliothèque Générale, Rabat
BRR	Bibliothèque Royale, Rabat (Ḥasaniya Archives)
BSOAS	*Bulletin of the School of Oriental and African Studies*
CPM	*See* AAE
DAR	Direction des Archives Royales, Rabat
Dozy	R. Dozy, *Supplément aux dictionnaires arabes*, 2 vols., Paris, 1967
EI	*Encyclopaedia of Islam*, 1st and 2nd editions
FO	Records of the Foreign Office, Public Record Office, London
GAL	Carl Brockelmann, *Geshichte der arabischen Litteratur* (GAL), 2 vols., Leiden, 1943–49; *Supplementbände* (S), 3 vols, Leiden, 1937–42
H-T	*Hespéris-Tamuda*
Harrell	R. Harrell et al., *A Dictionary of Moroccan Arabic: Arabic-English*, Washington, D.C., 1966

Hesp.	*Hespéris*
IB	H. A. R. Gibb, ed., *The Travels of Ibn Baṭṭūṭa*, 3 vols., The Hakluyt Society, Cambridge, 1958
MDM	*See* AAE
MM	Archives du Ministère de la Marine, Achives Nationales, Paris
RA	*Revue africaine*
RMM	*Revue du monde musulman*
S	*See* GAL
SEI	*Shorter Encyclopaedia of Islam*
TT	Muḥammad Dāwud, *Tārīkh Tiṭwān*, 8 vols., Tetuan, 1959–79

I

INTRODUCTION

Plate 1. The Prologue of the manuscript.

INTRODUCTION

Sometime in the spring of 1846, with the fresh and heady scent of orange blossoms filling the gardens surrounding his native Tetuan, Muḥammad aṣ-Ṣaffār, newly returned from travels in France, took up his pen and began to write. Before him was the thick bundle of notes reminding him of the people, places, and marvels seen and heard during his voyage. After invoking the blessings of God, he patiently set to work, recording his impressions in a careful, fluid hand steadied by years of practice.

At the beginning of September, when the blossoms of spring were ripening into golden orbs, aṣ-Ṣaffār wrote the closing lines of his manuscript, giving expression to the relief that often comes with finishing an arduous task: "This is all that it is possible for this poor insignificant self to do, given his muddled brain and the pressures of other work. Were it not for the sake of helping him whose request is hereby answered—for obedience to him is an obligation—I would not have completed it."[1] These words, and indeed the evident haste in which they were written, suggest that the request to which aṣ-Ṣaffār was responding came from the Sultan himself.

Why was Mulay ʿAbd ar-Raḥmān, Commander of the Faithful, descendent of the Prophet Muḥammad, head of a dynasty that had ruled Morocco for more than two hundred years, so eager to read Muḥammad aṣ-Ṣaffār's account? One reason may have been the expectation that its densely filled pages would contain answers to some troubling questions: What is the secret of French power? How

1. See page 220.

can it be acquired? How have they achieved mastery over nature in ways as yet unknown to us? How do they lead their daily lives, educate their children, treat their women and servants? What is the status of their learning, how do they amuse themselves, what do they eat? In short, what is the condition of their civilization, and how does it differ from ours?

The significance of Muḥammad aṣ-Ṣaffār's *riḥla*, or travel account, arises from the author's ability to offer answers to these questions and to capture his experience in finely drawn images that are profoundly human. He had the aptitude for opening a window on a world remote from his own and transmitting what he saw to others. Through his minute descriptions of the new (and almost everything is new), we feel the texture of the cultural encounter: in reading his travel account, we have the rare opportunity to "get inside the skin" of a literate Moroccan at a critical moment that tested his beliefs, sensibilities, and bearings.

Aṣ-Ṣaffār's "rendezvous" with the new, to borrow Barthes's phrase, evokes a far greater confrontation, in which his experience was magnified many times. In the background to his journey were events which had profoundly upset the Moroccan ruling elite's perception of its own power vis-à-vis the West. Indeed, aṣ-Ṣaffār's journey was part of an effort to try to correct the imbalance, and to gain insight into what had gone wrong. The age in which he lived was one of anxiety about Moroccan abilities against a militant West, and of fears about the impact of external affairs on a fragile domestic order. These larger issues are the antecedents to the voyage, casting it onto a higher plane of historical significance. In order to understand the *riḥla*, we must first see it within the setting of its times.

Morocco, France, Algeria

The watershed event of aṣ-Ṣaffār's generation was the French landing in Algiers in 1830. As the French coastal enclave grew into a full-scale occupation, the geographical continuum of Muslim states stretching from Egypt to Morocco, established in the first centuries of Islam, was abruptly broken. For Morocco, the French penetration meant that a Christian power now shared a long, exposed border of open plains and deserts, offering an open way into the Moroccan heartland. It was an unprecedented turn of events, and its effect was traumatic.

It was not the first time that invaders from Europe had threatened Morocco, but this was a threat of a new and different order. Iberian marauders in the fifteenth and sixteenth centuries had made inroads into the coast, but these occupations were for the most part transitory. By the seventeenth century, a static tension had developed between Morocco and Europe whose fault line was the sea; Moroccan and European-based corsairs would raid each other's shipping, enriching their respective coffers under the guise of religious faith.[2] By the middle of the eighteenth century piracy had slackened off, giving way to less violent forms of exchange. Occasional warfare was one feature of the Moroccan-European relationship; active trade and diplomacy was another. Under Sultan Muḥammad III (1757–90) a new port was built at Mogador (aṣ-Ṣawīra) on the Atlantic coast, in order to attract foreign merchants and to generate customs revenues for the treasury of the Makhzan.[3] Then came the French Revolution and the Napoleonic Wars, and a decisive break in relations with the West. Moreover, the death of Sultan Muḥammad III initiated a struggle for succession that unleashed countrywide spasms of warfare. Political life entered a period of excess that was unusual even in the weary eyes of the Moroccan chroniclers.[4]

2. J. Bookin-Weiner, "The 'Sallee Rovers': Morocco and its Corsairs in the Seventeenth Century," in *The Middle East and North Africa: Essays in Honor of J. C. Hurewitz*, ed. Reeva S. Simon (New York, 1990), p. 317.

3. Daniel Schroeter, *Merchants of Essaouira: Urban Society and Imperialism in Southwestern Morocco, 1844–1886* (Cambridge, 1988), pp. 11–20. *Makhzan* is the Arabic name for the Moroccan government, derived from the word meaning "storehouse."

4. Aḥmad b. Khālid an-Nāṣirī, *Kitāb al-istiqṣā li-akhbār duwal al-Maghrib al-aqṣā*, 9 vols. (Casablanca, 1956), 8:72–86.

It was not until the 1820s that both Morocco and Europe emerged from the time of troubles. On the continent, Europeans celebrated peace with a burst of growth and an assertive search for overseas markets and sources of supply. While Europe entered a new age, Morocco drew inward, and under Sultan Mulay Sulaymān (1793–1822) broke most of her European ties. In 1817 the Sultan disbanded what was left of the Moroccan fleet, and put an end to all maritime trade on Moroccan ships.[5] Ports were closed to foreign trade, and Moroccans were forbidden to travel abroad without permission of the Sultan.[6] His successor, Mulay ʿAbd ar-Raḥmān (1822–59), tried to redress the imbalance but failed, and Morocco returned to self-imposed isolation.[7] The near-total break in Morocco's relations with the West lasted more than a generation. During the interval, Western Europe metamorphosed in ways most Moroccans could not imagine.[8]

The French conquest of Algeria abruptly ended this phase and thrust Morocco once again onto the European stage. Against his will, the Sultan was drawn into the affairs of his Algerian neighbor. Morocco's involvement began with the Amir ʿAbd al-Qādir, an Algerian leader who in 1832 organized local resistance to the French. The Sultan helped him with arms and supplies, fulfilling his religious duty to respond to the Christian threat. But at the same time the

5. On the dismantling of the Moroccan navy in the early nineteenth century, see M. al-Manūnī, *Maẓāhir yaqẓat al-Maghrib al-ḥadīth* (Rabat, 1973), 1:3–8 (all references to this work are from the 1973 edition unless otherwise indicated). See also J.-L. Miège, "La marine marocaine au xixe siècle," *Bulletin de l'enseignement publique au Maroc* 237 (1956): 51–57.

6. An example is the *ẓahīr*, or proclamation, from Mulay Sulaymān to the Ḥājj ʿAbd ar-Raḥmān Ashʿāsh, dated 28 Shawwāl 1221/8 January 1807, granting him permission to travel abroad. *TT* 3:236.

7. J. Caillé, "Le dernier exploit des corsaires du Bou-Regreg," *Hesp.* 37, 3–4 (1950): 429–37.

8. For an overview, see J.-L. Miège, *Le Maroc et l'Europe*, 4 vols. (Paris, 1961), vol. 2: *L'ouverture*, pp. 19–258; L. Valensi, *Le Maghreb avant la prise d'Alger (1790–1830)* (Paris, 1969).

Sultan was wary of the Amir's undisciplined army and charismatic appeal, and feared he would arouse France to attack Morocco.[9]

This friendly, if uneasy, relationship continued as long as the war was confined to Algeria. But in 1841 the conflict suddenly entered a new phase. General Bugeaud, recently appointed chief of the French army, swore that "the Arabs will neither sow, reap, nor pasture without our permission," and pursued ʿAbd al-Qādir relentlessly, finally forcing him across the border into Morocco.[10] On 6 August 1844, without warning, a French fleet bombarded Tangier, and a few days later reduced Mogador to ruins. In one week the French had damaged the Sultan's two chief ports and severely impaired his customs revenues.[11] Meanwhile, General Bugeaud crossed the border and destroyed a Moroccan army at the River Isly. On land and sea, the Moroccans were in defeat.

Now France sought to make peace. "Now we can be generous without being weak," Bugeaud wrote, "because we have hit them hard."[12] The Treaty of Tangier of September 1844, and the Treaty of Lalla Maghnia the following March, solidified the French success while exacting a heavy price from the Sultan.[13] He had to agree to

9. On ʿAbd al-Qādir, son of Muḥī ad-Dīn al-Mukhtārī (1807–83), resistance leader from 1832 to 1847, see R. Gallissot, "La guerre d'Abd el Kader ou la ruine de la nationalité algérienne (1839–1847)," *H-T* 5 (1964): 119–41. P. de Cossé-Brissac, *Les rapports de la France et du Maroc pendant la conquête de l'Algérie (1830–1847)* (Paris, 1931), details diplomatic initiatives. For a postcolonial reinterpretation, see A. Laroui, *History of the Maghrib* (Princeton, 1977), pp. 299–301. A basic work is C.-A. Julien, *Histoire de l'Algérie contemporaine* (Paris, 1964), ch. 4. Paul Azan says ʿAbd al-Qādir gave the Sultan "the deference due to a seigneur by his vassal." Azan, *L'émir Abd el Kader* (Paris, 1925), p. 142.

10. Quoted in Julien, *Histoire*, p. 174.

11. An eyewitness account of these events is A.-H. Warnier, *Campagne du Maroc, 1844* (Paris, 1899).

12. Quoted in Cossé-Brissac, *Rapports*, p. 96.

13. Texts of both treaties are in H. M. P. de La Martinière and N. Lacroix, *Documents pour servir à l'étude du nord-ouest africain*, 4 vols. (Algiers, 1894–97), 2:517–21.

cooperate in the capture of ʿAbd al-Qādir, as well as to negotiate new border demarcations. In one fell swoop he was forced to abandon his opposition to the French, and to concede their presence in Algeria a de facto recognition it had never before had.

Meanwhile, the Makhzan tried to come to terms with the disaster. Moroccan writings of the time demonstrate, according to the Moroccan historian Muḥammad al-Manūnī, the "confusion of spirit" and the "muddled thinking" of the men of the court and the ulema.[14] Two motifs emerge: the first, a call to holy war; the second, a searching through the classical texts to find explanations for the catastrophe.[15] Both suggest that, at least initially, some members of the elite looked inward for guidance on how to react to the French threat in Algeria. But for others in the ruling circle, it was clear that inherited wisdom was inadequate, and that new information was needed. The doors of the Makhzan were far from hermetically sealed, and novel concepts were beginning to filter in. By the mid-1840s, curiosity about Europe had taken root in a small yet influential circle of men who became partisans, not exactly of reform, but rather of "inquiry" and of "seeing and hearing" (as aṣ-Ṣaffār put it) what the West had to offer.[16] Perhaps this curiosity was stirred by reports from travelers—Europeans, Moroccans, other Muslims—who brought news of the great scientific and technolog-

14. Al-Manūnī, *Maẓāhir* 1:13.

15. The first trend is exemplified by an exhortatory poem (*qaṣīda*) of the Minister Ibn Idris that begins: "Oh people of our Maghrib, it is time to sound the alarm! / To the jihad, to right what is wrong." Al-Manūnī, *Maẓāhir* 1:20. Also M. Lakhdar, *La vie littéraire au Maroc sous la dynastie ʿAlawide* (Rabat, 1971), pp. 316–17, 327–35. The second trend is seen in the work of Muḥammad b. ʿAbd al-Qādir al-Kilānī, known as al-Kardūdī, an *ʿālim* of Fes, who wrote *Kashf al-ghumma bi-bayān anna ḥarb an-niẓām* ("Unveiling the Sorrow, An Explanation of the War of Order"), BGR MS# D1281; quoted in al-Manūnī, *Maẓāhir* 1:13–15, and A. Laroui, *Les origines sociales et culturelles du nationalisme marocain (1830–1912)* (Paris, 1977), pp. 276–78.

16. Laroui, *Origines*, pp. 273–74, 278.

ical changes taking place in Europe; perhaps it was stimulated by the appearance of travel books such as the Egyptian aṭ-Ṭahṭāwī's voyage to Paris, which found its way into the library of the Sultan's First Minister Ibn Idrīs;[17] most certainly, it arose as a consequence of military defeat. Drawing on these sources, the idea of a mission to witness European civilization at first hand seems to have taken hold. It was a controversial idea, fraught with misgivings; nevertheless, it was an idea whose moment had come.

The Embassy of Ash'āsh

The idea of a Moroccan embassy was first raised during negotiations over the Treaty of Lalla Maghnia, when the French suggested that the Sultan send an envoy to France to implement "the modifications and changes that the new situation demanded."[18] These overtures were greeted with reserve by the Makhzan. Months passed with no answer, while factions within the court debated the idea. The Sultan's representative to the foreign consuls, Bū Silhām b. 'Alī Azṭūṭ, told a French intermediary that he favored conciliation with France but his views were not yet accepted at the court: "An alliance with France suits us," he is reported to have said. "This idea is not yet completely accepted by the Emperor . . . but it is germinating in his spirit; I will nurture it with all the means in my power."[19] Encouraged by this news, the French assigned Léon

17. For mention of Ibn Idrīs's library see ibid., p. 215 n. 63. On aṭ-Ṭahṭāwī, see note 132 below.

18. AAE/MDM 9/370, de La Rue to Ibn Idrīs, 22 March 1845.

19. AAE/CPM 14/119–22, Roches to Guizot, 24 August 1845. Abū Silhām b. 'Alī Azṭūṭ, governor of Tangier and Larache (popularly known as Bū Silhām), was the Sultan's representative to the European consuls resident in Tangier. Foreign relations were conducted through Makhzan officials residing in the North, who acted as go-betweens to shield the Sultan and the court from excessive contact with foreigners.

Roches, one of their most gifted and tenacious agents, to organize the mission.[20] Roches was in steady contact with Bū Silhām in Larache and with First Minister Muḥammad Ibn Idrīs at the court.[21]

Meanwhile, the French government's enthusiasm for a Moroccan embassy grew, especially as its political advantages became clear. The ambassador would be tangible proof to a divided French public that the goals of the long and costly Algerian war had finally been achieved: "The Emperor of Morocco must give our King a powerful weapon to withstand the opinion of his subjects," wrote Roches. "That weapon is the ambassador."[22] Also in the back of Roches's mind was another vision, of a Morocco tamed and chastened, and joining the ranks of Muslim states that had already submitted to the will of France. The Sultan would someday conclude an alliance like "that which exists between us and the Sultan of Constantinople, the Pasha of Egypt, and the Bey of Tunis. . . . You should come to our country to seek the instructors who will furnish magnificent battalions to Turkey, Egypt, and Tunis, and to study our science and industry."[23]

20. Roches began his career with the French army in Algeria in 1832, and in 1837, during a period of truce, became ʿAbd al-Qādir's personal secretary, taking the Arabic name ʿUmar b. ar-Rūsh. In 1839 he rejoined Gen. Bugeaud's staff and played a key role in the embassy of Ashʿāsh, accompanying the group to Paris. AAE, Personal Dossier, "Léon Roches"; M. Emerit, "La légende de Léon Roches," *Revue africaine* 91, 410–11 (1947): 81–105. Roches's memoir *Trente-deux ans à travers l'Islam*, 2 vols. (Paris, 1884–87), does not cover this period.

21. Muḥammad Ibn Idrīs (1794–1847), First Minister to Sultan Mulay ʿAbd ar-Raḥmān, was a poet and statesman of extraordinary ability. Originally staunchly anti-European, after Isly his attitude changed and he favored the sending of an embassy to France. See Nāṣir al-Fāsī, "Muḥammad Ibn Idrīs, wazīr Mulay ʿAbd ar-Raḥmān wa-shāʿiruhu," *Al-baḥth al-ʿilmī* 1 (January–April 1964): 157–80.

22. AAE/CPM 14/182, Roches to Ibn Idrīs, 12 September 1845. On the political debate within France over the Algerian war, see F. P. G. Guizot, *France under Louis-Philippe, 1841–1847* (London, 1865), pp. 117, 130.

23. AAE/CPM 14/182, Roches to Ibn Idrīs, 12 September 1845.

Compelling reasons led the Moroccans to negotiations at this time. First of all, there was the situation with ʿAbd al-Qādir; the French were pressing for his expulsion, but the Sultan needed more time. Roches argued that direct appeal for patience made in Paris would be more persuasive than indirect diplomacy in Morocco.[24] Then, there was the advantage of seeing France at first hand; some of the inspiration behind the embassy must have been the chance to gather intelligence directly, and through a trusted envoy, rather than through intermediaries whose loyalties were in doubt. Finally, the Sultan may have reasoned, negotiation in this case was the proper course. While holy war was one aspect of the relationship with the non-Muslim world, compromise and conciliation, *ṣulḥ* and *hudna*, were another, employed by Muslim rulers since the earliest times. As long as there was a consensus that it served the interests of the community, and as long as the agreements reached were seen as temporary and short-term, diplomacy with non-Muslims was an approved instrument of policy.[25]

24. AAE/CPM 14/152–53, Roches to Gen. de La Morcière, 3 September 1845. The Sultan wrote to Bū Silhām that the purpose of the embassy was "to demonstrate far and wide that [our] differences were over and we have returned to our former situation." He also wanted to "cancel the clause regarding ʿAbd al-Qādir," and "most important, obtain the release of Muslim captives in the hands of the enemy." This last objective is not mentioned in the French sources. DAR 17561, 22 Jumādā ath-Thānī 1261/28 June 1845.

25. The conditions under which travel to the non-Muslim world should take place were a matter of concern to devout Muslims. Islamic doctrine taught that travel should be *toward* the community of believers, not away from it. The essential meaning of *hijra*, "migration," was movement away from *dār al-kufr*, the territory of the disbelievers, to *dār al-islām*, the house of Islam. Thus travel to the West was inherently problematic, and a point of discussion among the ulema. See Dale F. Eickelman and James Piscatori, eds., *Muslim Travellers: Pilgrimage, Migration, and the Religious Imagination* (Berkeley and Los Angeles, 1990), and especially the essay by Muhammad Khalid Masud, "The Obligation to Migrate: The Doctrine of *Hijra* in Islamic Law," pp. 29–49. In the same volume, Moroccan travel is treated by

Precedent also dictated the conventions of Muslim diplomacy. Unlike European states, who watched over their foreign interests through resident consuls, most Muslim states in premodern times, including Morocco, had no corps of "professional" diplomats and no permanent embassies abroad. Negotiations were usually carried out by special envoys chosen by the ruler: they went abroad, performed their duties, and returned home as soon as the mission was completed. Nevertheless, to be chosen as an envoy was a mark of distinction, and diplomatic appointments were eagerly sought. So when the Sultan's intention of sending an ambassador to France became known, his choice became a subject of intense speculation.

Friends at the court told Roches how the topic of the embassy was on everyone's lips. Each faction had its own candidate; the French Consul at Tangier, Edme de Chasteau, reported that "Ibn Idrīs has come forth with one, Bū Silhām with another, and the Emperor is inclined toward a rich merchant of Fes."[26] Hoping to

---

Abderrahmane El Moudden in "The Ambivalence of *Rihla*: Community Integration and Self-definition in Moroccan Travel Accounts, 1300–1800," pp. 69–84. For more on this subject, see Laroui, *Origines*, pp. 320–21; M. El-Mansour, "Moroccan Perceptions of European Civilisation in the Nineteenth Century," in *Morocco and Europe*, ed. George Joffé, Center of Near and Middle Eastern Studies, School of Oriental and African Studies, University of London, Occasional Paper 7 (London, 1989), pp. 37–45; and A. al-Qadūrī, "Ṣuwar ʿan Urūbbā min khilāl thalātha riḥlāt maghribiya wa-baʿḍ al-murāsilāt ar-rasmiya," *Majallat kulliyat al-ādāb wal-ʿulūm al-insāniya* 15 (1989–90): 45–66. The ulema of Fes opposed contact with non-Muslims at any level, which led to conflicts with local merchants eager to conduct overseas trade. N. Cigar, "Socio-economic Structures and the Development of an Urban Bourgeoisie in Pre-colonial Morocco," *Maghreb Review* 6, 3–4 (May–August 1981): 67. For treatment of this issue in aṣ-Ṣaffār's account, see p. 76.

26. AAE/CPM 14/83–84, de Chasteau to Guizot, 3 August 1845. Initially Muṣṭafā Dukkālī and Aḥmad Timsimānī, both merchants with extensive foreign connections, were mentioned by the French as candidates. However, this was not the Sultan's intention. According to a letter in the Royal Archives, he preferred an envoy who was "knowledgable about

influence the choice, Roches invoked the days of Mulay Ismāʿīl and Louis XIV, when relations between the two nations were marked by "pomp, magnificence, and happy results," and urged the Moroccans to appoint "a man who combines all the advantages of an imposing exterior, an intelligent spirit, a noble origin, and an elevated rank in his government."[27]

Word finally came that the Sultan had reached a decision. Roches heard from "a friend at the court in Fes" that ʿAbd al-Qādir Ashʿāsh, the governor of Tetuan, had been selected. Roches immediately wrote a flattering description of Ashʿāsh to Foreign Minister Guizot that made up in enthusiasm what it lacked in accuracy:

> His ancestors were among the Moors chased out of Spain in the fifteenth century who settled where the city of Tetuan is now; that is to say, they were its founders. Since that time, the position of Pasha [governor] has fallen to the eldest of the family. This hereditary *pashalik* [governorship] . . . is without parallel in Morocco. Ashʿāsh is thus among the men of good breeding and distinction. Barely thirty-five years old, he is learned and has much worldly experience. He possesses all the confidence and friendship of the Emperor, has a considerable fortune, and has been to Mecca. . . . It would be quite impossible to find in Morocco a man more suitable than he.[28]

Ashʿāsh was the eldest son of a rich and powerful Tetuan family that had ruled the city for three generations. His grandfather, ʿAbd ar-Raḥmān Ashʿāsh, the first of his family to gain political prominence, had been governor of Tetuan at three different times; his father, Muḥammad Ashʿāsh, also a governor, was known as a man

Makhzan affairs and not a merchant." DAR 17571, Ibn Idrīs to Bū Silhām, 14 Rajab 1261/19 July 1845.

27. AAE/CPM 14/106–7, Roches to Bū Silhām, 10 August 1845.

28. AAE/CPM 14/253–54, Roches to Guizot, 20 October 1845. The Sultan chose Ashʿāsh because of his "polish, his good sense, and his excellent family." Sultan to Bū Silhām, #18 Shawwāl 1261/20 October 1845.

of powerful and autocratic personality. Greatly feared and respected, he was said to have ruled Tetuan with an iron hand. "In his day," says his biographer Muḥammad Dāwud, "it was safe for womenfolk to walk the streets day and night," in the classic metaphor for peace and security. His ruthlessness and loyalty to the Sultan allowed him to consolidate the hold of his clan over Tetuan, and at his death in 1845 the governorship passed directly to his eldest son, ʿAbd al-Qādir.[29]

ʿAbd al-Qādir Ashʿāsh had held office for only a few months when the prize of the ambassadorship was awarded to him. Moreover, he was younger than Roches estimated, probably twenty-eight years old. One wonders how a man of so little experience was chosen for such a demanding task. It was true that Ashʿāsh was no newcomer to public life; he had spent his formative years at his father's side, apprenticing in the subtle politics of town and court.[30] But more important than his background and capabilities was his enormous wealth, which allowed him to assume the expenses of the embassy himself. This seems to have been the deciding factor, and Ashʿāsh was regarded as a fortunate choice: dignified, skilled in public affairs, and endowed with a private fortune that would relieve the Makhzan of much of the heavy costs of the mission.[31]

The letter from the Sultan appointing ʿAbd al-Qādir Ashʿāsh also instructed him on how to prepare for the journey:

29. TT 3:276–94 describes the rule of Muḥammad Ashʿāsh over Tetuan.

30. He was not highly literate, however, corroborating Laroui's claim that Moroccan ambassadors sent abroad were often "uncultivated." *Origines*, p. 215. An undated note in his awkward hand is found in AAE/ADM/ "Voyage de Sidi Aschasch, Pacha de Tetouan, 1845" (noted hereafter as AAE/ADM/Voyage).

31. AAE/CPM 14/253–54, Roches to Guizot, 20 October 1845. Roches wrote: "The proposal that he made to bear all the expenses of the embassy decided the Sultan in his favor." His father had already promised the Sultan that if he were chosen as ambassador, he would bear all the costs of the embassy. DAR 10794, Mulay ʿAbd ar-Raḥmān to ʿAbd al-Qādir Ashʿāsh, 18 Ramaḍān 1261/20 September 1845.

Plate 2. Portrait of the Ambassador, Ḥājj ʿAbd al-Qādir Ashʿāsh.

Our most excellent servant, Ḥājj[32] ʿAbd al-Qādir Ashʿāsh, may God grant you success, may peace be upon you along with the blessings and mercy of the Most High. The request has been made repeatedly that we send an ambassador to the land of the French as a demonstration of the truce between us. We asked your father, God have mercy upon him, when he

32. *Ḥājj* is the title given to someone who has made the pilgrimage to Mecca.

was alive, and he agreed, saying that if another were [chosen] it would be necessary to provide for him, but if he were to go, nothing more would be needed.[33] No ambassador was sent at that time because of our situation with the French. However, today the need is greater than ever, and God advises us to send you as ambassador to Paris.

We judge you worthy of this mission because of your high rank and position, and your knowledge of rules and proper decorum. With the arrival of this letter, you should begin to prepare by choosing those who will accompany you. They should be men of intelligence, virtue, and piety, who are acquainted with the ways of other peoples. You should also take an *ʿālim*[34] to attend to religious matters such as prayers and reading from the Koran, for the French examine Muslims closely about the mysteries of their beliefs both in general and in particular.

In order that you may all leave together, you should begin to prepare now. Ten days before the festival of ʿĪd al-Fiṭr,[35] come to our presence and spend it here. Then you may leave on your mission, taking with you the gifts we have readied for them, such as lions and the like.

This is not a difficult mission, for you are not required to bind or loosen a contract, but are merely charged with delivering a letter and returning with a response, if God is willing, and it is He who will recompense you. Peace.[36]

33. A reference to the elder Ashʿāsh's willingness to pay the costs of the journey.

34. A learned man (plural *ulema*). For portraits of the type in the Moroccan context, see E. Burke III, "The Moroccan Ulama, 1860–1912: An Introduction," and K. Brown, "Profile of a Nineteenth-century Moroccan Scholar," both in *Scholars, Saints, and Sufis: Muslim Religious Institutions in the Middle East since 1500*, ed. Nikki R. Keddie (Berkeley, 1972), pp. 93–125, 127–48.

35. The holiday of the "breaking of the fast" at the end of Ramaḍān, the Muslim month of fasting.

36. DAR 17564, Sultan to ʿAbd al-Qādir Ashʿāsh, 4 Ramaḍān 1261/6 September 1845.

It had taken nearly a year from the time the embassy was first proposed to the moment when Ashʿāsh and his suite were ready to depart. As the time drew near, Roches's confidence that his diplomacy was succeeding grew. Elated with his success, he wrote that "a revolution is taking place at the court. . . . This revolution is entirely in our favor, and we are at the point of establishing the influence of France over that of all other nations, if we know how to profit from it."[37]

The Météore

The first week of November 1845, the steamer that was to take the mission to France arrived in Tangier. Originally equipped as a hospital ship, the *Météore* had seen continual service in the Algerian campaign, carrying fresh troops from Toulon to Oran and returning home with a load of sick and wounded. The French Consul made a tour of inspection and wrote an indignant letter to Foreign Minister Guizot in Paris. The ship was too small, he complained, and its commandant, Lieutenant Geoffroy, was a "subaltern"; both were inadequate for the mission.[38] But grander vessels were in short supply because of the war, and nothing could be done. Roches set out for Gibraltar on a shopping trip to outfit the *Météore* properly. There he bought linens, furniture, hangings, and rugs to decorate the ambassador's suite in "oriental" style, with low tables and rugs on the floor. Despite their small size, it was reported that the apartments were made comfortable and pleasing.[39]

37. AAE/CPM 15/169–76, Roches to de Chasteau, 5 November 1845 [?], marked "confidential." See also J. Caillé, *Une mission de Léon Roches à Rabat en 1845* (Casablanca, 1947).

38. AAE/CPM 15/52–55, de Chasteau to Guizot, 5 November 1845.

39. AAE/CPM 15/68–69, Roches to Guizot, 13 November 1845; AN/MM/BB4–642, 1846, "Missions particulières, *Météore*, Mission à Tanger,"

Early in December 1845, the small group of Frenchmen who would accompany the Moroccan embassy to France assembled in Tangier. Their leader was Léon Roches, and with him was Auguste Beaumier, "a young man full of intelligence who speaks a bit of Arabic,"[40] who was secretary to de Chasteau. They left Tangier by sea on December 6th and reached Tetuan later the same day. On entering the town, they found the streets and rooftops jammed with curious onlookers. Ashʿāsh awaited them in the garden of his residence, and favorably impressed the French party with his appearance. "His smile is agreeable and his manners distinguished; I think that the government of the King will be satisfied with the ambassador," wrote de Chasteau.[41]

It soon became apparent that the Moroccans would not be ready to leave until the next day. During the night a violent wind blew up, and the *Météore* had to put to sea to ride out the storm. The bad weather prevented its return for several days. Finally, the morning of December 13th, the Moroccan suite assembled on shore and Commandant Goeffroy sent his longboats to fetch them. The landing craft were "invaded by a horde of Moroccans who positively wanted to come on board," Goeffroy wrote in his journal. Meanwhile, others took touching leave of the ambassador: "One person kissed his robe, another his shoulder, while a third kissed his hands." With the Moroccans on board, the *Météore* weighed anchor.

---

report of Commandant Goeffroy (unpaged). Aṣ-Ṣaffār's impressions of the sea voyage are found on pp. 85–86; see illustration, p. 80.

40. Born in 1822 in Marseille, he studied Arabic and became the private secretary of the French consul de Chasteau in 1839. After the embassy, he spent most of his diplomatic career in Morocco, serving as vice-consul in Rabat and consul in Mogador, where he died in 1876. He had scholarly interests (see AAE/MDM 4/209–22), wrote articles for the *Bulletin de la Société de Géographie*, and translated into French the *Al-anīs al-muṭrib bi-rawḍ al-qirṭās* by Ibn Abī Zarʿ (d. 1325), a history of Fes. AAE, Personal Dossier, "Beaumier." See also J. Caillé, "Auguste Beaumier: Consul de France au Maroc," *Hesp.* 37 (1950): 53–95.

41. AAE/CPM 15/189–93, de Chasteau to Guizot, 12 December 1845.

The entire first day, the ambassador and his party stood on the bridge gazing out to sea in quiet contemplation.[42]

The passenger list of the *Météore* for this journey indicates that in addition to the ambassador, the Moroccan group included his father-in-law, Muḥammad al-Libādī, an older gentleman who suffered severely from seasickness. Ashʿāsh showed great concern for his comfort throughout the journey. Then there was Ashʿāsh's brother-in-law, Ḥājj al-ʿArabī al-ʿAṭṭār, according to Goeffroy "a charming and gay fellow, forty to forty-two years old," who spoke Spanish and seemed to understand French. He had already made several trips to Gibraltar in addition to a pilgrimage to the Holy Places. The third person in the inner circle was Muḥammad aṣ-Ṣaffār, the "savant," aged about thirty-five. To Commandant Goeffroy, aṣ-Ṣaffār seemed "very reserved and much less affable than the others." Only these three had the privilege of taking meals with the ambassador. A fourth person, Aḥmad al-ʿAyāṭ, was described as "the chief officer of the Ambassador's household." He was not allowed at the ambassador's table, but shared his apartment. In addition, there were nine Moroccan soldiers who accompanied them as servants.[43]

Once the initial strangeness had passed, life at sea settled into a routine. At mealtimes, Ashʿāsh and his intimates shared the captain's table. Commandant Goeffroy planned adequate stores for his guests, but Ashʿāsh had seen to his own provisioning: "Two bulls, forty sheep, six hundred chickens . . . eggs, vegetables, apples, and raisins in great profusion" had been put on board the *Météore* in

42. AN/MM/BB4–642, report of Goeffroy. APT/2C201/Journal du bord, *Météore*, 13 December 1845.

43. They were, according to the quaint spelling of the passenger list of the *Météore*: Abbou el-Aattitar, Ahmad el-Zghal, Hajj Ahmed el-Yakoubi, el-Tahir Brioul, Abu el-Salem el-Amri, Mohammed el-Kerassi, Hadj Abd el-Rahman Choulon, Mohammed Elou el-Dressi, and Mohammed Mokhtar, the last-named designated as an "interpreter." APT/IC 2754/1845, *Météore*, Rôle d'equipage, "passagers à la table du commandant."

Plate 3. The house of Governor Ashʿāsh at the port of Martil. Watercolor by Lt. Bellaire. Angus collection, Old American Legation, Tangier.

Tetuan. Moreover, the Moroccans showed little enthusiasm for French cuisine, preferring instead to prepare their own,

> especially the famous dish called couscous, which they cannot do without and which is served to them every evening. They are very religious and rigorous observers of the Koran. They never drink wine, but do not appear scandalized when we take it in front of them, and perhaps would not be ill-disposed to give it a try. . . . Someone once joked with the savant, saying that with all his knowledge, he should find a verse in the Koran that permits drinking.[44]

Apart from meals, there was little else to do. Trying his best to make the voyage pleasant, Goeffroy planned nightly entertainments such as fireworks to amuse his guests. By December 17th the coast of France had been reached, and on the 19th they arrived in Marseille, where they rested before leaving for Paris. The ambassador and his suite were invited to visit the city but Ashʿāsh refused, insisting on departing for the capital without delay. His reluctance to engage in tourism puzzled his French hosts, who had set notions about how "oriental" visitors should behave. One of the Frenchmen explained the ambassador's strange attitude as yet another manifestation of Muslim religious zeal: "Like all Muslims, he understands that his first duty on arriving in a country is to present himself to the sovereign, who is, in their eyes, the unique and absolute master of his subjects."[45]

They left Marseille on December 21st, traveling overland by coach along the route northward through the valley of the Rhône,

44. AN/MM/BB4–642, report of Goeffroy.

45. AAE/CPM 15/215–16, Pourcet to Guizot, 19 December 1845. Compare with the seventeenth-century Moroccan voyager to Spain, the Wazīr al-Ghassānī, who refused invitations to rest before he reached "the city to which we are going and the king to whom we are sent." *Riḥlat al-Wazīr fī iftikāk al-asīr*, trans. and ed. A. Bustani (Tangier, 1940), p. 9. References are to the Arabic text.

and on the 27th they arrived in Orléans, where they spent the night before entering Paris. The next morning, the fifteenth since their departure from Tetuan, they took a special train from Orléans to Paris, the first documented journey by rail made by Moroccans. Arriving in Paris at midday, they were taken directly to lodgings prepared for them at 66, avenue des Champs-Elysées.

Seeing Paris

Paris in the 1840s had the air of the grande dame of Europe. London may have been the financial capital of the world, but Paris was its cultural epicenter, exuding the self-confidence of a beauty come of age. Her domain was style, and she reveled in her preeminent position as its arbiter and judge. The swarms of visitors who came to see her industry, art, fashions, and luxury reminded Parisians of the degree of progress that French society had attained.

Yet the arrival of the Moroccan embassy in Paris captivated even the most jaded Parisians, used to the appearance of foreign potentates. There was a special aura about the envoy from the Sultan, relating to the peculiar place of Morocco in the popular imagination—a country so close geographically yet so distant in manners and mentality that "a Moroccan looks quite like a Chinese."[46] And there was the graceful and striking figure of the ambassador himself, which conjured up visions of adventure and romance. "The envoy from Morocco has caught . . . the imagination of Paris. Everything about him recalls the court of the Moorish kings of Granada and the brilliant Abencerages of whom he is a descendent."[47]

46. *L'Illustration*, 3 January 1846, announcing his arrival, promised "the fullest and most curious details about the ambassador."

47. Ibid., 10 January 1846. Heroes of a romantic-tragic tale by François-Auguste-René Chateaubriand (1768–1848), author of *Les aventures du dernier Abencerage*, set in fifteenth-century Spain (Paris, 1826). Hassan Mekouar, *Washington Irving and the Arabesque Tradition* (Ph.D. dissertation, Brown University, 1977), pp. 30–31; *EI* 1, s.v. "Abencerages."

Details of his dress were noted, from the stuff of his headcloth to the shape of his slippers:

> The Ambassador is a young man of twenty-eight years; his form is pleasing and regular, his features fine, his eyes kind and expressive. His hands are small and beautifully shaped. He wears . . . a *sarbouch*,[48] pointed at the end, around which is wound a turban of fine muslin. His head is encircled by a scarf of red cashmere. . . . Over several short jackets he wears a [garment] . . . with wide, floating sleeves. This is the *jellaba*, the national dress of Morocco. A belt secures the jellaba around him. When the Pasha goes out, he puts on two more burnooses,[49] one of wool and the other of a heavy gray material. He wears lovely hose of white silk, and yellow *babouches*[50] which he always wears with the backs pushed down.[51]

Shortly after their arrival, *L'Illustration* printed a series of sketches of the ambassador and his suite. Now visual images reinforced the picturesque prose, as Paris threw itself headlong into making the Moroccans the chief attraction of the winter social season. Invitations to balls, charitable events and "spectacles," requests for money, gifts and offerings of poetry, even letters of advice and caution flowed in. Auguste Beaumier, the young secretary assigned to the delegation, struggled to keep the ambassador's household running smoothly and his social schedule in order. Here is Beaumier's description of a typical day, 17 January 1846:

> Some petitioners awaken me at eight, after which I respond to a score of letters addressed to the ambassador of Morocco, which must be answered politely. . . . Then a dozen valets ar-

48. A cap of felt material. In Arabic *sarbūsh*, which Dozy calls a "coiffure distinctive des émirs." *Dictionnaire détaillé des noms des vêtements chez les Arabes* (Beirut, n.d.), pp. 222–24.

49. A hooded floor-length cape.

50. Leather slippers, usually yellow and pointed at the tips.

51. *L'Illustration*, 10 January 1846.

> rive for the orders of the day, and I do the accounts of the previous day. Following that, a visit to the ambassador and his suite, and a general review to see that all is well: who is in need of a doctor, a barber, or a bath. Then everyone is called to lunch, while I act as interpreter for the invited guests. After that, instructions to go directly to the Champ-de-Mars. Roches arrives in time to take charge of arranging the ambassador and his officers in the carriages. We cross Paris in the midst of a parade of the curious. Arriving at the Ecole Militaire, we go up onto a balcony. At three o'clock, we return with the ambassador and I write the necessary letters of thanks. . . . Later, I go over the events planned for the evening, . . . and give an accounting of the day's expenses, insofar as possible. . . . Dinner next, two deadly hours but a first-class meal—600 francs per day! I take some coffee, converse in Arabic for a time, take a carriage to the Théâtre-Italien. . . . Return at midnight . . . and then to bed.[52]

After six weeks of this hectic schedule, Beaumier expressed his longing "to return again to the tranquility of Tangier and my little room, for all my strength is gone."[53]

The ambassador's first days in Paris were spent fulfilling his role as emissary. On December 30th he presented his credentials to the King at a ceremony at the Palace of the Tuileries, and delivered to him the letter from the Sultan.[54] The letter dealt mainly with the

52. AAE/ADM/Voyage, no date. During his stay in Paris, Beaumier wrote regularly to de Chasteau in Tangier. Drafts of these letters and other miscellanea collected during the journey are found in this dossier. For aṣ-Ṣaffār's view of the day's activities, see pp. 190–194.

53. Ibid., Beaumier to de Chasteau, 8 February 1846.

54. Ash'āsh's letter of introduction is in 'Abd ar-Raḥmān Ibn Zaydān, *Itḥāf a'lām an-nās bi-jamāl akhbār ḥāḍirat Miknās*, 5 vols. (Rabat, 1929–33), 5:170; also *TT* 3:295. A French translation is in AAE/MDM 4/123–25. Ash'āsh wrote to his brother about the audience (*Wathā'iq* 2:119:21), and de Chasteau passed on news of events in Paris in a letter to Ibn Idrīs at the court. DAR 17570, 28 Muḥarram 1262/26 January 1846.

question of ʿAbd al-Qādir, asking for patience while the Sultan implemented a plan to eject him from Morocco. "By using policy to expel him, that is, causing the people to forsake and abandon him until he stands alone," the letter argues, "he will leave without further exhausting effort." The letter also criticized the new border arrangements with Algeria, and ended with a sharp protest against French incursions along Morocco's southern coast.[55]

It took more than a month for Guizot to reply. In his letter, the Foreign Minister suggested that instead of reviewing old grievances, "it would be better to throw a veil of forgetfulness over the past."[56] In his view, the purpose of Ashʿāsh's mission to Paris was to place the Moroccans on display, and nothing more. In his *Mémoires* Guizot glosses over the political aspects of the visit, representing it instead as a spectacle devoid of substance. Ashʿāsh was "a young Arab of agreeable person, serious, modest, and gentle, of mild and elegant manners, anxious to show himself scrupulously attached to his faith, respectful, with dignity, more concerned with obtaining a good reception for himself and the sovereign he represented than intent on any distinct political object." He was sent to Paris "as a demonstration of the friendly relations between France and Morocco."[57]

Guizot's comment reveals how, in French eyes, the embassy was made to fit in the framework of a European-centered view of events, in which the element of demonstrating French superiority was predominant. The courtesy of their Moroccan guests, indeed, their very presence, were taken as signs of France's success in pursuing a foreign policy whose purpose, in the words of Guizot, was

55. The letter from the Sultan to Louis-Philippe is dated 7 Muḥarram 1262/6 January 1846; written in aṣ-Ṣaffār's handwriting, it is AAE/MDM 4/145. The French incursions were near the River Nūn in the south, on the trade route from Mogador to Timbuktu. AAE/MDM 9/297–99, "Mission d'exploration des côtes de Wadnoun (1843)"; Miège, *Le Maroc* 2:146–54.

56. AAE/MDM 4/155–60, Guizot to Ashʿāsh, 14 February 1846.

57. Guizot, *France under Louis-Philippe*, p. 222.

"to secure the safety of our possessions in Africa."[58] The visit had been a success, he felt, because it seemed to bring the Moroccans even closer to accepting France as a permanent feature in the region. His reading of the event prevailed, and the embassy has gone down in French history as one more charming episode of *petite histoire*, "collected" by colonialist historians as testimony to the "grandeur of France" and the inevitability of its rule in North Africa.[59]

His political responsibilities completed, Ashʿāsh and his suite devoted themselves to enjoying Paris. Contrary to aṣ-Ṣaffār's claim that "we rarely ventured out," the Moroccans led a busy social life under the watchful eyes of their French hosts. Some invitations were refused because they were considered beneath the ambassador's rank: "We could have been commonplace by coming and going frequently," aṣ-Ṣaffār explains, "but we were opposed to that." Beaumier always replied with a note, and in many cases a token of the ambassador's generosity. Among Ashʿāsh's contributions were 5,000 francs "for the poor people of Paris . . . whatever their religion may be." The press remarked on the ambassador's "princely generosity," calling him a "nabob" with "his hands filled with presents."

The most magnificent presents were for the King. Before leaving Paris, Ashʿāsh handed over six Arabian horses and a troop of wild animals at a ceremony at the Tuileries. The animals, destined for the Jardin des Plantes, included a lion, two ostriches, three gazelles, and a "mouton à manchettes," a variety of Barbary sheep hitherto unknown in Europe. The press had little difficulty in recasting the gift-giving in an Arabesque mode: "Once the descendents

58. Ibid., p. 204.

59. J. Caillé, "Un ambassadeur marocain à Paris (1845–1846)," *Le monde Français* 16, 49 (October 1949): 86; see also, by the same author, "Ambassades et missions marocaines en France," *H-T* 1, 1 (1960): 65–67. French historians have been unaware of aṣ-Ṣaffār's account, although J.-L. Miège suggested that the embassy of Ashʿāsh has "not been sufficiently emphasized." *Le Maroc* 2:205 note 1.

Plate 4. Presentation of gifts from the Sultan to Louis-Philippe. From *L'Illustration*, 21 February 1846.

Plate 5. A Barbary sheep given to the Jardin des Plantes. From *L'Illustration*, 21 February 1846.

of Moorish kings brought diamonds and perfumes," commented *L'Illustration*. "Today the son of the desert bestows on us lions and gazelles."[60]

The Return

Ashʿāsh and his party said their farewells and left Paris on 17 February 1846. Heading south, at their hosts' insistence they made a detour via Toulon, the home port of the French Mediterranean fleet;

60. 10 January 1846.

here they inspected a warship that, unknown to them, had taken part in the bombardments of Tangier and Mogador in 1844.[61] Finally they reached Marseille, where they stopped for several days to make numerous purchases of silks and gold brocades for the Sultan and his First Minister.[62] On March 2nd the group boarded the *Météore*, reaching Tetuan five days later. Scenes of wild joy greeted them on their return. A Frenchman who was present gave an account of their reception:

> All the religious corporations and the ulema of the various mosques lined the streets, waving the colorful flags of the marabouts. . . . The Pasha approached each group, one by one, and recited words of the Koran with them, while the sacred standards drooped to surround him with the benedictions of the Prophet. . . . Women, children, and old people ran up onto the terraces; they were dressed in clothing reserved for feast days. The Jewish quarter especially presented a gorgeous sight, with the embroidered dresses and jewels of its women. They saluted the Pasha with their "you-yous" and "vivas," while the menfolk lining the sides of the street respectfully kissed the knees and burnoose of the Pasha.[63]

Before entering his house, Ashʿāsh went directly to the mosque where the remains of his father were buried, to give thanks for the happy outcome of his mission.

61. The Moroccan suite visited the warship *Jemmapes*, anchored in the port of Toulon, on 25 February 1846. AAE/CPM 16/35–37, Pourcet to Guizot, 2 March 1846. This vessel took part in the bombardment of Tangier, where it was "positioned opposite the Casbah and within rifle-shot of the town." Warnier, *Campagne du Maroc*, p. 96.

62. Ashʿāsh left France with forty-six pieces of baggage weighing 2,064 kilos. AAE/ADM/Voyage, "bill of lading."

63. AAE/CPM 16/71–74, Pourcet to Guizot, 13 March 1846. The Jews of northern Morocco are mostly Spanish-speaking, tracing their ancestry to Spanish exiles of the late fifteenth century.

Plate 6. The house of Governor Ashʿāsh in Tetuan. Watercolor by Lt. Bellaire, 1844. Angus collection, Old American Legation, Tangier.

Almost immediately, the ambassador set out for Marrakesh to report to the Sultan.[64] On 22 March 1846 the British Consul, John H. Drummond Hay, also en route to Marrakesh, met him in Rabat and had tea with him. Hay noted in his journal that Ashʿāsh "is the best style of Moor I have seen, and appears to have rubbed off the usual quantum of Moorish fanaticism on his visit to Paris."[65] According to Hay, Ashʿāsh was received at court with honor, a sign that the Sultan approved of his conduct abroad.

Ashʿāsh returned home to his post as governor. But he did not forget his French hosts, and according to documents in the French archives, wrote to de Chasteau: "If you have any desire, make it known to me, and with the help of God I will carry it out."[66] Throughout the spring and summer of 1846, he provided the French Consul with valuable information about local affairs.[67] Soon other partisans of France appeared, and the circle of those receiving payments from the French widened to include the highest officials of the Makhzan: according to French sources, the First Minister, Ibn Idrīs, received 29,920 francs in Spanish doubloons; Bū Silhām was given 10,360 francs, which he accepted after swearing to "undying secrecy"; and Bin Abū, the governor of the Rif, was promised 18,000 francs yearly, "as long as he continued to act in the interests of France."[68] Roches's prediction had come true: a revolution had

64. Family Archive. Ibn Idrīs to Muḥammad ar-Razīnī, 20 Rabīʿ al-Awwal 1262/18 March 1846.

65. J. H. D. Hay, *Journal of an Expedition to the Court of Marocco in the Year 1846* (Cambridge, 1848), p. 45.

66. AAE/CPM 16/68, Ashʿāsh to de Chasteau, 10 March 1846.

67. AAE/CPM 17/212, de Chasteau to Guizot, 27 September 1846, for a report originating with Ashʿāsh about the arrival of a British flotilla in Tetuan.

68. AAE/CPM 18/160–65, de Chasteau to Guizot [?], 12 February 1847. Laroui says that certain families began receiving large sums of money and became "faithful allies of European interests." *History*, p. 322. Such bribery was already commonplace in the Ottoman Empire in the eigh-

taken place at the court, and for the moment the position of France was predominant. The British Consul Hay wrote: "Not a day passes that I do not see the decrease of our influence and an increase of the French."[69]

The Moroccans also viewed the embassy with satisfaction. Not long after Ashʿāsh's return, Guizot decided to relieve the pressure on the Sultan, and allow him to deal with ʿAbd al-Qādir at his own pace.[70] Deprived of Moroccan support, the latter eventually gave himself up and went into exile. But the congruity of interests between Morocco and France was only temporary, and was swept away with the Revolution of 1848. In the aftermath of the upheaval, European imperialist ambitions were to reemerge with new vigor, placing the two states again in bitter contention.[71]

As for the dour "savant," Muḥammad aṣ-Ṣaffār, shortly after his return he began to write his travel account. Perhaps he had intended to write from the beginning, for he had kept a journal; perhaps, too, he was urged to write by Ashʿāsh, who wanted a written record of the journey to present to the Sultan. What is certain is that the most abiding outcome of the embassy is the *riḥla*. And while the name of the ambassador and the purpose of his mission have receded with time, the name of the secretary, Muḥammad aṣ-Ṣaffār, has endured.

---

teenth century, where it was "integral to the transaction of business." Thomas Naff, "Ottoman Diplomatic Relations with Europe in the Eighteenth Century: Patterns and Trends," in Thomas Naff and Roger Owen, eds., *Studies in Eighteenth Century Islamic History* (Carbondale, 1977), p. 95.

69. Public Records Office, FO 99/31, Hay to Palmerston, 4 November 1846, quoted in F. R. Flournoy, *British Policy toward Morocco in the Age of Palmerston* (Baltimore, 1935), p. 116.

70. Guizot, *France under Louis-Philippe*, pp. 198–206. In the *Istiqṣā*, vol. 9, an-Nāṣirī documents the steady deterioration in relations between the Sultan and the Amir; the latter's "corruption of the tribes" (p. 50); his "rebellion against the Sultan" (p. 56); and his final capture, greeted with official rejoicing in Morocco (p. 58).

71. The aftermath of the embassy and developments in French-Moroccan relations are described in Miège, *Le Maroc* 2:214–20.

The Author

His full name was Abū ʿAbd Allāh Muḥammad b. ʿAbd Allāh aṣ-Ṣaffār, al-Andalusī by origin, Tetuani by birth.[72] His ancestors came from the town of Jaén in Andalusia, and his father bore the *laqab*, or agnomen, of Jayyānī. Like many of his contemporaries, his birth date is not known, nor are the circumstances of his early life. However, the house in which he was born is still standing in Tetuan. A plain, two-story structure, its interior boasts none of the elegant flourishes of the houses of the wealthy.[73] Its simplicity tells us that aṣ-Ṣaffār's family was a modest one, perhaps rich in culture and distinguished ancestry, but not in worldly goods.

The aṣ-Ṣaffār family came to Tetuan with the wave of emigrants that fled the Reconquista at the end of the fifteenth century, joining the colony of Spanish Muslims who rebuilt Tetuan as a base for counterattacks on Spain and on the foreign enclaves at nearby Ceuta and Tangier. Part of the family emigrated to Fes, but the Tetuan branch took root and prospered in the peculiar soil of that northern Moroccan city. Muḥammad aṣ-Ṣaffār's self-image was bound to his native town, and the poetic feeling he expresses on leaving it is a sign of his deep attachment.[74]

Every Moroccan city has its own unique character, and Tetuan is no exception. Sprawled across a plateau between the mountains and the Mediterranean, it beckons to the hinterland more than to the sea. Over the centuries, the old core of Andalusian nobility was

72. The main source for aṣ-Ṣaffār's life is *TT* 7:78–98. Other sources consulted include: *Taqyīd fī tarjamat al-wazīr aṣ-Ṣaffār*, unsigned, BRR #12419 (noted here as the "Anonymous Taqyīd"); Aḥmad ar-Ruhhūnī, *ʿUmdat ar-rāwīn fī tārīkh Tiṭṭāwīn* 6:523–33, Bibliothèque Générale, Tetuan; al-ʿAbbās b. Ibrāhīm al-Murrākushī, *Al-iʿlām bi-man ḥalla Murrākush wa-Aghmāt min al-aʿlām*, ed. ʿAbd al-Wahāb Bin Manṣūr, 10 vols. (Rabat, 1974–83), 7:34–35; Muḥammad Gharrīt, *Fawāṣil al-jumān fī anbāʾ wuzarāʾ wa-kuttāb az-zamān* (Fes, 1347/1928), pp. 70–71.

73. Visit of May 1973.

74. See p. 78.

joined by an influx of mountain people from the Rif and the Jabala, tempted by its bustling markets and emerald gardens. Its nearby port of Martil now lies in sultry disuse, but once was aswarm with activity. Though not the busiest port in Morocco, it was nevertheless an important link in the trade routes to the east and south. A rich merchant class, typified by the *tājir*[75] in his spotless white jellaba and burnoose, flourished there. Benefiting from their relative remoteness from the centers of Makhzan power, the people of Tetuan sought above all else "to increase their wealth by trade, and to enjoy in peace the joys of the arts and letters."[76]

The richness of the town was a temptation, and from time to time Tetuan was the scene of violence and disorder. In 1236/1820, tribal partisans of Mulay Ibrāhīm, a rival claimant to the throne held by Mulay Sulaymān, entered the town and "took possession of the wealth of the port and of the storehouses of the Sultan."[77] At other times, the Sultan himself intervened in Tetuan's freewheeling mercantile life by "eating up" the wealth of merchants whose prosperity had become too apparent.[78] But usually the pattern of local life was serene, with times of troubles an occasional counterpoint to the otherwise steady rhythm of prosperous trade.

This trade sometimes took Tetuanis far from home; from the port of Martil they sailed into the Mediterranean and beyond. Some

75. In Moroccan usage, a successful merchant, often involved in international trade.

76. G. S. Colin, *EI* 1, S.V. "Tīṭṭāwīn." See also J. D. Latham, "The Reconstruction and Expansion of Tetuan: The Period of Andalusian Immigration," *Arabic and Islamic Studies in Honor of Hamilton A. R. Gibb*, ed. G. Makdisi (Leiden, 1965), pp. 387–408; A. Joly, "Tétouan," part 2, "Historique," *AM* 5 (1905): 198–264, 313–18.

77. An-Nāṣirī, *Istiqṣā* 8:152.

78. In 1242/1826 the governor Muḥammad Ashʿāsh, acting on the orders of Sultan ʿAbd ar-Raḥmān, imprisoned two leading merchants of Tetuan and "seized their wealth and sent it all to the Sultan." *TT* 3:278–79.

had been to Algeria, and a few even to Europe. In 1212/1797, the merchant ʿAbd ar-Raḥmān Madīna received a notarized document from the *umanāʾ*[79] of Tetuan, confirming his intention "to travel by sea to the Christian lands, for the purpose of profitable trade, if God wills it," along with an accounting of the money he was taking with him: "4,570 riyals, 36 doubloons, and twenty ducats."[80] Muḥammad aṣ-Ṣaffār describes one of his companions on the voyage, the Ḥājj al-ʿArabī al-ʿAṭṭār, as "skilled in dealings with other peoples and . . . parts."[81] The al-ʿAṭṭār family were prominent Tetuani businessmen accustomed to following business opportunities abroad. Tetuanis, then, had the business acumen generally ascribed to the people of Fes; but in addition they had a cosmopolitan air and a skill in dealing with foreigners that was rare in early nineteenth-century Morocco.

But contact with foreigners did not necessarily imply acceptance. The nearby enclave of Ceuta was an outpost of Christian encroachment that rubbed sorely on Tetuan's side, and the not distant town of Tangier was seen as a source of foreign contamination.[82] Proximity to Europe bred in the people of Tetuan complex feelings of familiarity and contempt. A special brand of militancy developed in the town, and many Tetuanis regarded themselves as standardbearers in the war against Christian occupation. In 1791 Tetuanis supported Mulay Yazīd's insurgence against his father, Muḥammad III,

79. Plural of *amīn*: the inspectors of finances in the port.

80. *TT* 3:236.

81. See p. 76.

82. Captured by the Portuguese in 1415, Ceuta has been under foreign control ever since. It passed to Spain in 1580, was seized by the British in 1810, and returned to Spain at the close of the Napoleonic Wars. Tangier, the residence of the consuls, was held in suspicion by other Moroccans. See A. Rey, "Le Maroc et la question d'Alger," *Revue des deux mondes* 24 (1840): 618, where the Minister Ibn Idrīs is quoted as saying: "C'est la ville des chrétiens"; Rey continues, commenting: "Ce n'est plus le Maroc, ce n'est pas encore l'Espagne."

largely because of the latter's indifference to the Spanish presence in Ceuta. Yazīd laid siege to the Spanish enclave and, though he failed in his effort, kept the loyalty of Tetuan while the rest of Morocco scorned him.[83]

The attachment to militant Islam received encouragement from another source. From the late eighteenth century on, Tetuan was the focus of intense religious activity centered on the recently formed brotherhood of the Darqāwa, which began near Tetuan and spread from there to the rest of Morocco. The main lodge, or *zāwiya*, of the Darqāwa was the scene of pilgrimages, nightly gatherings, chanting, and other ecstatic practices associated with the worship of saintly folk that is characteristic of Moroccan Islam. Soon the influence of the Darqāwa brotherhood was paramount in the town. When Sultan Sulaymān actively opposed saint worship for political and religious reasons, he stirred local resentment. All segments of Tetuani society, including devotees of the brotherhoods, merchants, notables, and ulema, joined to support his rival Mulay Saʿīd. When in 1822 the Sultan abdicated in favor of his nephew Mulay ʿAbd ar-Raḥmān, ending the campaign against the brotherhoods, Tetuan is said to have rejoiced.[84]

This, then, is the background to aṣ-Ṣaffār's Tetuan: a city where side by side one found the luxurious refinement of Andalus and the crude roughness of the Rif; the urbane tastes of the rich merchant and the militancy of the holy warrior; the scholarly erudition of the mosque and the intense devotionalism of the *zāwiya*. These contrasts animated the world around Muḥammad aṣ-Ṣaffār and shaped his consciousness.

He began his education in Tetuan, studying "under the sheikhs

83. *TT* 3:191.

84. See *TT* 3:206–24, 258–65, for this episode in Tetuan's history. On the Darqāwa brotherhood, see *EI* 2, s.v. "Darḳāwa." Another cause of displeasure was the tight rein Sulaymān kept on foreign trade, which cut into the profits of local businessmen. J. Brignon et al., *Histoire du Maroc* (Paris, 1967), p. 281.

of his day," although their names are not known to us.[85] Then he went to Fes to "read the sciences" at the mosque-university of the Qarawiyīn in the company of his lifelong friend, Muḥammad ʿAzīmān, who later become the *qāḍī*, or judge, of Tetuan.[86] There was no fixed length to the course of study at the Qarawiyīn, but most students generally stayed only four or five years. Aṣ-Ṣaffār, however, remained in Fes more than eight years, immersing himself in the study of law, Hadith, and Arabic grammar with the noted scholar Ibn ʿAbd ar-Raḥmān al-Hujrātī.[87] He must also have taken part in the evening sessions held outside the mosque, where exceptional students studied rhetoric and style to gain full mastery of literary Arabic. When he finally returned to Tetuan in 1252/1836, he had earned the title of *faqīh*, showing that he had excelled in the sciences of law and jurisprudence.

Aṣ-Ṣaffār acquired more than the tools of the legist's trade in Fes. Having completed his course of study with distinction, he was ready to enter the upper ranks of Moroccan society, the *khāṣṣa*, or people of standing, as opposed to the *ʿāmma*, or common folk.[88] Association with the Fes scholarly establishment was an "intense

85. *TT* 7:78. Aṣ-Ṣaffār did not leave behind a *fahrasa*, or "spiritual autobiography," which would have listed the names of his teachers and the works he studied with them.

86. Ibid. The traditional education system in Morocco is the subject of a study by D. Eickelman, "The Art of Memory: Islamic Education and Its Social Reproduction," *Comparative Studies in Society and History* 20, 4 (1978): 485–516 (see bibliography cited).

87. Abū al-ʿAbbās b. Muḥammad b. ʿAbd ar-Raḥmān al-Filālī al-Hujrātī, *shaykh al-jamāʿa* (senior scholar) of the Qarawiyīn mosque, regarded as the most learned man of his generation. He died in 1303/1886. Muḥammad b. Jaʿfar al-Kattānī, *Salwat al-anfās wa-muḥādathāt al-akyās bi-man uqbir min al-ʿulamāʾ waṣ-ṣulaḥāʾ*, 3 vols. (Fes, 1898), 2:206, 3:9; Lakhdar, *La vie littéraire*, p. 357 note 193.

88. Terms used by both medieval and modern Arabic writers to broadly distinguish the elite from ordinary people. *EI* 2, s.v. "al-Khāṣṣa wa'l-ʿĀmma."

socializing experience"[89] that offered the young man of modest yet genteel background direct entry into the provincial urban elite. Armed with letters of recommendation from his prestigious teachers, aṣ-Ṣaffār quickly found a suitable position, and slipped easily into the dignified if modest life of a notary (*ʿadl*) in the law court of Tetuan, where he gave testimony about the character of witnesses and supervised the drawing up of legal contracts.[90] Notaries were esteemed by the community for their knowledge of the law, and respected for their integrity. Aṣ-Ṣaffār was highly regarded on both counts, according to Dāwud, and soon became one of the foremost notaries of Tetuan. He was also occupied with giving legal opinions, and occasionally substituted for the *qāḍī* in making decisions. His aspiration was to rise eventually to the position of judge in the court of Tetuan.

In addition to his duties as notary, aṣ-Ṣaffār taught in the mosque of the Upper Fountain in Tetuan, specializing in Hadith and jurisprudence.[91] He gave public lessons every morning in *muʿāmalāt*, or social relations, and every afternoon in *ʿibādāt*, or religious practice. No doubt these were years of contentment for him. Held in respect by his fellow Tetuanis, he immersed himself in the comfortable atmosphere of his native city, occupied with the tasks of teaching and administering justice. Aṣ-Ṣaffār also settled down in his family life,

89. Eickelman, "Art of Memory," p. 496.

90. The *ʿadl*'s function was to witness contracts between parties and notarize them with the *qāḍī*'s seal. He also knew legal language and could draw up documents correctly. This post was known as the *shahīd* in the eastern Muslim world. Dozy 2:103.

91. Among his pupils was the Sheikh Mufaḍḍal ʿAfīlāl, a well-known Tetuani of that time, who left a diary mentioning that he began reading the *Mukhtaṣar Khalīl* with aṣ-Ṣaffār in 1258/1842, the *Lāmiyāt al-Afʿāl* of Ibn Mālik in 1259/1843, and the *Alfiya* in 1260/1844. *TT* 7:78–79. The *Mukhtaṣar* was a "summary" of Imām Mālik's *Muwaṭṭa'* by Khalīl b. Isḥāq al-Jundī, *GAL S* 2:96; the *Lāmiyāt* is a work on philology by Jamāl ad-Dīn b. ʿAlī Ibn Mālik, *GAL S* 1:526; the *Alfiya*, also by Ibn Mālik, is a basic manual on grammar, *GAL S* 2:522.

marrying the Sharīfa al-Mubāraka, daughter of the muezzin; with her he had two daughters, both of whom married in Tetuan and whose descendents still live there.[92]

This calm and settled life was disrupted and eventually terminated by aṣ-Ṣaffār's association with the governor of Tetuan, Muḥammad Ashʿāsh, and after his death, with his son, ʿAbd al-Qādir Ashʿāsh. Reluctantly, the sources say, he was drawn away from his career in teaching and jurisprudence and pressed into the governor's service. Valued in this provincial setting for his thorough knowledge of Arabic language and Islamic law, he became Ashʿāsh's counselor, advising him on matters of legality and proper form. Aṣ-Ṣaffār's entry into his new vocation is reported as follows:

> The Sultan ordered all the governors of his domain to employ secretaries who were proficient in composition and the art of letter-writing. Letters had been coming to his court in the handwriting of country scholars who did not know the proper forms of address, were deficient in their responses, and showed no knowledge of grammar or language. One of these governors was Ḥājj ʿAbd al-Qādir Ashʿāsh of Tetuan, who asked the Faqīh aṣ-Ṣaffār to reply to the letters which came to him from the court. Aṣ-Ṣaffār at first refused, but Ashʿāsh persisted until he finally won him over. When [aṣ-Ṣaffār's] first letter arrived at the court, the Sultan was greatly pleased and said, "At last Ashʿāsh has taken on a secretary!"[93]

When the Sultan instructed Ashʿāsh to prepare for his voyage to France by choosing an *ʿālim* who could "attend to religious matters," Ashʿāsh naturally turned to Muḥammad aṣ-Ṣaffār. In France,

92. After aṣ-Ṣaffār left Tetuan he established a second household in Fes, where he married additional wives up to the Koranic limit of four. Several concubines are also named in his will.

93. *Anonymous Taqyīd*, unpaged. Aṣ-Ṣaffār actually began his employment in the time of Ashʿāsh's father, Muḥammad Ashʿāsh, according to ar-Ruhhūnī.

aṣ-Ṣaffār showed a lively curiosity and took detailed notes. He tasted the food, the luxury, the strangeness of European life, and marveled at its variety. Beaumier wrote to de Chasteau in Tangier that "the savant . . . is making the most of his time. He is gifted with an uncommon intellect and is carrying out research. He writes volumes."[94] In the pages of the *riḥla*, he comes alive and sharply into focus. We see him in a deeply private mode, stimulated by the beauty of women, contorting during his ritual ablutions, suffering with boredom at endless dinners. His opinions and ideas leap out from every page, some prosaic and conventional, others startlingly original. For him, the journey was more than a catalogue of curiosities—it was a transforming experience. But after fifty days abroad, he longed for Tetuan and home—"the seat of our happiness, the comfort of our daily lives, the pillow of our heads, the nest of our youth, the abode of our joy and vitality."[95]

In Tetuan once again, aṣ-Ṣaffār resumed his position in the judiciary and his teaching in the mosque, along with his secretarial duties for Ashʿāsh.[96] In addition to all this, he busied himself in writing his report to the Sultan. Once the onerous task was completed, he returned to obscurity, and for the next few years we hear nothing of him.

This phase came to an abrupt end in the month of Ramaḍān 1267/June 1850, when ʿAbd al-Qādir Ashʿāsh fell into royal disfavor and aṣ-Ṣaffār found himself in grave difficulty because of their association. During the feast of ʿĪd al-Kabīr,[97] the Sultan ordered

94. AAE/ADM/Voyage, Beaumier to de Chasteau, 29 January 1846.

95. See p. 78. cf. also Beaumier's comment: "The ambassador and his suite are . . . beginning to miss their country." AAE/ADM/Voyage, Beaumier to de Chasteau, 8 February 1846.

96. Dāwud found documents bearing aṣ-Ṣaffār's *ʿalāma*, or official signature, dating from 1263/1846, indicating that he continued to work in the judiciary after his return from France.

97. *ʿĪd al-Aḍḥā*, or *ʿĪd al-Qurbān*, celebrated on the 10th of Dhū al-Ḥijja, the day on which pilgrims to Mecca sacrifice in the valley of Mina. *SEI*, s.v. "ʿĪd al-Aḍḥā."

the governor of Tetuan to the court at Fes to present the customary gifts due on the occasion. Unsuspecting, Ashʿāsh made his way to Fes, taking Muḥammad aṣ-Ṣaffār with him. Dāwud recounts the ensuing events:

> When Ashʿāsh arrived in Fes with aṣ-Ṣaffār, his secretary, the two of them were invited by the Faqīh Sīdī al-Kabīr al-Fāsī to have lunch at his house.[98] But Ashʿāsh excused himself, saying that he had to go to the palace to present his gift to the Sultan. Aṣ-Ṣaffār remained with Sīdī al-Fāsī, and it was a blessing from God that he did so. For when it came time for the midafternoon prayers and he rose to leave, the master of the house detained him until the time of the gift-giving had passed. Finally, aṣ-Ṣaffār left the house and came to the Saffarin, where he heard the news about the seizing of Ashʿāsh and all those with him. Aṣ-Ṣaffār went directly to the Zāwiya Fāsiya to seek sanctuary.[99]

During his confinement in the *zāwiya*, aṣ-Ṣaffār tried to negotiate his release. Perhaps influential friends at court from his days in

98. ʿAbd al-Kabīr b. al-Majdūb al-Fāsī (d. 1296/1879), a descendent of a distinguished Fāsī family, *khaṭīb*, or preacher, in the sanctuary of Mulay Idrīs. E. Lévi-Provençal, *Les historiens des Chorfa* (Paris, 1922), p. 346. Dāwud's source was the Qāḍī Sīdī ʿAbd Ḥafīẓ al-Fāsī, grandson of Sīdī al-Kabīr. The gift, or *hadīya*, was a token of homage in money or goods presented to the Sultan by local officials on important occasions.

99. *TT* 7:79–80. Tombs of certain saints were "sacred zones" where asylum could be sought. The sources do not agree on aṣ-Ṣaffār's choice of sanctuary. Dāwud says he went to the Zāwiya Fāsiya, and the *Anonymous Taqyīd* agrees. Ar-Ruhhūnī assumed he fled to the shrine of Mulay Idrīs, the customary place of sanctuary in Fes. The Zāwiya Fāsiya is the religious lodge (*zāwiya*) of Sīdī ʿAbd al-Qādir al-Fāsī (d. 1680), located in the Qalqaliyīn quarter of Fes. N. Cigar, *Muhammad al-Qadiri's 'Nashr al-Mathani': The Chronicles* (London, 1981), p. 132 and note 7; Lévi-Provençal, *Les historiens*, pp. 264–65.

The Saffarin is a small square in the heart of the Fes medina near the Library of the Qarawiyīn, named for the many metalworkers (*ṣaffārīn*) there.

Fes intervened for him; perhaps the Sultan himself remembered the author of the travel account. In any case, aṣ-Ṣaffār was soon given a safe-conduct to leave the sanctuary. Not only was he pardoned for his ties with Ashʿāsh, but he was invited to join the Sultan's entourage.[100]

The fate of ʿAbd al-Qādir Ashʿāsh was less fortunate. While aṣ-Ṣaffār remained in the safety of the *zāwiya*, Ashʿāsh was taken off to prison along with his entire family. All their possessions were seized and sold, the profits going to the Makhzan. The reasons for their ruination are not entirely clear, but Dāwud reproduces a detailed inventory of confiscated property showing that the family's resources were substantial and no doubt had aroused the cupidity of the Sultan.[101] Eventually Ashʿāsh was released from prison and allowed to return to Tetuan, where he lived quietly. In 1862 Sultan Muḥammad IV reappointed Ashʿāsh as governor; but soon he was in difficulty again, and had to be removed from his post. Ashʿāsh spent the rest of his life as a minor functionary in Meknes, where he died in 1282/1865–66. The once-proud Ashʿāsh family never regained the prominence it once had held in Tetuan affairs.[102]

The second phase of aṣ-Ṣaffār's life, his period of government service, is the most elusive from the biographer's point of view. During his years in the Makhzan, his life becomes veiled in secrecy, his own individuality engulfed in the larger entity of the Sultan, the court, and the cadres of functionaries clustered around the center. Outwardly, every aspect of court life was subject to strict rules of protocol, the *qāʿida*, which governed all behavior from the pouring of tea to the greeting of foreign embassies. Coming from far-flung parts of the country, the officials who joined the Makhzan were molded by the *qāʿida* into one cohesive social category. Each left

100. *TT* 7:79. Dāwud says the Wazīr Ibn Idrīs "looked favorably" on the letters of appeal and helped gain his release.

101. *TT* 3:303, 309–34.

102. *TT* 6:11; 88–91.

behind his regional loyalties and became a new type devoted to the royal institution alone. Their isolation from the rest of the population was heightened by their rootlessness, for the Sultan and his court assumed a nomadic existence, moving from one place to another, sometimes housed in one of the Sultan's palaces, at other times living under canvas.

In return, the court official received certain benefits. He was relieved of all worries about his own upkeep, and given free food and lodging. In the time of Sultan ʿAbd ar-Raḥmān, even the highest officials were unsalaried. In theory, they were dependent on the Sultan for everything, awaiting presents of houses, clothing, property, and even money. In practice, however, they used the power of their office to increase their personal wealth, and the life of the high official was generally one of comfort and luxury.[103]

The attractions of court life would have been difficult to resist, even if one were given a choice. As it happened, aṣ-Ṣaffār had none; deprived of his patron in Tetuan, dispirited by his period of confinement, he decided to throw his lot with the Makhzan. For the next thirty years he lived in the innermost circle, his individual actions woven into a larger tapestry, the strands of his life nearly inseparable from the rich fabric of the whole.

When Muḥammad aṣ-Ṣaffār came to the court, he was not integrated into the ranks of secretaries engaged in endless letter-writing. Instead, the Sultan entrusted him with tutoring the royal princes, including the future Sultan Ḥasan I. In return he was provided "with meals from the Sultan's table both morning and night." This arrangement placed him within the family circle of the Sultan, and in a short time the extent of aṣ-Ṣaffār's talents became clear. The relationship between them developed as follows:

103. Descriptions of nineteenth-century Moroccan court life can be found in E. Aubin, pseud. (Léon Descos), *Morocco of To-day* (London, 1906), ch. 12; E. Michaux-Bellaire, "Au palais du Sultan marocain," *RMM* 5, 8 (August 1908): 647–62; and by the same author, *EI* 1, s.v. "Makhzen." The best Arabic source is ʿAbd ar-Raḥmān Ibn Zaydān, *Al-ʿizz waṣ-ṣawla fī maʿālim nuẓum ad-dawla*, 2 vols. (Rabat, 1929–33), vol. 1.

> Sometimes the Sultan himself was present at these lessons with the royal princes, that is, the sons and grandsons of the Sultan, and he would ask [aṣ-Ṣaffār] to lead the prayer if his ranking prayer-leader was not present. Also he would spend much time with him in conversation. Then he made him his special secretary to carry out the duties which he wished to confer only on someone in whom he had perfect confidence and trust.[104]

Advancing from teacher to confidential secretary, aṣ-Ṣaffār rose finally to the rank of First Minister (*wazīr al-awwal*) at the end of the reign of Sultan ʿAbd ar-Raḥmān. This was the highest position to which an official of the Makhzan could aspire.[105] His task was to sit at the Sultan's side, executing his orders and staying in touch by correspondence with local officials. Although the relationship between the Sultan and his Minister varied, one fact is clear: the Minister had to enjoy the full confidence of the ruler in order to remain in his post. The most telling insight into aṣ-Ṣaffār's character is that for nearly three decades he remained at the center of power, a remarkable record of durability in the volatile world of Makhzan politics.

When aṣ-Ṣaffār became First Minister, he lost no time in eliminating rivals and taking advantage of his new position. According to Muḥammad Gharrīṭ, there was at that time a chief of protocol[106] who was "all-powerful and kept the monopoly of influence for himself. He took charge of all matters of supply, as well as the sources

104. *TT* 7:81, 92.

105. The sources do not agree about the date of this appointment, varying by as much as two years, because aṣ-Ṣaffār was filling the duties of the office informally long before his official appointment began. *TT* 7:80–81.

106. *Qāʾid al-mashwar*. The *mashwar* is the large galleried court at the entrance to the royal palace. This official was head of the external palace guard, and master of ceremonies at official events such as military reviews and the greeting of ambassadors. Ibn Zaydān, *ʿIzz* 1:133–34 and glossary, p. 412.

of income and expenditures, without referring to aṣ-Ṣaffār." Aṣ-Ṣaffār complained to the Sultan, who removed the offending official. Thereafter, Gharrīṭ continues, aṣ-Ṣaffār took over, "milking the udder and selecting the seed, amassing his wealth in Tetuan."[107]

The sources tell us little about the remainder of aṣ-Ṣaffār's career in government, and he emerges into view only fleetingly. In the summer of 1859, for example, Sultan ʿAbd ar-Raḥmān was failing, and the succession was in doubt. The anchor of the Makhzan was Muḥammad aṣ-Ṣaffār. "Two English doctors were called to Meknes for consultation in August," the French archives report, "and pronounced him close to the end. The Minister aṣ-Ṣaffār was the real master of affairs."[108] Aṣ-Ṣaffār was also instrumental in assuring the smooth election of his successor, Sultan Muḥammad IV (1859–73), who was an advocate of reform.[109]

107. Gharrīṭ, *Fawāṣil al-jumān*, pp. 70–71. The *Anonymous Taqyīd*, on the other hand, cites numerous examples of aṣ-Ṣaffār's honesty. Aṣ-Ṣaffār became wealthy during his service with the Makhzan. His Tetuan residence, acquired later in life, is beautifully decorated with fine tiles and carved woodwork. His position provided opportunities for gain, as it was customary for plaintiffs to give the *wazīr ash-shikāyāt* (Minister of Complaints, see note 110 below) gifts of money "proportionate to the importance of their claim," according to Michaux-Bellaire; "Un rouage du gouvernement marocain: La beniqat ech chikaïat de Moulay Abd el Hafid," *RMM* 5, 6 (June 1908): 252.

Aṣ-Ṣaffār's will—a document measuring some 30 cm wide and 6 m long—lists all of his heirs, property, debts, and assets. It indicates that he left over thirty pieces of property in Tetuan, Fes, Zerhoun, and Marrakesh worth 42,883 *riyāls*. He also left 2,600 *riyāls* in debts, which were forgiven after his death by order of Sultan Ḥasan I. Aṣ-Ṣaffār family archives, Tetuan.

108. Miège, *Le Maroc* 2:359 note 4.

109. Ibid. Later, in 1873, aṣ-Ṣaffār was said to have been instrumental in quelling the "tanners' revolt" in Fes, dissuading Sultan Ḥasan I from bombarding the town by saying: "Fes is the crown jewel of Morocco; if we destroy it, where will we find another?" *TT* 7:89; al-Manūnī, *Maẓāhir* 1:299–300.

One of the new Sultan's objectives was to rationalize the state structure, and alongside his First Minister he created another position, the Minister of Complaints (*wazīr ash-shikāyāt*), who acted as his eyes and ears in responding to grievances from the local level. To this post he appointed Muḥammad aṣ-Ṣaffār. The new Minister's task was to receive all kinds of complaints, answering some himself "according to the Sultan's will," referring others to the ruler. Once a week, the Sultan in person would hear plaintiffs, affirming his traditional role of chief judge and final court of appeal.[110] We have a glimpse of the conduct of the office from Ibn Zaydān's *Itḥāf*:

> The custom of the sovereign in apportioning the days of the week was to receive on Sunday those who had a complaint. The Minister delegated to hear the grievances would come forward with a register of plaintiffs and their complaint . . . listing their name, their *nisba*,[111] their place of residence, and a statement of the claim. The Sultan would take the register and call them up one by one, examining each until he had seen them all. . . . He followed the claimant's problem closely, sorting out his words until the truth came clear; then he acted accordingly. All the while the Minister of Complaints stood behind the Sultan, holding a similar list.[112]

Aṣ-Ṣaffār remained in this position throughout the reign of Muḥammad IV and into that of his successor, Sultan Ḥasan I, until his death in 1298/1881.

110. See Laroui, *Origines*, p. 113; Mohamed Lahbabi, *Le gouvernement marocain à l'aube du XXe siècle* (Rabat, 1958), pp. 173–81. The Ministry of Complaints was created to relieve the social distress that mounted after the Spanish invasion of Tetuan in 1859. On this office, see Ibn Zaydān, *'Izz* 1:50–54; al-Manūnī, *Maẓāhir*, 2nd ed. (Casablanca, 1985), 1:43; and note 107 above.

111. A name denoting one's family, tribe, or place of origin.

112. This account is a description of the office under Ḥasan I, who succeeded Muḥammad IV. *Itḥāf* 2:516.

The loyalty and discretion that marked aṣ-Ṣaffār's career at its outset were sustained to the end. Unlike others who fell athwart the royal pleasure and ended their years in banishment, aṣ-Ṣaffār's last days were lived in the same closeness to the center as his first. Despite his growing age, he still followed the Sultan's entourage on its travels around Morocco. On one of these expeditions, as the royal party passed through the remote mountain area between Fes and Marrakesh, he became ill. Mulay Ḥassan's concern for him was so great, it is said, that he gave him his own litter, because the minister was too sick to ride. When they reached the region of the Ibn Ziduḥ clan near Tadla, aṣ-Ṣaffār died.[113] There the Sultan ordered him prepared for burial, and attended the prayers for him. Then his body was returned to the Sultan's litter and carried to Marrakesh, where aṣ-Ṣaffār was buried in the garden of the shrine of Sīdī Yūsuf Bin ʿAlī, outside of Bāb Aghmāt, one of the great gates of Marrakesh.[114]

The final burial near the saint was performed at the order of the Sultan, as a reward for a life spent in the service of the Makhzan. Paradoxically, it was aṣ-Ṣaffār's devotion to the institution he served so long that kept his name alive, while his achievements as a travel writer were soon forgotten. His biographers poured his life into a seamless mold of pious virtue, smoothing over the rough textures that made it unique. No one makes more than passing reference to his trip to France, with the exception of Muḥammad Dāwud;[115] and no one speculates on the effect the journey may have had on the rest of his life or work. Nor do we learn from them if his foreign experiences influenced Makhzan policy, although he lived in an age

113. The Ibn Ziduḥ were an important family who supplied governors for the Tadla region.

114. Sīdī Yūsuf b. ʿAlī, a Sufi saint of the twelfth century, one of the seven patron saints of Marrakesh. G. Deverdun, *Marrakech: Des origines à 1912*, 2 vols. (Rabat, 1959–66): vol. 1, pp. 378–79; vol. 2, plate 39.

115. Dāwud's account of the embassy is in *TT* 3:295–309. Al-Murrākushī erroneously said the *riḥla* was to England, a mistake corrected in the Bin Manṣūr edition. See *Al-iʿlām* 7:35 note 1.

when reform along Western lines was the paramount issue of the day.

We do learn that the skills of observation and elegance of expression evident in the travel account were also qualities needed in the Makhzan, and that the intelligence and tact that helped him make his way in France were also virtues in the palace of the Sultan. But in order to discover the singularity of the man and of his experience, we must turn to the *riḥla* itself. Just as an account of aṣ-Ṣaffār's life complements our understanding of the voyage, the reading of the voyage deepens our knowledge of the man.

Meanings in the Encounter

The significance of aṣ-Ṣaffār's journey to France lies both in its uniqueness and in its universality. In the pages of the *riḥla*, a mute voice from the past comes alive in all its nuances, giving us entry into a world otherwise inaccessible. If the value of the travel account lies in its literalness and its "continual reference to actuality,"[116] then here we find ourselves in the presence of the real. The fact that illuminates, the impression based on a clairvoyant naïveté, contain within them the humanness of the account. Given our limited knowledge of the times, and the absence of other voices that speak with equal clarity, it is the particularity of the *riḥla* that enlarges our understanding.

But the voyage also strikes chords that go beyond the concrete, especially when the text is examined through prisms other than the strictly historical. In this section, I shall propose ways of interpreting aṣ-Ṣaffār's *riḥla* that evoke deeper levels of meaning. Anthropologists have had insights into the nature of the travel experience,

116. Paul Fussell, *Abroad: British Literary Traveling between the Wars* (New York, 1980), p. 203. It will be evident the extent to which Fussell's critical work has influenced my own reading of aṣ-Ṣaffār.

and literary critics have elaborated on the structure and content of its narrative expression; both inform my effort.

Critic Paul Fussell has said that travel literature is a genre that bridges two modes of perception: first, the actual, nonfanciful, physical world; second, an imaginative mode, where the specific becomes the general, fact becomes figure, and observation is transformed into vision. "A travel book is like a poem in giving universal significance to a local texture."[117] His subject is British travel writing between the two world wars, but his comment applies with equal force to the *riḥla* of Muhammad aṣ-Ṣaffār, suggesting that the best examples of this genre, regardless of their particular cultural matrix, possess corresponding qualities of universality.

For most of us, travel to distant places is a magical and transforming life event. Anthropologists have long noted the effect travel has on human perceptions and behavior, and especially its ability to transport us out of the ordinary, or "profane," into a time and space that become endowed with "sacred" qualities.[118] Whether for pleasure or duty, travel is an interlude that interposes itself into daily life, separating the humdrum from the marvelous; indeed, the very alternation between the two states of ordinary and extraordinary can become a measure of the passage of time itself. One way we count the stages of our lives, says Nelson Graburn, is through fluctuations between the sacred and the profane. Travel helps define time for us, by composing life into segments marked by rituals of leaving and returning.[119]

117. Ibid., p. 214.

118. Nelson H. H. Graburn cites the writings of Durkeim, Mauss, Leach, and Van Gennep as important in shaping concepts of the sacred and the profane in relation to travel. See his "Tourism: The Sacred Journey," in Valene Smith, ed., *Hosts and Guests: The Anthropology of Tourism*, 2nd ed. (Philadelphia, 1989), pp. 24, 26. Also V. Turner and E. Turner, *Image and Pilgrimage in Christian Culture: Anthropological Perspectives* (New York, 1978), ch. 1.

119. Graburn, "Tourism," pp. 24–25.

These two events, the wrenching departure and the ecstatic return, bracket the voyage and transport it to the level of the uncommon. Fussell notices the "tripartite" structure of the travel account, in which the protagonist, like a romantic hero, leaves the familiar and wanders into the unknown: "First, the setting out, the disjunction from the familiar; second, the trials of initiation and adventure; and third, the hero's return and reintegration into society."[120] The voyage is like a "microlife, with a bright beginning, a middle, and an end . . . marked by rituals that thrust us irreversibly down life's path."[121]

In aṣ-Ṣaffār's *riḥla*, the setting out from the ordinary, and the transition to a heightened intellectual and emotional state, come through with special clarity. Although the Moroccan scholar is an unlikely figure for a heroic adventurer, he nevertheless undergoes an extraordinary experience, and his words give an indication of his excitation. On leaving Tetuan, he aches at the parting: "O my splendid Tetuan," he poetizes, "will fate allow us to come home, and will we meet again . . . after the crashing waves, will we be reunited?"[122] The pain of separation is compounded by his fear of the sea. The ocean voyage is more than a passage to the unknown, it is a flirtation with death, and here the emotion is also archetypal, for often in the back of the traveler's mind is the fear of dying far from home.

The return is also fraught with difficulties. Stepping back into the familiar, the traveler is caught in emotional ambivalence. Coming home not only means rejoining missed loved ones; it also means returning to the constraints of normal life and leaving behind the magic of the journey.[123] In the *riḥla* there is no description of the homecoming; nevertheless, there is an emotional climax. On the final page of the manuscript, aṣ-Ṣaffār takes leave of France by say-

120. Fussell, *Abroad*, p. 208.
121. Graburn, "Tourism," p. 26.
122. See p. 78.
123. Graburn, "Tourism," p. 27.

ing: "May God forgive me for what my hands have committed, for the repulsive abominations my eyes have witnessed, and for the abhorrent blasphemies and confused mutterings of the misguided that my ears have heard."[124] This remark represents closure: it is both an acknowledgment of the wonders seen, and a disavowal of association with them. With it, aṣ-Ṣaffār consciously breaks away from the enchantment of the sacred experience, and begins the reentry into the ordinary.

The threefold structure of the journey elevates it into "an allegory of human life itself,"[125] and like life, it has moments high and low. Some of what aṣ-Ṣaffār saw in France concerns the mundane, but much also relates to his meeting with the strange, the bizarre, and the unexpected. The novelty of the subject is the source of its difficulty as well as its fascination. In the culture from which aṣ-Ṣaffār came, the unprecedented was suspect, the new could be dangerous. Franz Rosenthal notes that, in the manuscript age, "the ultimate success of new ideas which did not fit in with dominant systems of thought was . . . uncertain. If a new idea did not find the approval of a comparatively large group of scholars in a comparatively short interval of time, it was likely to be buried in a library, with an infinitesimal chance of subsequent rediscovery."[126] For one who had to report on so much that was unfamiliar, the issue of credibility loomed large. In order for his ideas to be accepted, they had to be cast in forms that were recognized and approved by the keepers of tradition. Fearing that his report would be rejected by his learned peers, aṣ-Ṣaffār knew that to make the new wine most palatable, it had to be served in old bottles.

Other realities weighed on him as well. It may be recalled that

124. See p. 221.

125. Fussell, *Abroad*, p. 209.

126. Franz Rosenthal, *The Technique and Approach of Muslim Scholarship*, *Analecta Orientalia* 24 (Rome, 1947), p. 57. Such was the fate of aṣ-Ṣaffār's manuscript, suggesting it may have been labeled "secret" by the Sultan. Laroui, *Origines*, p. 215.

the Sultan was interested in the project, thus raising it to a higher level of seriousness. The report would be scrutinized and discussed at court, and perhaps would be read by Mulay ʿAbd ar-Raḥmān himself. Some in the entourage would be friends from student days; others would be related through family or patronage; all would be men of his own social class. In order not to disgrace himself or his patron Ashʿāsh, he had to perform well. His account had to be endowed with qualities of erudition, respect, and ideological correctness that would commend it to the inner circle; moreover, it had to have the accuracy, literary elegance, and proper form expected from a man of letters. It is not surprising that aṣ-Ṣaffār struggled with the task.

What elements of style gave it the "right" qualities? First of all, there was aṣ-Ṣaffār's decision to cast the report as a *riḥla*, a time-honored literary form having roots deep in the classical tradition. While travel accounts have been written in many places and times, the genre flourished to a luxuriant degree in Spain and the Maghrib. Devout in their faith, yet distant from its sources in Arabia, Maghribis were dutiful in performing the pilgrimage, or *ḥājj*, to the holy cities of Mecca and Medina. The pilgrimage account, by which the pilgrim shared his adventure with others, was the archetypal sacred story: the invocations to God, the stages of the journey, the dangers passed, the achievement of the distant goal, were recognized points in a formalized narrative structure. Reaching the Holy Places was the emotional high point in which all events in the journey were subsumed; its attainment gave form and purpose to the voyage and rendered it meaningful in a way that a simple chronological account could not. In time, the genre of the *riḥla* expanded to include accounts of journeys for other purposes, such as study or diplomacy, but the most perfect model for travel and its narration remained the pilgrimage to the Holy Places of the Hijaz.

The Maghribi tradition of the *riḥla* was a part of aṣ-Ṣaffār's cultural apparatus, providing the logical form in which to cast his travel experience. More important, it was also known to his readers—so much so that reading the Prologue of his text, which recalls the opening words of the pilgrimage account, must have been as reassuring as the incantation of a sacred text.[127]

But here there is a problem. The highest and purest form of journey is to the sources of Islam, to the holiest shrines of the faith. A journey to the West, on the other hand, is an inversion: it is a voyage to the unholy and the impure. In the West, the Muslim traveler was subjected to the rules and temptations of a society that was at its core corrupt. There, it was a trial to carry out the duties of the faith; there too, the threat of pollution was omnipresent. The problem for aṣ-Ṣaffār (as well as for other Muslim travelers to Europe) was how to shake off the clinging odor of the impure, and to justify the undertaking to those left behind.

Aṣ-Ṣaffār was conscious of this problem, and his solution is to

127. On Arabic *riḥlāt* see M. Hadj-Sadok, "Le genre 'Rihla,' " *Bulletin des études arabes* 8, 40 (1948): 195–206; *GAL S* 3, index, s.v. *riḥla*. Also *EI* 2, s.vv. "Djughrāfiyā," "Ḥadjdj." On travel to the West, see B. Lewis, *The Muslim Discovery of Europe* (New York, 1982); I. Abu-Lughod, *The Arab Rediscovery of Europe: A Study in Cultural Encounters* (Princeton, 1963); and Henri Pérès, *L'Espagne vue par les voyageurs musulmans de 1610 à 1930* (Paris, 1937), a useful, if dated, overview. On Muslim travel, see the *Dictionary of the Middle Ages*, vol. 12, s.v. "Travel and Transport, Islamic," by Richard Bulliet, and the magisterial work by André Miguel, *La géographie humaine du monde musulman jusqu'au milieu du 11ᵉ siècle*, 4 vols. (Paris, 1967–88), vol. 1, ch. 4 and vol. 2, ch. 7. Also see note 25 above.

For Moroccan travel accounts, see ʿAbd as-Salām Ibn Sūda, *Dalīl muʾarrikh al-Maghrib al-aqṣā*, 2 vols. (Casablanca, 1960–65), 2:333–70. He mentions about 240 works, mostly unpublished accounts of pilgrimages to Mecca. Other sources are M. al-Fāsī, "Ar-riḥla as-safariya al-maghribiya," *Al-Bayyina* 1, 6 (October 1962): 11–24; "Ar-raḥḥāla al-maghāriba wa-āthāruhum," *Daʿwat al-ḥaqq*, 2, 4 (January 1959): 22–25, by the same author; the introduction to *Al-iksīr fī fikāk al-asīr*, by M. b. ʿUthmān al-Miknāsī, ed. M. al-Fāsī (Rabat, 1965), and Lakhdar, *La vie littéraire*, passim. Also M. al-Manūnī, *Al-maṣādir al-ʿarabiya li-tārīkh al-Maghrib*, part 1 (Casablanca, 1983) and part 2 (Mohamedia, 1989); see the indices s.v. *riḥla*. Published Moroccan *riḥlat* are indicated in my bibliography by an asterisk (*).

invoke the formula of *maṣāliḥ al-umma*, "the welfare of the Islamic people." The journey, according to this argument, merits the approval of the community because it conforms to religious values of protecting the faithful. Aṣ-Ṣaffār says that the Sultan dispatched the mission because he was "mindful of his duty to watch over the . . . affairs of all our people"; indeed, he goes on to say that the protection of the Islamic community has always been a concern of its leaders. "The Prophet . . . sent out the best from among his companions on missions, providing an example followed by the rightly guided caliphs and imams."[128] No higher authority than this—the precedent set by the early followers of the faith—could be invoked to set a seal of approval on the venture. The concurrence of the community in the voyage is an essential element in travel, says Graburn, so that the expenditure of time and effort that could be devoted to other social purposes is justified.[129] By associating his effort with the sacred pilgrimage, and by invoking the beneficial results of diplomacy in the past, aṣ-Ṣaffār seeks approval by locating the undertaking within the mainstream of a long tradition.

Although aṣ-Ṣaffār had no prior direct experience of France, he most certainly had preconceived notions about Europe from others who had traveled, and from his own knowledge of social organization in general. His education not only provided him with the literary model of the *riḥla*, it also gave him concepts about the way society is structured, derived in large measure from the writing of Ibn Khaldūn, the fourteenth-century Maghribi historian, philosopher, and social theorist. Ibn Khaldūn's *Muqaddima* was the rich and abundant source from which aṣ-Ṣaffār drew his ideas about geography, society, and the nature of political authority.[130]

128. See p. 76.

129. Graburn, "Tourism," p. 28.

130. References to the *Muqaddima* are from F. Rosenthal, *The Muqaddimah: An Introduction to History*, 3 vols. (Princeton, 1967). Vol. 1 contains a biography. Ibn Khaldūn's theory of the state is summarized in E. I. J. Rosenthal, *Political Thought in Medieval Islam* (Cambridge, 1968), ch. 4; see Ali Oumlil, *L'histoire et son discourse* (Rabat, 1982), for a Moroccan perspective.

Ibn Khaldūn was concerned with culture (*ʿumrān*) and the way it manifested itself in society. For him, the most efficient way for mankind to live is in groups, and the survival and prosperity of the group is dependent on the degree of cooperation among its members. When aṣ-Ṣaffār says France is a "center of civilization," he sees the Khaldunian ideal in action—large numbers of people working industriously and in harmony. Aṣ-Ṣaffār also adopted Ibn Khaldūn's notions of political power. The Maghribi philosopher believed that men in their natural state are selfish and aggressive, and have to be restrained by force. The well-run society is characterized by a strong king and army, and sound finances to support them. Aṣ-Ṣaffār's concern for military and money matters in the pages of the *riḥla* is not only a reflection of Morocco's predicament; it is also a projection of his belief, based on his reading of Ibn Khaldūn, that they are the twin pillars of the secure state.

Ibn Khaldūn's theories of social organization provided aṣ-Ṣaffār with a blueprint for the productive society. The landscapes filled with houses and buildings, the workshops humming with activity, the plowed and cultivated fields that aṣ-Ṣaffār saw in France were signs of the advanced civilization he recognized from the pages of the *Muqaddima*. Even the Sultan's "speech from the throne" on New Year's Day is an expression of Khaldunian notions of royal authority.[131] These ideas were part of the body of tradition transmitted from one generation of Moroccan scholars to the next in the restricted milieu of higher learning; familiar to the well-educated, they reverberated and evoked recognition in the minds of those who read the *riḥla*. The invocation of his Maghribi predecessor allowed aṣ-Ṣaffār a certain amount of latitude; by casting his vision of France in the Khaldunian mode, he could express admiration for the French and their achievements, while staying within the bounds of the culturally permissible. He was able to do this because French society, at least in its outward aspects, seemed to him to conform to a fourteenth-century Islamic idea of the well-run state.

131. See p. 181.

If Ibn Khaldūn contributed the scaffolding for aṣ-Ṣaffār's narrative, it was aṭ-Ṭahṭāwī who provided material for construction. One oblique mention of the Egyptian writer is all that is made, but a comparison of the two voyages shows that aṣ-Ṣaffār borrowed much from the Egyptian.[132] Whether aṣ-Ṣaffār read aṭ-Ṭahṭāwī's *Takhlīṣ* while he was still in France, or found a copy of it in Morocco after his return, is impossible to tell. But at some point the book lay open before him, and he took extensive notes. Similarities in style, format, details, even turns of phrase betray a borrowing that would be deemed plagiaristic by Western standards, but in the Islamic tradition merely indicates confidence in a reliable source.

An *ʿālim* like aṣ-Ṣaffār, aṭ-Ṭahṭāwī fulfilled a similar role: to provide spiritual guidance to a group of Muslim laymen in a foreign culture. The two men were steeped in the same sources and shared a worldview; although they never met, they enjoyed a spiritual kinship that made aṣ-Ṣaffār's borrowing that much simpler. Aṣ-Ṣaffār esteemed aṭ-Ṭahṭāwī for yet another reason. The Egyptian had spent nearly five years in Paris, the Moroccan only fifty days. By his own admission, aṣ-Ṣaffār was deficient in his knowledge of

132. Rifāʿa Rāfiʿ aṭ-Ṭahṭāwī (1801–73) was born in Ṭahṭa in Upper Egypt, and studied at al-Azhar. In 1826 he was sent to Paris by the Khedive Muḥammad ʿAlī to serve as *imām* (prayer-leader) to a group of Egyptian students. He stayed in Paris for five years, learned fluent French, and summarized his impressions of France in his *Takhlīṣ al-ibrīz fī talkhīṣ Bārīz*, printed at Bulaq shortly after his return. The book enjoyed great popularity and was translated into Turkish; it was also known to Moroccan literati. A recent French translation is by Anouar Louca, *L'or de Paris: Relation de voyage, 1826–1831* (Paris, 1988). On aṭ-Ṭahṭāwī see A. Hourani, *Arabic Thought in the Liberal Age, 1798–1939* (London, 1967), pp. 69–83; J. Heyworth-Dunne, "Rifāʿah Badawī Rāfiʿ aṭ-Ṭahṭāwī: The Egyptian Revivalist," *BSOAS* 9 (1937–39): 961–67, 10 (1940–42): 399–415; A. Badawī, *Rifāʿa Rāfiʿ aṭ-Ṭahṭāwī*, 2nd ed. (Cairo, 1959); Abu-Lughod, *Arab Rediscovery*; and Anouar Louca, *Voyageurs et écrivains égyptiens en France au XIXᵉ siècle* (Paris, 1970), ch. 2. Aṣ-Ṣaffār's mention of aṭ-Ṭahṭāwī (as "Rifāʿa Effendi") comes at the beginning of ch. 3 of the present work.

French society. What he lacked in his own experience he sought in aṭ-Ṭahṭāwī.

However, there are limitations to the similarity between the two accounts, for circumstances made them quite different. When aṭ-Ṭahṭāwī left Egypt for France in 1826, the movement for reform in his country was already well under way, backed by the iron will of the Khedive Muḥammad ʿAlī.[133] Patterns of change taking shape in Egypt were not yet considered in Morocco, nor would they be for decades. Many of the Egyptian's comments on French philosophy, politics, social mores, and scientific learning were incomprehensible to the Moroccan, and certain topics mentioned in the *Takhlīṣ* are simply absent in aṣ-Ṣaffār's account. It should be recalled that aṭ-Ṭahṭāwī was sent by a leadership on the offensive; aṣ-Ṣaffār was dispatched by a leadership in retreat. Aṭ-Ṭahṭāwī's aim was to be an advocate for reform; aṣ-Ṣaffār's intention was merely to observe and report. Aṭ-Ṭahṭāwī's *riḥla* was commissioned by an admiring Khedive; aṣ-Ṣaffār's was read by a limited coterie within the Makhzan whose attitude toward change was dubious at best. In the final analysis, these divergent factors determined the shape of each work and made them different.

Aṣ-Ṣaffār's singularity stems not only from background conditions, but also from the immediacy of his observations. He saw France through the lens of a value system that favored knowledge gained from direct, "lived" experience over knowledge gained from books, and his voyage is filled with vivid firsthand impressions. The notion of personal observation, or *ʿiyān*, meant learning without mediation; it was considered the purest form of knowing by the classical traveler.[134] Aṣ-Ṣaffār invokes this principle explicitly and

133. On the Egyptian reform movement, see A. L. as-Sayyid Marsot, *A Short History of Modern Egypt* (Cambridge, 1985), pp. 54–66.

134. "The transmission of things one has observed with one's own eyes is something more comprehensive and complete than the transmission of information and things one has learned about. A habit that is the result of [personal observation] is more perfect and firmly rooted." *Muqaddimah*

demonstrates it by example. He tells us that "there is no other way of obtaining useful information except by mixing with people,"[135] and in his narrative he regales us with details to convince us he was actually there. Even when the function of the thing described is not fully understood, it is depicted in full, for the fineness of detail is a value in itself, and an apprehension of truth. Thus the tedious explanations of arcane scientific experiments, the precise counting of candles in the dining room, the faithful rendering of the structure of a bridge: aṣ-Ṣaffār reports these details, not so that the thing itself may be replicated, but rather to assure us of the reality of his presence. Although conformity to tradition was still the main criterion for truth in aṣ-Ṣaffār's milieu, his emphasis on the individuality of his own experience signals the beginning of a new, more realistic literary style, which brought together the teller and the thing told more intimately than in the past. Not merely mind-numbing minutiae, these details are an assertion of the self, reminding us of the authenticity of the encounter.[136]

Moreover, aṣ-Ṣaffār makes careful distinctions between what he sees and what "they" tell him, which further enhances his credibility. "They claim," "they say," and similar phrases indicate that the information to follow is at second hand, perhaps from an interpreter, and we immediately take it in with a jaundiced eye. He realized that his hosts manipulated what they showed. Kept within their control, the Moroccans were led from one tourist site to another in order to receive "the best impression of the grandeur and

2:346. See also Eickelman, "Art of Memory," p. 501 note 20, and A. Miquel, *Géographie humaine* 1:135 and passim, for references showing the importance of "lived truth" for the medieval traveler.

135. See p. 77.

136. See, for example, al-Ghassānī's *Iftikāk*, in which descriptions of the observed world are minimalist as compared with aṣ-Ṣaffār. For relevant discussion of the growth of realism in English letters in the eighteenth-century novel, see Ian Watt, *The Rise of the Novel: Studies in Defoe, Richardson and Fielding* (Berkeley, 1957), ch. 1.

power of France."[137] Aṣ-Ṣaffār resents the long, uncomfortable detour to Toulon in order to see the French fleet, and he chafes with chagrin at the military display on the Champ-de-Mars. A hierarchy of truth is implicit in the text, with direct observation at the highest level, transmitted knowledge from Muslim sources in the middle, and information from his Christian hosts at the bottom. Aṣ-Ṣaffār is deft at making explicit the precise value of each.

Despite his ardor for truth, aṣ-Ṣaffār can only give us a partial impression of France. He was limited by what he saw and what he understood. Like aṭ-Ṭahṭāwī, France for him was largely Paris, a city of the salon, the boulevard, and the *spectacle*.[138] He saw little of the seamy underside of Parisian life—the poverty and suffering, the armies of destitute workers and prostitutes, the shocking inequalities between rich and poor—that animated the contemporary literature of social protest.[139] For him, Paris was populated by chaste women and industrious men who labored in the interests of a just and well-ordered state. Paris was the place of magic, the symbolic as well as physical locus where the purpose of the journey would be fulfilled. By idealizing Paris, aṣ-Ṣaffār elevated it to the sacred, and intensified the dialogue with home that forms a distinct subtext of his journey.

For the alternation between the sacred and the profane in travel

137. The quote is from Guizot's instructions to Pourcet and Urbain, AAE/CPM 15/23 November 1845. The idea is stated even more clearly by Louis-Philippe in his letter to Mulay ʿAbd ar-Raḥmān summing up the visit: "My ministers were ordered to show [the ambassador] whatever we had in the way of wonders (*ʿajāʾib*) in art and industry." DAR 17575, 13 February 1846.

138. The French Orientalist Silvestre de Sacy observed that aṭ-Ṭahṭāwī judged all the French "d'après les habitants de Paris." Louca, *L'or*, p. 218.

139. In 1842 Eugene Sue's *Les mystères de Paris* was serialized in the *Journal des débats*, introducing the reading public to the "frightening underworld of poverty and violence in Paris." David Pinkney, *Decisive Years in France, 1840–47* (Princeton, 1986), p. 97.

creates an inevitable tension in the traveler's consciousness, a tension between the place visited and the place left behind. Even if we try to forget home, countless moments on the journey remind us of it.[140] The travel experience is like a two-sided mirror: one side reflects the new, the other preserves the image of the known. Inevitably, one begins to think in terms of contrasts, both favorable and unfavorable, with home. The speed and comfort of travel in France stirs poignant memories of the difficulties of travel in Morocco; the fertile pastures seen from the window of the carriage are reminders of the more verdant fields at home.

At these points of divergence, the writer brings us closest to grasping the nature of the imaginative process that underlies the journey. These are the moments when the subdued counterpoint between the external and internal worlds becomes sufficiently audible for us to listen in. In *Tristes Tropiques*, Claude Lévi-Strauss notes that travel means dislocation in three dimensions: time, space, and social relations.[141] For the medieval Muslim traveler, according to André Miquel, the dissonance of the journey to non-Muslim lands created an incomparable opportunity to transcend the banality of everyday experience and to challenge the imagination.[142] In order to truly understand the dynamic of the cultural encounter, one must enter into the consciousness of the traveler at the point of disorientation, where cumulative values no longer apply, where the shock of the new refreshes thought. "We look for evidence of culture," says Alan Trachtenberg, "at those minute points of contact between new things and old habits, and we include in our sense of history the power of things themselves to impress and shape and evoke a

140. I. de Sola Pool, "Effects of Cross-national Contact on National and International Images," in H. Kelman, ed., *International Behavior, A Social-psychological Analysis* (New York, 1965), p. 122.

141. Miquel's observation (*Géographie humaine* 1:115), based on his reading of the chapter "The Quest for Power" in Lévi-Strauss's *Tristes Tropiques*, trans. J. Russell (New York, 1970), pp. 38–46.

142. *Géographie humaine* 1:115, 120.

response within consciousness."[143] Thus the journey of aṣ-Ṣaffār can be looked at from another perspective—that is, as a set of lively interactions "between new things and old habits" that represent the intensity of his responses to phenomena at their very moment of newness. We shall now examine this juxtaposition of feeling and object in the three categories Lévi-Strauss identifies as most susceptible to dislocation during the voyage: time, space, and social relations.

From the moment of his arrival in France, aṣ-Ṣaffār's senses reeled with sights and sensations that were totally unfamiliar. The most immediate disorientation was in the relationship of time and space, created by the disparities in technology between France and Morocco. He came from a world where the normal form of travel was by foot or on horseback; he went to Europe at the moment when it was making the transition from animal to mechanical power. In Morocco, the traveler might cover three or four miles in an hour, depending on the terrain; in France, the distance/time ratio, even by animal-drawn transport, was twice as great. The French stagecoach of the 1840s moved at about six miles an hour, but to a Moroccan its velocity seemed tremendous.[144]

Aṣ-Ṣaffār first meets these new dimensions of speed on the journey by coach from Marseille to Orléans. On entering, the coach seems deceptively familiar, furnished "like a room"; but suddenly, on the open road, the horses begin to move at a speed that is "breakneck, like a cavalry charge." In an instant, the comfortable room is transformed into a rocketlike projectile hurtling through space, subverting previous notions about the capability of the human body

143. Quoted in the preface to Wolfgang Schivelbusch, *The Railway Journey: The Industrialization of Time and Space in the 19th Century* (Berkeley, 1986), p. xv.

144. See Laroui, *Origines*, pp. 54–55, for the speed of travel in Morocco. Pinkney, *Decisive Years*, p. 53, is the source for data on France. The following discussion of the early railroad and its psychological effects on riders was inspired by Schivelbusch, *Railway Journey*, ch. 4.

to cover distance. When aṣ-Ṣaffār rides the railroad between Orléans and Paris, his distance/time disorientation is complete. Even at this early period in the development of the railroad, the cars moved much faster than the stagecoach, at about thirty miles an hour.[145]

Aṣ-Ṣaffār describes his sensation: he is carried along at "a speed [I] had never experienced, almost like a bird flying through the air. . . . When we looked at the sides of the road, we could not see what was there; it looked like an endless ribbon moving along with us, and we could not distinguish . . . anything."[146] The feeling of flying—which, incidentally, was not unique to the Muslim traveler, for European travelers used almost identical language to describe their first train ride—had the effect of collapsing time and space to nothingness. In two and a half hours, a journey that would have taken days in Morocco was over. We know that perceptions of space and time and the connections between them are culturally determined; we also know that those relationships can be relearned through repeated experience. Such was the case with the railroad ride, which eventually became routine for both Westerners and non-Westerners. The virtue of aṣ-Ṣaffār's account is that we are present at the crux of newness, experiencing the event unalloyed with prior knowledge or sensation.

The *riḥla* records other delicate subversions of fundamental space/time relations. During his journey to France, aṣ-Ṣaffār made the transition from a world in which time was measured by ritual to a world in which time, for the most part, was measured by the mechanical ticking of a clock. In Morocco, and indeed in all the lands of Islam, the passage of the day is punctuated by the times of prayer. One rises for the morning prayers, dines after the noon prayers, ends the day with the evening prayers. In the traditional Muslim male world, meetings were set, business arranged, and contracts concluded according to the fixed points of prayertime; in-

145. Pinkney, *Decisive Years*, p. 53.
146. See p. 115.

deed, one is continually reminded of the time of day by the calling of the muezzin from the mosque. The most dependable clock is the rhythm of ritual, denoted by sounds and visual signs (the faithful walking to the mosque carrying their prayer mats) that mark time as intelligibly for the Muslim as the chiming of Big Ben does for the Londoner.

Far from home in a non-Muslim land, aṣ-Ṣaffār found himself suddenly deprived of these culturally determined time markers. The meeting with King Louis-Phillipe, he tells us, will take place at "ten in the morning"; the reception at the palace is on New Year's Day, "the first day" of the Christian year. France was the land of the clock and the Christian calendar, of time measured in odd intervals. In Morocco there were clocks too, but usually they were for decoration.[147] European travelers saw them in the homes of the well-to-do, but the hands were rarely correct—not because Moroccans were ignorant of clock time (for they were not), but because they were not especially sensible to it.[148] What mattered most to aṣ-Ṣaffār was not the precise hour of the day, but rather religiously consecrated time as embodied in the predictability of prayer.

Another basic defining category of daily life, and an arena in which we again see aṣ-Ṣaffār's confrontation with the new, is the boundary between private and public space. Space, says Michael Gilsenan, "is not a kind of pure, given form but is a set of structures and relations that have to be learned . . . and constantly acquired in daily life."[149] Human needs and activities differ from one culture to

147. Except, of course, the clocks in the palaces of the Sultan, and those in the important mosques, which were kept on time to determine the correct hour of prayer. Ibn Zaydān, *'Izz* 1:138–39.

148. Describing a comfortable house in Rabat, J. H. D. Hay remarked: "[It] was furnished in good Moorish style, with carpets of all kinds, looking-glasses and clocks, which latter indulge generally in the hour they please." *Journal*, p. 43.

149. Michael Gilsenan, *Recognizing Islam: Religion and Society in the Modern Arab World* (New York, 1982), p. 187.

another, and space is the stage on which those varying functions are acted out. For the stranger, learning the complex codes that define space and its changing social functions can be among the most difficult trials of the journey. The traveler must be initiated into them by instruction or by example, and failure to learn them can lead to painful embarrassment. Most travelers abroad have acquired at least one story of cultural misunderstanding based on a misinterpretation of signs that set boundaries.

While in France, aṣ-Ṣaffār met with difficulties in his understanding of socio-spatial relations. For example, he describes the typical French house as "quite different from ours: they do not have a courtyard, a ground floor, and upper stories . . . such as we have; rather, their courtyard is outside the house, where the carts and draft animals stand." He goes on to say that "the rooms . . . have very large windows which look out onto the street."[150] The contrast with the traditional Moroccan house was striking: at home there were no windows looking onto the street, no point at which the outside could look in. The interior of the house is the ultimate private domain; the courtyard is an arena of family life, not a place where animals stand. In other words, a space that is the nexus for intense social interaction within the Moroccan household is missing in France.[151]

In Morocco, the courtyard is also the space where the stranger may stand without violating the privacy of the interior, or compromising the women within who may not wish to be seen. To enter directly into the interior of a house without benefit of the mediating stage provided by the courtyard was a peculiar experience for aṣ-Ṣaffār. Moreover, once having entered the house, he found the inside virtually open to the outside because of the large windows. Light floods the interior, exposing its contents to view. The open-

150. See p. 135.

151. Ernst Rackow, *Beiträge zur Kenntnis der materiellen Kultur Nordwest-Marokkos: Wohnraum, Hausrat, Kostüm* (Wiesbaden, 1958), p. 5 and Tafel 4, a plan of a typical Tetuan house.

ness and display of the family and its treasures to the casual viewer are a new phenomenon, quite unlike the wall-like protectiveness surrounding family life at home. Clearly, concepts of public versus private in domestic arrangements would have to be revised in the context of France.

Aṣ-Ṣaffār's perception of spatial boundaries is disrupted even further as he begins to explore the nuances of social praxis. The bathhouse, for example, is a subject of wonderment, and he describes it at length: "There is . . . [a] structure made of wood, which is their public bathhouse. Inside it are small rooms that are enclosed, each with a large tub that may be filled with hot or cold water, or both. . . . It is their *ḥammām*; they do not have a *ḥammām* like ours."[152] Other aspects emphasize the seclusion of the act of bathing; there is a small glass window with a filmy curtain that lets in light but keeps out prying eyes. One can even take a bath in one's own room, by ordering a servant to bring water. In other words, among the French, the bath is a private affair, included in that brief list of physical activities that, for reasons of shame or modesty, one conducts in total isolation.

The *ḥammām* or public bathhouse in Morocco was an entirely different matter. Bathing was done in a large, open room, not in private cubicles; it often took hours and was a prime social event of the day.[153] Gossip was exchanged in the bathhouse, business discussed, plans made. The ritual of the bath was an engaging social experience for both men and women, even while it was sexually segregated, like most social events. The nonenclosure of the bathing space, the free circulation and meeting of individuals while unclothed, was considered right and proper; bathing, in other words, was very much part of the public domain. Fascinated by the technology of the bath, aṣ-Ṣaffār remained unconvinced of the need for uncompromising isolation in the act of bathing. Indeed, he hints

152. See p. 129.
153. Rackow, *Beiträge*, p. 7.

that the technology may even be misplaced, for in the situation where such an installation would be most useful—in performing the ritual ablutions—it was unavailable.

The disorientation about spatial boundaries became more serious when it spilled over into relations between men and women, where the codes differed radically from those at home. Aṣ-Ṣaffār learned these lessons quickly, and he is eager to share his knowledge with us. Playing the role of practiced guide, he advises us about how to treat women properly if we find ourselves in France: "If you enter a man's house and a woman is present," he tells us, "you are not considered gracious or well-mannered unless you approach her with greetings and friendly speeches in a tone of modest gentility. Her husband will delight in that and his esteem and love for you will increase."[154]

This is indeed a world that is topsy-turvy. Coming from a culture where a meeting with strange females was a rare and stylized event, aṣ-Ṣaffār found the multiple possibilities for interaction with French women a subject of fascination and delight. In Morocco, in the street, women were veiled and made invisible; at home, they were kept behind closed doors which no incidental visitor could penetrate. In France, no such physical boundaries prevailed. In the salon, women mixed freely with strange men, wearing garments, it seemed to him, that left them half-naked, with their hair, upper arms, and bosoms exposed; in the street, their faces were uncovered, their eyes roamed freely.

The effect on him of the proximity of women was intoxicating. When describing their deportment and dress, he suddenly breaks into poetry. He also uses the device of *sajʿ*, or rhymed prose, to ornament the text and express his rising emotions. Beneath the flowery rhetoric, we feel a deep longing for the sensual experience. Many of the images, to be sure, are stereotyped, but others hint at a suppressed eroticism that seems eminently human. Yet, as in all things, aṣ-Ṣaffār exhibits restraint, and unlike aṭ-Ṭahṭāwī, who had

154. See p. 161.

a rather low opinion of French women, the Moroccan finds them on the whole to be "virtuous." Aṣ-Ṣaffār, of course, did not understand French. But he seems to have grasped that the physical and spatial barriers placed between men and women in his own society had their counterpart in France in the elaborate verbal rituals, or *politesse*, that surrounded the male-female encounter. He concentrates, therefore, on initiating others into the correct performance of greeting and leavetaking, so that in this vital area of social relations one will make no mistakes.

The strange, the new, and the marvelous permeate the voyage and greet the traveler at every turn. But even the strange has its own internal logic. France for aṣ-Ṣaffār is the land of *niẓām*, of order. Everywhere he looks he sees evidence of putting things in their proper place. The trees grow in straight rows, fields are plowed in perfect furrows, streets are tidy, libraries are neatly arranged, the soldiers march in even ranks, horses obey their masters, even the ladies part their hair with precision. France is the home of the straight line and the perfect landscape, of nature tamed and man made obedient. He laments the contrast with home:

> In comparison with the weakness of Islam, the dissipation of its strength, and the disrupted condition of its people, how confident they are, how impressive . . . how competent they are in matters of state . . . how capable in war . . . not because of their . . . bravery, or religious zeal, but because of their marvelous organization, their uncanny mastery over affairs, and their strict adherence to the law.[155]

Even while aṣ-Ṣaffār admits to a French "mastery" in the appearance of reality, he also grasps that the surface order is emblematic of a far deeper plan, a plan in which all of society is harnessed in the service of production. Herein lies the mystery of that pervasive yet indefinable power that non-Europeans sensed in the European order of things. The disciplined children and straight rows of trees are

155. See pp. 193–194.

superficial representations of a social organization that he suspects may be inimical to his own. It appears to him as rational, relentlessly efficient, and organized around economic rather than religious imperatives. Needless to say, it also seems so all-encompassing and powerful that the mere thought of competing with it induces in him a sense of despair.[156]

In Europe, aṣ-Ṣaffār had a vision of another world. He saw what the human spirit could achieve when left to its own inventiveness. But it was a world beyond reach. True, there are innovations in France that he regards as useful, and in matters of technology and everyday life, he freely admits, they are superior. But in matters of religion they are still infidels. "They know well what is apparent to the life of this world," he says, "but are completely ignorant about the hereafter."[157] Their science may be admirable, their manners perfect, their houses clean. Yet they have this one insurmountable moral flaw: with regard to their belief in God they are corrupt. This is no mere prudent declaration of loyalty; rather, it is a statement of profound conviction. Nor was aṣ-Ṣaffār alone in proclaiming his faith in Islam at the end of his voyage, for other Moroccan travelers to the West did the same: "Everything in their way of thinking impelled them to deny reality, or at least not to acknowledge it. This is your world, and ours is different, they seem to say."[158]

Which leads us to our final point. The voyage of aṣ-Ṣaffār, and indeed other Arabic travel accounts of this era, can be read in several ways. First, they are useful sources of information for reconstruct-

156. See Timothy Mitchell, *Colonizing Egypt* (Cambridge, 1988), ch. 1, on the impact of European ideas of order on nineteenth-century Egypt.

157. See p. 220.

158. Laroui, *Origines*, p. 228. The "disclaimer" was also a feature of medieval Christian pilgrimage accounts, where curiosity about the strange "put the pilgrimage in bad repute"; the "ideal" Christian pilgrim traveled "with his eyes to the ground," according to D. R. Howard, *Writers and Pilgrims: Medieval Pilgrimage Narratives and Their Posterity* (Berkeley, 1980), pp. 23–24.

ing a particular conception of reality, serving as repositories of facts to contextualize scenes distant in time and place. Second, as we have seen, this kind of writing gives us glimpses into the human experience of the voyage, offering access to moments of contact between the voyager and the outside world which illuminate the interior sensations of the journey. There is yet a third dimension which travel writing can assume, which becomes especially meaningful as we struggle to understand the workings of cultures other than our own. As involved companions along the road, we are not only engrossed in *what* the traveler saw in Europe, but also *how* he saw it, and how it resonated in his consciousness and reminded him of home. France and Paris are the mirrors in which we read aṣ-Ṣaffār's vision of more distant locales; the green fields, crowded streets, *bals*, and *soirées* are the tableau on which another image is etched, of a place less familiar to us but even more engaging. That place is the Morocco of aṣ-Ṣaffār's imagination.

Finally, and on yet another plane, these accounts transcend the fact of traveling and begin to take on moral intonations, reinforced by the universality of the act of displacement. Here the journey becomes a metaphor, the voyager a mythmaker, and the story a fable. It is not only the paradigm of its structure—the departure, the adventure, the return—that makes the travel account universal, but also the meanings construed from the voyage by the voyager himself. In aṣ-Ṣaffār's case, the parable is quite explicit: he tells us that one can go to the land of enchantment, the abode of both good and evil, immerse oneself in it, and return home wiser yet unscathed.

This is the lesson of the voyage; but whether his tale convinced those who read it in his own time, we cannot tell. The *riḥla* was undoubtedly circulated and discussed within the narrow confines of the court, then consigned to the Royal Library, where it languished in obscurity for over one hundred years. Never did aṣ-Ṣaffār think, one would imagine, that his manuscript would sleep for so long and than reawaken to bring enlightenment and pleasure to readers of another age.

II

THE TEXT

1

PROLOGUE

In the name of God, the Merciful and Compassionate, God bless our Prophet Muḥammad and his Companions and grant them salvation.[1]

Praise be to God, mover of creation on land and sea, opener of ways and means for whoever wished to follow to places both populous and desolate. Thanks to Him, whoever put concern for his fellow man first found that his affairs profited and his efforts yielded the highest return. But whoever was destined for a life of misery would lose his way and find that his dealings were unsuccessful. "*If God had wished, He would have made you one* umma."[2] Praise be to God who proclaimed His uniqueness by means of His Oneness, His authority by means of His divine attributes, His absolute distance from earthly time, place, and relationships by irrefutable proofs which no man of reason can doubt. "*For how could He have a child, when He has no wife?*"[3]

1. The *riḥla* begins with a *khuṭba,* or "invocation to God," in which the author asks for His blessings on the enterprise, mentions his patrons, and states the main themes of the work.

2. Koran 16:93. *Umma* here refers to human groups bound by ties that may be ethnic, linguistic, or religious; usually *umma* refers specifically to the community of Islam. *SEI,* s.v. "Umma."

3. Koran 6:101.

We testify that there is no God but Allāh, nor has He any associate.[4] He is alone in creating this world, and His skill is unprecedented. There is no one like Him. He made the towns and the settled places, the open country and the wastelands, and the cities large and small, dispersing among them people of various tongues, colors, creeds, and religions, so that men of intelligence would increase their understanding, and men of good sense their insight. The proof of His omnipotence is manifest in His great works.

Oh how astonishing!
How can the unbeliever reject God or deny him?
In all things He has given a sign
Proving that He is the One.

Praise be to God who separated all creation into monotheist and polytheist, imprinting upon the hearts [of believers] the unshakable truths of monotheism. To some He gave a good life in this world, and for others He reserved the pleasures of the hereafter, raising the lowly on high in reward for their good deeds. "*He will not be tested about what He does; rather, it is they who will be tested.*"[5]

We testify that our Master, prophet, and protector Muḥammad, His servant and messenger, Lord of the Arabs and the non-Arabs, confirmer of His miracles, was sent to the other nations to spread His message over the world from West to East. Whoever responded was saved, but whoever resisted had the sword of God raised over his neck. Thus the strength of God broke the noses of tyrants, and His true religion eclipsed all others. God bless [Muḥammad], his family and his companions, his wives and his descendents, and grant them salvation. May His blessing be perfect, holy, and everlasting. May we reach the highest places and be well-received there,

4. Associating another with God (*shirk*) is considered a form of polytheism by Muslims. The rejection of *shirk* is usually expressed along with a statement about the Oneness of God, as here. *SEI*, s.v. "Shirk."

5. Koran 21:23.

following His unswerving path until we arrive in the presence of our noble Master, the Merciful, the Compassionate. There is no Lord other than He, and no hope other than in His goodness.

Let us continue. After that, God opened the heart of our Sire,[6] pillar of our religion and of this world, the great, majestic, celebrated Sultan, that lofty and venerable believer in God, the mightiest and most protective of his people, the sword of the Islamic community, the pride of Islam, the greatest of the great.

King of all time and delight of the eye,
Full moon and hidden pearl.
A king who beautifies with majesty
And whose being radiates great knowledge and wisdom.
Issue of Sultans [?][7] from the seed of Muḥammad,
Most great in his glory and worship of the Merciful One.

He is a *sharīf* by descent, *ʿAlawī* in rank and relation, *Ḥasanī* by birth, a branch of the Lord of the Arabs and the non-Arabs.[8] May God make him victorious and sustain him in his faith. May He make his future easy, until free men become the slaves of their slaves. May He provide him with his full share of blessings, according to his portion. May He make his sword triumphant over the necks of the evildoers, and spread the carpet of his happiness over the earth. May He bestow on him possessions whose like will not

6. *Mawlā*, or *Mulay* in the Moroccan dialect. One of the titles of the Sultan of Morocco (Dozy 2:624). The reference is to the reigning Sultan, ʿAbd ar-Raḥmān b. Hishām (1822–59).

7. Word not clear in manuscript.

8. Titles for rulers of Morocco, who claim descent from the Prophet Muḥammad. A *sharīf* is a relative of the Prophet. In Morocco, most *sharīfs* are from the branch of the Prophet's grandson al-Ḥasan, son of ʿAlī and Fāṭima; thus " ʿAlawī" and "Ḥasanī." C. E. Bosworth, *The Islamic Dynasties* (Edinburgh, 1967), pp. 38–41; *EI* 2, s.v. "Ḥasanī," and table.

be seen again, and make "caliphate" a word that will remain with his children.[9] May [God] bless his days and provide for his people.

[The Sultan] was inspired to send an envoy to the King of the French,[10] so that some benefit might result from it for Muslims and for Islam. He decided on it according to sound judgment and good sense, mindful of his duty to watch over the orderly affairs of all our people, both highborn and low. It has always been a concern of the leaders of our community to protect the people of our faith. The Prophet, God bless him and grant him salvation, often sent out the best from among his companions on missions, providing an example followed by the rightly-guided Caliphs and Imams,[11] as we know from the sources.

The Sultan, may God render him victorious, had a high opinion of his servant,[12] the wise and successful fruit of his planting, advocate of his sound policies and executor of his authority, guardian of the well-being of his flock, the most illustrious and happy Qā'id[13] and Ḥājj ʿAbd al-Qādir, son of the deceased Qā'id Muḥammad

9. Moroccan sovereigns laid claim to the spiritual title of "Caliph" along with the temporal title of "Sultan." Their official title of *Amīr al-Mu'minīn* ("Commander of the Faithful") underscored the fact that their legitimacy rested not only on family and political power but also on religious authority. On the Caliphate, see H. A. R. Gibb, "The Sunni Theory of the Caliphate," in *Studies on the Civilization of Islam*, eds. Stanford J. Shaw and William R. Polk (Boston, 1962), pp. 141–50; *SEI*, s.v. "Khalīfa."

10. Literally, "to the exalted one of the French people" (*li-ʿaẓīm jins al-faransīs*). Louis-Philippe's official title was *Roi de France*, but aṣ-Ṣaffār usually refers to him as "Sultan" rather than "King" (*malik*), following the usage in Makhzan correspondence.

11. *Al-khulafā' ar-rāshidūn wal-a'imma al-muhtadūn*, a reference to the revered immediate successors to the Prophet, who served as models of behavior to subsequent generations of believers.

12. *Khadīm*. High officials in the Makhzan were called "servants," even those who served in the upper ranks. Dozy 1:354; Laroui, *Origines*, p. 117.

13. The *qā'id* was a Makhzan official appointed by the Sultan who had various functions; here, the governor of a large town. Ibn Zaydān, *ʿIzz*, 1, glossary, p. 412.

Ashʿāsh, may God be his protector and his sustenance. The Sultan chose him because of his excellent qualities, and ordered him to take along two bright and intelligent *amīns*[14] from families of distinction and piety in Tetuan, as well as whatever *ṭālibs*,[15] servants, and helpers he needed to demonstrate the superiority of Muslims and Islam over the worshippers of idols and the proclaimers of fatherhood and sonhood. As it says in the Hadith: "God have mercy on him who shows strength at the right time."[16]

Then the Qā'id chose from among the men of the first rank his distinguished son-in-law Muḥammad b. al-Ḥājj Muḥammad al-Libādī, who is known far and wide, and the bright and sincere Ḥājj al-ʿArabī b. ʿAbd al-Karīm al-ʿAṭṭār, who is skilled in dealings with other peoples and has traveled widely in other parts. He also showed good sense by choosing a secretary to accompany him, since he found no shortcomings in him and was in need of his specialty.[17] It is wise for those who go far from home to record everything they see and hear, since they may find some knowledge and value in it. There is no better way of obtaining useful information than by mixing with people. According to a wise saying of the ancients: "The eye never tires from seeing, nor the ear from hearing."

Therefore, I decided with the help of God to blacken these pages with what I saw and heard during this voyage, be it clear or obscure. For I am but a woodgatherer of the night, the one who lags behind, a horse who is out of the race. You should not judge me too harshly, for I am only doing it as a reminder to myself, and to inform others

14. A Makhzan official entrusted with fiscal responsibilities. The *amīns* in Tetuan were inspectors in the port, charged with collecting customs revenues and making payments on orders from the Sultan. Ibn Zaydān, *ʿIzz*, 1, glossary, pp. 396–97.

15. Literally, a student of Islamic studies, but in Morocco, a title also applied to an educated man who earned his living through commerce. Laroui, *Origines*, pp. 90, 441.

16. The Hadith are collections of sacred traditions about the life of the Prophet and his companions. *SEI*, s.v. "Ḥadīth."

17. This was Muḥammad aṣ-Ṣaffār.

who may ask me from among my fellow countrymen. Let the masters of composition and rhetoric excuse me, and let the burdens of the men of metaphor and allusion be lifted from me. I beseech God to cover my mistakes. May He help me complete the task and be pleased with me, for I say, I take my hope from Him.

Our departure from the seat of our happiness, the comfort of our daily lives, the pillow of our heads, the nest of our youth, the abode of our joy and vitality, our Tetuan, may God keep it safe forever, took place early Saturday morning in the month of Dhū al-Ḥijja al-Ḥarām, in which exactly thirteen nights had already passed. It was the year 1261.[18]

At the start of the journey, the caravan leader bridled the animals and composed these verses, the words giving him comfort:

O my splendid Tetuan, will fate allow us
To come home, and will we meet again?
Will your face appear and draw near, after
The crashing waves, will we be reunited?
May torrential rain sweep your quarters and refresh
Your sheltering walls, after the horses have run the course!
I commend to your care my loved ones, and I
Hold their memory dear, even though I am far away.

We rode out of town to the port. A huge vessel had been sent for us, one of the ships of fire known as *bābūr*.[19] They had chosen one of their very best for us, as a sign of their friendship and good faith. We rode to the larger ship in small boats and then went down into its belly just as one goes down into a grave of the dead. The captain settled us in the best quarters, separate from the crew. His people greeted us with friendly smiles and kind attentions. They put us in a cabin[20] with fine clean rugs and low comfortable beds, and their

18. 13 December 1845.

19. Here, a steamship, from the Spanish *vapor*. Ibn Zaydān, *'Izz*, 1, glossary, p. 414.

20. Arabic *qamra*, from the Spanish *cámara*, a room or cabin on a ship. Dozy 2:403.

spokesman said to us: "Be at your ease, for we wish you to be as comfortable as possible." When everything was ready, we took our leave from those who had come to bid us farewell.

Then the ship raised its anchor, its parts stirred into motion, and we prayed: "Keep us from the cursed Satan. In the name of God, let us reach our destination and put safely into port, for the Lord is compassionate and merciful." Cannons of rejoicing were fired and the sea accepted us into its tranquility. We put ourselves into the hands of the eternal life, for there is no defense or refuge other than Him, praise be unto Him. "*If the evil in the sea touches you, there is no help other than from Him.*"[21] As Ibn al-ʿArabī[22] said, "Whoever is willing may be assured that God alone is the First Cause, and [other] reasons pale [beside Him]"; so ride upon the sea and it will be as he said. And it is said: "Whoever sails the sea puts his life in jeopardy, but even greater is the danger for him who counsels the Sultan unwisely." There is no doubt that he who travels by sea is nothing but a worm on a piece of wood, a trifle in the midst of a powerful creation. The waters play about with him at will, and no one but God can help him.[23] Our goal was the city of Marseille, which is on the northern shore of this sea.

You should know that this sea is called the Sea of Rūm because of the great number of countries of Rūm along its shores,

21. Koran 17:67.

22. Muḥammad Ibn al-ʿArabī, celebrated Sufi mystic of Andalusian origin, who died in Damascus in 638/1240. *SEI*, s.v. "Ibn (al-)ʿArabī."

23. The Greeks and Romans idealized the sea, but Arabic writers often spoke of it with loathing. ʿAmr b. al-Ās, the Arab conqueror of Egypt, reportedly wrote to the Caliph ʿUmar that "the sea is a great creature upon which weak creatures ride, like worms on a piece of wood." Aṭ-Ṭabarī, *Annales*, ed. M. J. de Goeje et al. (Leiden, 1879–1901), 1:2821, anno 28 [648–49], quoted in the *Muqaddimah* 2:39. Abū al-Ḥasan ʿAlī at-Tamgrūtī (Tamgrouti), author of *En-nafkhat el-miskiya fi-s-sifarat et-tourkiya: Relation d'une ambassade marocaine en Turquie, 1589–1591*, trans. H. de Castries (Paris, 1929), used a similar expression (p. 39). Despite their proximity to the sea, Moroccans rarely chose seamanship as an occupation, and local folklore reflects a fear of it. See L. Brunot, *La mer dans les traditions et les industries indigènes à Rabat et Salé* (Paris, 1921), pp. 1–12.

Plate 7. The Moroccan suite on board the *Météore*. From *L'Illustration*, 28 February 1846.

especially to the north.[24] It used to be called the Sea of Shām because it ended in the land of Shām;[25] also [it was called] the Middle Sea. But today it is known among most people of Morocco as the Small Sea in contrast to the Surrounding [Sea], which we call the Great Sea.[26] It begins at the narrow opening between Tangier and Tarifa, which is about twelve miles wide and commonly known to us as *būghāz*.[27] In the south, the straits are between Ceuta and Qaṣr al-Jawāz, also known as Qaṣr aṣ-Ṣaghīr;[28] in the north, between Algeciras and Tarifa. The [Small Sea] has no other outlet to the Surrounding Sea than this. The straits are in the fourth zone.[29]

The explanation of this is that the shape of the earth, according to the ancients, is spherical, and is surrounded by the element of water, like a floating grape. The water withdrew from some

24. *Rūm* was the medieval Arabic term for Greek Byzantium; by extension, *Rūmī* meant Christian, and the "lands of Rūm" meant Christian Europe. According to S. D. Goitein, *Rūmī* was used by Arabic-speaking Egyptian Jews (in the Geniza documents) "well into the twelfth century"; thereafter, the word *Ifrānjī* emerges (from "Frank"), with a distinction made between Europeans in the East (*Rūmīs*) and the West (*Ifrānjīs*). After the thirteenth century, *Fransā* is used in the Geniza letters to designate France. Goitein, *A Mediterranean Society*, 5 vols. (Berkeley, 1967–88), 1:43.

In Morocco, Europeans are commonly known as *naṣārā*, or "Nazarenes." Aṣ-Ṣaffār uses the following terms: 1) *bilād ar-Rūm*, by which he means all the lands of Christian Europe; 2) *bilād al-Faransīs*, the "land of the French"; and 3) *Fransā*, France. For further discussion, see Lewis, *Muslim Discovery*, pp. 20, 140; *IB* 2:415 note 14.

25. *Ash-Shām*, the medieval Arabic term for the land of Syria.

26. The Atlantic Ocean.

27. The Moroccan word for "straits." Harrell, p. 14. At-Tamgrūtī says it is Turkish. *En-nafkhat*, p. 43.

28. Qaṣr aṣ-Ṣaghīr was the departure point for expeditions against Spain; hence the name Qaṣr al-Jawāz, "the fort of the passage." E. Michaux-Bellaire, "El-Qçar Eç-Çeghir," *RMM* 16, 12 (1911): 350.

29. The word for "zone" (*iqlīm*) comes from the Greek *klima*, meaning a latitudinal section of the earth's surface. *Muqaddimah* 1:111.

parts of it, about one-half of the surface of the sphere. Therefore the earth has a spherical form surrounded on all sides by a body of water called the Surrounding Sea.[30] This sphere is divided into two halves by a long line extending from east to west, called the equator. If you stand on this line and face east, everything on your right will be south, everything on your left north. Next to the equator in the southern direction it is almost completely wasteland, because of the excessive heat and the very slight inclination of the sun there from the equinoxes. The inhabited area to the north of the equator is sixty-four degrees [wide]. The rest is barren and uninhabited because of the freezing cold.

Thus the settled land on the exposed part of the earth is equal to one-fourth of it. This cultivated area was divided by the ancients into seven parts, each part called a "zone."[31] This is what is meant by the seven zones. These zones are equal in width but unequal in length, because their length goes from west to east and their width from north to south. The first zone is longer than the second, the second longer [than the third], and so on until the seventh, which is the shortest of all, because of what happens when you divide a hemisphere. The beginning of the first zone is the length of the equator, and its width extends in the northerly direction. It runs along the equator from west to east, bordering the equator in the south and the second zone on the north. The beginning of the second zone is where the first zone ends. Its extent is also from west to east and on the south it borders the first zone, and on the north the third zone, and so on. The first [zone] is the longest and the last the shortest, because the longest line around any sphere is that which goes around its middle, and we have already said that the equator

30. Ibn Khaldūn: "The earth has a spherical shape and is enveloped by . . . water. It may be compared to a grape floating upon water. The water withdrew from certain parts of (the earth) . . . [about] one-half the surface of the sphere. . . . [It] is surrounded on all sides by . . . a sea called 'the Surrounding Sea.' " *Muqaddimah* 1:94–95.

31. See note 29 above.

divides [the earth] in two. Then they divided each zone lengthwise from east to west into ten equal sections. That is why you hear someone say that such-and-such a place is in the fourth or fifth section of the first zone or the second.

The Small Sea begins at the abovementioned straits, which are in the [ ][32] section of the fourth zone. It terminates at the end of the fourth section of the fourth zone at the coast of Syria, 1,160 parasangs from its starting point.[33] After leaving the straits, the Small Sea heads eastward and spreads out toward the north and the south, entering the third zone in the south and reaching as far as the fifth zone in the north, according to what Ibn Khaldūn says.[34] On its southern shore are Tangier, Ceuta, Tetuan, then the coast of the Rif where Melilla and Badis, both owned by the Spanish, are located.[35] Then Oran and Algiers and the rest of that province, which is now in the hands of the French. Then Tunis, Sfax, and Sousse and the rest of the coast of Ifrīqīya,[36] then Jerba, which is in the bay there. Then Tripoli and Maserata, the place where Sīdī Aḥmad Zarrūq,[37]

32. Aṣ-Ṣaffār left a blank space, probably because he did not know; nor did Ibn Khaldūn provide the information.

33. A parasang, from the Persian *farsang*, originally the distance covered on foot in one hour. According to Ibn Khaldūn, it measures 12,000 cubits or about three Arabic miles, hence 3.5 English miles. *Muqaddimah* 1:96 and note 19.

34. This section is based on Ibn Khaldūn's Second Prefatory Discussion, updated with contemporary place names and more recent historical data. *Muqaddimah* 1:129–33, 139–43.

35. Melilla was captured by the Spanish in 1497; Badis was ceded to the Spanish in 1564. C.-A. Julien, *History of North Africa: Tunisia, Algeria, Morocco* (London, 1970), pp. 206, 226, 253.

36. The medieval Arabic term for Tunisia. Zakariya b. Muḥammad b. Maḥmūd al-Qazwīnī, *Āthār al-bilād wa-akhbār al-iʿbād* (Beirut, n.d.), pp. 148–49.

37. Abū al-ʿAbbās Aḥmad b. Muḥammad b. ʿĪsā al-Burnūsī al-Fāsī, known as Zarrūq (b. 846/1442), a famous jurisconsult revered throughout North Africa. Al-Qadiri (trans. Cigar), *Nashr*, p. 160 and note 13; Lévi-Provençal, *Les historiens*, p. 187 note 3.

may God be of assistance to us, is buried. Then the bay known as the Bay of Kibrīt,[38] then Derna and the other lands of Barqa,[39] then Alexandria. Then one passes on to the land of Shām.

On its northern shore are Tarifa, then Algeciras, then Gibraltar, then Malaga, then Almeria, and the rest of the shore of Andalus, now known as Spain. All of it belongs to the Spanish except for Gibraltar, which is English. Then comes the country of France. The first port after Spain is a small one called Port-Vendres, then Marseille, then Toulon, and the rest of the coast of France. Then comes the land of Italy. Among its cities are Genoa, which belongs to Sardinia, Livorno, which belongs to the Livornese, then the great city of Rome, which is not on the coast but is inland. Then comes Naples, which belongs to the Neapolitans. It is on a mountain which extends into the sea; at its tip is the island of Sicily. Between them is a small opening called the Straits of Messina, which also belongs to the Neapolitans. Then the sea enters a gulf beyond Naples called the Gulf of Venice, which ends in the land of Austria, to which both Venice and the straits of the above-mentioned Gulf belong.

On the coast of this Gulf after Austria and opposite Naples is the land of the Turks and Albania. Numerous islands are crowded together there. Then following the land of the Turks along this shore comes the Peloponnesus, which belongs to the Greeks. After the Peloponnesus the sea enters a small bay and emerges again in the land of the Turks. It ends at the narrow straits known as the Straits of the Dardanelles,[40] which open out directly to the city of Constan-

38. The location is the Gulf of Sidra (*khalīj surṭ*), but the name *kibrīt* which aṣ-Ṣaffār uses could not be found in any of the standard geographical dictionaries. *Kibrīt* is sulphur, important for making gunpowder and medicaments; perhaps this region was a source of it. *EI* 2, s.v. "Kibrīt."

39. A word applied by the medieval Arab geographers to the town of al-Marj and the region surrounding it, located in ancient Cyrenaica; present-day Libya. *EI* 2, s.v. "Barḳa."

40. In Arabic *shāna qalʿa*, from the Turkish *çanakkale*, which is a combination of *çanak*, a Turkish word meaning "pot," and *qalʿa*, Arabic for "fort."

tinople the Great, which is Istanbul.[41] Then it leaves by the straits known as the Straits of Constantinople and ends in the land of Moscow. That sea, which is surrounded by land, is generally known as the Black Sea, and the Turks call it *kara deniz*, which is two words, *kara* signifying "black" and *deniz* meaning "sea" in Turkish, that is, the Black Sea, with the adjective coming first according to the rule of structure in languages other than Arabic. From here it leaves through the Straits of the Dardanelles and goes on to the city of Izmir, where many of the peoples of Rūm and of the Turks [live], and so on until it reaches the land of Shām, where it turns back in the direction of Alexandria and comes to an end. In this sea are many inhabited islands, among them the islands of Ibiza, Majorca, and Minorca, all belonging to Spain and close to it. Also the island of Sardinia, which belongs to the Sardinians, and the island of Corsica, which belongs to the French, and the island of Ṣiqillīya, which belongs to the Neapolitans and is called Sicily nowadays, as we have mentioned.[42] Also, the famous island of Malta, which is under English rule, and the island of Crete facing the Peloponnesus, and the island of Cyprus opposite Syria, and many other small islands, especially [between] the Peloponnesus and the land of the Turks.

Returning to where we were, for four days we traveled in the greatest comfort and luxury. Sometimes the waves lifted us up; at

41. Moroccan travelers used both names. Ibn Baṭṭūṭa (fourteenth century) explained that "one of the two parts of the city of Constantinople is Aṣṭanbūl. It is on the eastern bank of the river." *IB* 2:508. At-Tamgrūtī (sixteenth century) referred to it as Constantinople. *En-nafkhat*, p. 43. For theories regarding the origin of the name, see D. J. Georgacas, "The Names of Constantinople," *Transactions of the American Philological Association* 78 (1947): 366–67; *EI* 2, s.v. "Istanbul."

42. Conquered by the Aghlabids in the ninth century, Sicily remained under Arab dominion for almost two hundred years. Al-Qazwīnī, *Āthār al-bilād*, pp. 215–16; P. Hitti, *The History of the Arabs* (New York, 1967), pp. 602–6.

other times, when the wind subsided and the weather became pleasant, they set us down. As the distance grew shorter our joy increased, for we were in dread of the terrors of the sea and our voyage was in the month of December.[43] But God kept us safe from its trickery, although each of us received a share of its motion. On Thursday, some small disturbances began, but we had already entered into the Gulf of Lions, where the crossing is almost always difficult. Moreover, the ship had an urgent need for coal, so it was decided to put in at Port-Vendres, the first French port [on this coast], where we anchored on Wednesday afternoon.[44] Our insides settled down and our excitement abated; each of us regained vitality, our dizziness stopped, and we returned to life.

This is a small port, but due to the skill and exactitude of its design and the excellent construction of its entranceway and shores, it is equal to or even better than a large one. There are no winds or waves inside it, and the ship sailed as if it were in a basin. When we reached the shore, they tied ropes [from the ship] to heavy iron rings nailed into the great rocks from which the shores are built. Fortifications for cannon guard its entranceway, and huge beacons sit upon the mountain to illuminate the darkness and lead [ships] into port. There is a small town here of the same name, with houses and shops along the shore where one can buy foodstuffs such as bread, meat, fruit, and vegetables. It also has many vineyards, for it belongs to the countryside and is not a large city. In the port the only goods we saw were vats of wine, perhaps because this is the country of the grape.

43. The migratory character of the Muslim lunar calendar made it impractical for agricultural purposes, and in Morocco the months were known by their Latin names even in precolonial times. The Roman months were used in everyday speech, while the Muslim calendar was reserved for dating government documents and religious events. A. Joly, "Un calendrier agricole marocain," *AM* 3, 2 (1905): 301–19; Dozy 1:425.

44. "A shortage of water and coal, in addition to a very strong wind, made the commanding officer decide to put in here." AAE/CPM 15/213, Roches to Guizot, Port-Vendres, 17 December 1845.

We spent the night there and the ship took on what it needed, and with the coming of the day, we raised anchor and reentered the Gulf of Lions. There we met calm going, which was unusual, except that during three hours of the last night something or other hit us. On Friday we awoke in the port of Marseille, and we thanked God for our safe arrival, for we had covered the distance and reached our goal. The length of our journey by sea apart from the stopover in Port-Vendres was five days.

After the sun rose, the most important man in the town came aboard to greet us, showing much friendliness and goodwill. We disembarked amidst ceremony and rejoicing while they fired off cannon, filling the air with news of our arrival for listeners both near and far. When we entered the town, we were greeted with respect and solicitude, for the chief of the militia had ordered the cavalry and infantry to line up for us in an honor guard. They transported us in fine coaches[45] pulled by elegantly fitted horses until we arrived at a luxurious house, where we stayed in the greatest comfort.[46] We remained there the day of our arrival and the next day, Saturday. Early Sunday morning we decided to leave for the city of Paris, the home of their Sultanate and the seat of their kingdom.

45. The word for coach is *kudshī* (pl. *akdāsh*), from the Spanish *coche*. The word had been known in Morocco for some time; it appears in al-Ghassānī's *Iftikāk*, a report of travels in seventeenth-century Spain (p. 9). In the late eighteenth century, L. Chenier wrote that Sultan Muḥammad b. ʿAbd Allāh (1757–90) "never appears in public but on horseback, or in his calesh." *The Present State of the Empire of Morocco*, 2 vols. (London, 1788), 2:307–8.

46. They stayed at the Hôtel d'Orient. AAE/CPM 15/215–16, Pourcet to Guizot, 19 December 1845. See also DAR 17578, Ashʿāsh to Sultan Mulay ʿAbd ar-Raḥmān, 20 Dhū al-Ḥijja 1261/20 December 1845.

2

OUR JOURNEY BY LAND FROM MARSEILLE TO PARIS

You should know that according to the rules of the road in this country, the traveler need not carry with him either food or bedding, or any of his worldly possessions. He need only take with him his *dirhāms*, *riyāls*, or gold, for he can buy whatever he wants along the way.[1] This is because most of the way is populated and the traveler leaves one settled place only to enter another. In each town, he will find a marketplace where everything he needs is sold, and a place to spend the night, called either a *locanda* or a *posada*.[2] If there

1. Travel in Morocco was described by foreigners as dangerous and exhausting. Those journeying under the auspices of the Sultan received the *mūna*, or provisioning by local officials; however, the *mūna* was not always forthcoming, and voyagers often had to carry their own food, buy it, or forage for it. Hay, *Journal*, p. 17. Carrying money was also risky because of the prevalence of brigands. Laroui, *Origines*, p. 36. The *dirhām* and the *riyāl* (from the Spanish *réal*) were basic units of Moroccan coinage. See Ch. 3 note 21, below.

2. In Arabic, *al-uwkanṭa* (vocalized in aṣ-Ṣaffār's text), from the Italian *locanda*, a tavern with rooms for lodging. Aṭ-Ṭahṭāwī describes it as a "restaurant . . . sometimes including places to sleep." *Takhlīṣ*, p. 114; *L'or*, p. 148. Aṣ-Ṣaffār says it is a place for sleeping, with food bought outside, which was closer to Moroccan practice. James Grey Jackson described an

is a place for sleeping and eating, it is the second; but if there is only a place for sleeping and one must bring food from the marketplace, it is the first.

This is a large house with many rooms, each with windows as tall as a man, which overlook the streets and markets below. In each room are one or more beds with sheets, a cover, and a mattress, all very soft and clean. The floor is usually carpeted with a fine rug which one walks on while wearing shoes, for it is not their custom to remove them except when getting into bed. The windows are covered with a curtain made of something like silk. There are also chairs for sitting, for they know nothing about sitting on the floor, nor would their clothing allow it because of the tightness of their trousers. In the middle of the room is a table of fine wood or marble for writing or reading. There is also a wardrobe made of wood that shines like a mirror and has drawers for keeping clothes or other things of value. Under each bed is a little box, and inside is a clean pot for relieving oneself.

Most of the large rooms are lit by many candles held in a cluster like stars. They also have one or two large mirrors on the wall, each so clear and tall that someone not paying close attention would think it an open way. Each room must have a pitcher for water set in a basin along with small, clean, folded towels for washing. In most of the rooms are pictures of the countryside, trees, people, animals, boats and the sea, and the like. This is a very important matter with them and they do not leave any place bare. The room

inn (*funduq*) of Fes as follows: "Three stories high, . . . [with] 50 to 100 apartments. . . . As the mode of travelling is to carry bedding with one, they do not provide beds in these inns, but leave you to make use of what you have got, providing only a mat; and if you want any refreshment you cannot order a meal, but must purchase it at a cook's shop, or procure it at the butcher's." *An Account of the Empire of Marocco and the District of Suse* (Philadelphia, 1810), p. 123. The *funduq* was mainly for country folk; people of aṣ-Ṣaffār's class usually stayed in private homes when visiting another city. The Spanish *posada* (Arabic *būṣāḍa*) was a place where travelers spent the night and changed horses.

might also have vases of flowers made of paper and covered with glass, so that their color will never fade, and sometimes a piano,[3] which is one of their amusements and ways of making music.

Each room must also have a small stove[4] built of marble or the like in a pleasing shape, where a wood fire burns in cold and rainy weather. It has a chimney open to the outside. The room is not bothered by smoke in the least because the chimney is well made and the wood is clean and dry. This is a necessity in every room, whether its owner is humble or well-to-do. The room may also have an inkpot and pen and other implements for writing. All these things are the furnishings of their rooms, although there may be variations depending on the owner's wealth.

In this place are many servants, both male and female, as well as cooks and a kitchen[5] containing all sorts of cooking equipment. When someone enters they take him upstairs to one of the rooms. If he desires food, he orders the servant to bring what he wants in the way of main dishes, fruits, and sweets. When he finishes eating and is ready to leave, the servant gives him a paper telling the price he must pay. If he wants a place to stay, he may choose whatever room he likes, according to his means. The servant brings everything and it is not necessary to call him for every small task, or to move from one's place when doing so. Inside every room is a rope, and each rope is connected to another. When it is pulled, its movement causes a bell to sound, bringing the servant quickly. The servant recognizes from which room it comes by a sign known to him.

As we have mentioned, travelers in that country need not carry provisions with them. Another rule is that travelers do not ride on the backs of saddled animals, or journey on foot, unless they are

3. *Sanṭīr*. Dozy 1:694.

4. *Kānūn*, a charcoal brazier, placed in the center of the room to heat it in winter; also a grill for cooking meat. Harrell, p. 60; L. Brunot, *Textes arabes de Rabat*, 2 vols. (Rabat, 1952), 2, glossary, p. 703.

5. *Qashīna*, from the Spanish *cocina*, "kitchen." Dozy 2:473.

soldiers or poor people. Travel is by stagecoach or wagons[6] drawn by horses. There are various kinds. One type is square and holds four people sitting two-by-two on benches facing each other, so that they can stretch out their legs underneath the opposite bench. It has windows of clear glass so the traveler can see the road, the world, and the people along the way. He can open them if he does not mind the heat or cold or the dust; but if he is bothered by them, he can close them, and the light and the view will stay with him. On each bench is a small cushion, and inside [the bench] is a place for putting a few small things. Everything is made from fine, unblemished wood—the floor, the sides, even the ceiling. In fact, it is like a room, and the rider need not fear wind or rain, heat or cold, because he is inside his room. If he wants to hide himself so that no one will see him, or if he is annoyed by the rays of the sun, he may lower the curtain over the windows.

Outside in front is a place for the driver, and in the rear a seat for another person, perhaps the driver's helper, or the servant of one of the passengers. The height [of the coach] is about two cubits[7] from the ground, so that it is higher than that [type of] small cart[8] which is hitched to one or more horses. The driver can also ride one of the horses drawing the coach. He holds a switch in his hand to spur the animals to a fast gallop, for their speed is breakneck, like a cavalry charge.

6. *Karrūṣa,* from the Spanish *carroza.* A four-wheeled cart drawn by a horse. Dozy 2:456. Nineteenth-century travelers to Morocco remarked on the absence of wheeled vehicles. J. H. D. Hay saw "on the road-side a wretched wheeled vehicle, ruder even in construction and form than a very ancient Egyptian cart which I saw shortly after its discovery on the banks of the Nile. This is the only wheeled carriage I have met with in all Morocco." *Western Barbary: Its Wild Tribes and Savage Animals* (London, 1861), pp. 121–22.

7. Arabic *dhirāʿ*, literally "forearm," the distance between the elbow and the tip of the middle finger, equal to about half a meter.

8. *Karrīṭa,* from the Spanish *carreta.* A small two-wheeled cart. Dozy 2:453; al-Ghassānī, *Iftikāk*, p. 39.

There is a long type [of vehicle] which accommodates a large number of people going in the same direction. If a person wishes to get off along the way, the driver will let him get down and then he will go on with the others. Most people who travel together in this way are related, such as a man and his wife, his children, and relatives, or a fellow and his friends, so they remain together during the journey. This type may have two levels, one on top of the other, or even separate compartments. They sometimes put the traveler's personal belongings or his wares on top, covering them to protect them from the elements. Another type accommodates just two people, and of this type there are many different kinds.

Yet another type is for carrying goods and heavy loads. It has no roof, but they cover it to keep off the rain by skillfully making arches from thin strips of wood and then stretching over them a heavy cloth, like the cloth for [making] sails. This cloth is then pulled tight and nailed down so that the goods are sheltered from the rain, as if they were in a tent. The driver also makes a place for himself under this covering, and the rain does not bother him either. In short, rain does not hinder travel in this country in any way, for it disturbs neither the traveler nor his goods; nor does it affect the road, as I am about to mention.

Other carts are made for carrying heavy loads such as stones or iron or the like. These are pulled by many horses hitched together, the number of horses depending on the quantity of weight to be drawn. This is not a great toil or labor for them. Even if the load is extremely heavy, only one person is needed to harness the animals or unhitch them. As for transferring goods, it is not necessary to unload them except at the end of the journey, for their weight rests on the cart harnessed to the draft animals and is pulled along by them.

Thus they handle huge loads easily, without difficulty or strain, and they carry nothing on the backs of animals. What one animal carries on its back, another could pull ten times over provided that the road is good. This is one of the sciences which they engage in—

the science of pulling heavy loads—and they have books written on it. Along their roads you hear only the sounds of heavy loads and the rattling of the chains used to draw them. The movement of freight is slow, unlike the movement of the passenger vehicles, which is very swift.

Speed is easy for them because of the smoothness of the roads, and their excellent state of repair. This is a great concern of theirs and a guiding principle in all matters. Their roads are like the floor of a room, with no bumps, holes, brambles, or stones to be seen. Wherever it begins to loosen up, they hurry to fix it, for they do not neglect its maintenance. Everywhere we passed we found piles of stones on both sides of the road to be used for repair. They crush them into jagged bits to strengthen their bond. If there is a hole somewhere, they fill it with these stones. The carts smooth out the road by grinding the stones into place when they pass, making it even firmer than before.

If the sides of the road have a slope, they build supports into them, and in most places the edges are planted with great trees which shade the road. There is not a river, ditch, or canal that does not have a bridge over it, and the entire length of our way we did not see one person fording a river on foot or on horseback.[9] You will not find any obstacles on the road either. All is smooth and level, with nothing to upset an animal or a cart. Their concern about this is so great that in certain places we found people with brooms

9. Bridges were rare in Morocco in the 1840s, but not entirely unknown. On his trip to Marrakesh in 1846, J. H. D. Hay passed two well-constructed bridges, a five-arched one reportedly built by a Spanish mason in the Shawiya region, and another closer to Marrakesh that had twenty-five arches. But most rivers and streams had to be forded or crossed by boat. Moving his small party across the Wad Sebou near Mehdiya took an entire day: "The embarkation immediately commenced of both horses and baggage in . . . one wretched boat. . . . The river is a wide and rapid stream, and the boat has only two oars, so that each passage has occupied upward of two hours; and though we commenced at break of day, we had not finished until sunset." Hay, *Journal*, p. 20.

in their hands, smoothing over the tracks of the carts, lest others follow in them and make ruts that would ruin the road.

Another example of their concern is that nearly every town has scales to weigh the wagons. The way they do it is with a thick wooden board mounted on something underneath that feels the weight, and descends according to it. They have marks for one *qinṭār*,[10] for two, and so on up to ten. As the weight increases, the board goes down. Every cart arriving at that place must pass over this board. The horses are taken off, and the wagon is weighed. Then they examine the wheels[11] [to see] if they are proper for carrying that weight, because they have a limit for the wideness of the rim in proportion to the weight it bears. If the rim of the wheel is narrow and the load heavy, the wheel leaves a deep rut that will eventually cause damage to the road. They have another purpose in weighing carts, and it is to see whether the load is more or less than they say. The reason for this is that they have to pay taxes on certain goods on entering or leaving a town.[12] They weigh them to make sure they do not carry anything hidden on which no tax was paid.

10. From a Greek word meaning "hundredweight" (cf. Latin *centenarium*). In Morocco it was equal to 100 *raṭls*, or about 50 kilograms. The weight of a *raṭl* changed from one region to another, and could vary according to the item being weighed; usually it meant a weight of about 500 grams. Laroui, *Origines*, pp. 49–50; Dozy 2:413.

11. In Arabic, *nāʿūra*, literally "noria" or "waterwheel." Since wheeled transport was rare, there was no commonly used Arabic word for cart wheel; the local word for "wheel" was often taken from the word for waterwheel. G. S. Colin, "La noria marocaine et les machines hydrauliques dans le monde arabe," *Hesp*. 14 (1932): 22–49; Thomas Glick, *Islamic and Christian Spain in the Early Middle Ages* (Princeton, 1979), pp. 236–39.

12. The word aṣ-Ṣaffār uses here is *maks*. In Morocco, the *maks* was a special duty imposed by the Sultan, separate from the Koranic taxes on land and income. Usually it was a "gate tax," levied on goods entering and leaving town, and thus aṣ-Ṣaffār associates it with the French *octroi*. The Moroccan *maks*, like the *octroi*, was greatly resented, especially by urban dwellers; often it was the spark that ignited popular uprisings. Al-Manūnī, *Maẓāhir* 1:297–301; *SEI*, s.v. "Maks"; E. Michaux-Bellaire,

There are agents (*wukalā' wa-nuqabā'*) along the road responsible for its upkeep; they have no task other than this, and usually their houses are alongside. Another indication of their concern is that wherever a road divides, they erect a signpost, writing on it where each road leads, and the condition of what lies ahead. At the sides they have marked the miles[13] in chalk so that the traveler may know how much [distance] has passed since the point of departure, and how much lies ahead.

It happens that travel in this country is easy both day and night, with no strain or toil, because there is complete security.[14] The traveler need not be afraid of thieves or brigands, and for that reason you will not see anyone carrying weapons other than a soldier. The good condition of the roads allows people to travel any time of night or day, even deep in the countryside, because their towns do not close their gates and have only a night watch. Indeed, most of the towns do not have an enclosing wall or gate, so that whatever time you arrive, you may enter.

Nor are the animals exhausted, for the horses and drivers are changed every hour. On the road are stables[15] that they call in their language the *poste*, where many horses are kept. When a traveler arrives here, he leaves his horses and takes fresh ones, along with a

"L'organisation des finances au Maroc," *AM* 11 (1907): 181, 189, 206–7, 213–16.

13. *Mīl*, used also in Arabic. Ibn Khaldūn says it equals 4,000 cubits, about two kilometers, or 1¼ English miles. *Muqaddimah* 1:96 and note 19.

14. A sign of the capable ruler was security on the roads. *Muqaddimah* 2:3. Travelers often had to depend on local authorities to provide security. Hay reported that the Moroccan countryside "is said to be infested with robbers. The Sultan has obliged two or three tribes to pitch their tents near the road so as to guard travellers from them." *Journal*, p. 52. But when the Sultan traveled, the movement became a demonstration of royal power: see J. Dakhlia, "Dans la mouvance du Prince: La symbolique du pouvoir itinérant au Maghreb," *Annales: Economies, Sociétés, Civilisations* 43, 3 (May–June 1988): 735–60.

15. *Iṣṭabl*, from the Latin *stabulum* (Spanish *establo*). Dozy 1:26; *EI* 2, s.v. "Iṣṭabl."

[new] driver. They go for an hour or so to another posthouse, where horses and driver are changed once again, so that the horses are always rested and may continue at the same fast pace. On our trip from Marseille to Paris, more than eight hundred horses were changed. We were in three coaches, each one drawn by ten horses: three, three, and four.

Nor does the journey keep the traveler from sleeping, because he is at his ease inside the coach—although not entirely, because he cannot stretch out fully. But no matter what the circumstances, travel is always a bit of torture, just as it says in the Hadith, for it keeps you from the full enjoyment of sleep, among other things.

[A Hadith:] One day when the Prophet was sitting in front of the Kaʿba[16] he was asked: "Why is travel a bit of torture?" And he answered at once: "Because of separation from one's loved ones." The Hadiths of Ibn ʿAbbās and Ibn ʿUmar[17] agree that travel is a bit of torture. One version has it: "Travel and profit from it!" while another says: "Travel and earn your livelihood!" and yet another says: "Travel and enjoy good health!" But travel does not have to improve one's health, so long as one has some benefit to show for it. Then it is not a bit of torture, but [simply] a hardship.

Whoever follows this road, traveling day and night, will arrive in Paris from Marseille in about three days. Letters and correspondence going from one city to the other take three days or less, even though the distance between them for a person traveling on horseback is close to a month.

16. The cultic center of Islam, located in the great mosque at Mecca, housing the sacred Black Stone. *SEI*, s.v. "Kaʿba."

17. Ibn ʿUmar and Ibn ʿAbbās were figures in early Islam. ʿAbd Allāh b. ʿUmar (d. 693) was the eldest son of the Caliph ʿUmar and one of the Prophet's closest companions; his contemporary, ʿAbd Allāh b. al-ʿAbbās (d. 687), was the cousin of the Prophet and famous for his sweeping knowledge of law and tradition. *SEI*, s.vv. " ʿAbd Allāh b. al-Abbās" and " ʿAbd Allāh b. ʿUmar b. al-Khaṭṭāb."

On our way we passed towns and villages, hills and valleys, and rolling countryside. You should know that these people do not have tents or huts[18] for dwellings, for they know only buildings and nothing else, although the [style] of buildings in the countryside differs from that in the cities. In reality, their villages are like most of the [larger] towns, for one finds in them whatever is found in the big city in the way of marketplaces and goods for sale. On our way we witnessed at first hand unmistakable evidence of their foresight and all-consuming concern for the matters of daily life, for improving their means of livelihood, and for mastering their affairs. They are very diligent about filling up the landscape with buildings and plantings. They do not follow the easy path or stay in the company of laziness or neglect. You will not see any wasted or barren land, or ruined buildings.[19] Wherever the soil is poor, they move good soil to it from another place. They give every kind of land what it needs. Land that will benefit from plowing is plowed, [land] that is good for planting is planted. Furthermore, they make a distinction in planting between what thrives in heavy soil and what grows in light, and earth and stones good for building are set aside for that.

Their trees are almost entirely cultivated, even if they are at the tops of mountains or deep within gullies.[20] They leave no spot bare, and even plant trees by ditches and streams and on the banks of rivers, yet they are not swept away. They do not neglect their up-

18. *Nawwāla*: a hive-shaped dwelling made out of sticks and thatch, seen especially in the countryside in northern Morocco.

19. Between Tangier and Rabat, Hay observed that the countryside was "almost uninhabited," but further south he found that "the country was better cultivated than any we had yet seen, the barley and wheat . . . looking splendid." *Journal*, p. 54; see also Laroui, *Origines*, pp. 34–38.

20. Forests were endangered in Morocco because of overgrazing and overuse: "The goats do their best to devour the young shoots, while the people of the country have the reprehensible custom of cutting down the trunks to make charcoal, and the thorny branches to fence in their fields." Aubin, *Morocco*, p. 12.

keep, and prune them whenever necessary. Nor is their concern limited to fruit-bearing trees, for they are few in number compared with others. Most trees bear no fruit, their only benefit being shade, firewood, and lumber. As for fruit trees, the olive is plentiful in the region of Toulon and Marseille, but it does not become overgrown as it does in Morocco.[21] Usually [the trees] are harvested from the ground and deliberately kept small so the fruit will grow large and the limbs strong. The oil is exceptionally sweet and clear. In fact there is a saying about French olive oil that goes like this: "Take a little of it to other parts because of its sweetness."

There are also many almond trees, particularly in the region of Marseille and its environs. They have both the sweet and the bitter almond, and their appreciation for the bitter is the same as for the sweet, or perhaps greater, for they use it in pastry and in soap-making, among other things. They have many walnut and mulberry trees, but the male of the species is more common there than the female.[22] Also there are apples, pears, plums, peaches, and cherries, but few apricots, according to what we saw. They keep fruit throughout the year by drying it and preserving it with sugar; no table would be without it. Likewise, fig trees are sparse, and we saw only a few in the region of Marseille and Toulon.

Orange trees are plentiful there, but they keep them in boxes.[23]

21. Aṣ-Ṣaffār refers to his country as *al-Maghrib*, "Morocco"—not meaning "the Greater Maghrib" (which included Algeria and Tunisia), because elsewhere he refers to Algeria as *al-Jazā'ir* and Tunisia as *Ifrīqīya*. On the Moroccan sense of national identity in the nineteenth century, see Laroui, *Origines*, pp. 57–59.

22. In Arabic, *tūt dūd al-ḥarīr*, the mulberry. The reference to male and female is not clear. Some mulberries bear no fruit; perhaps this is what he meant by the "male" of the species. *Encyclopaedia Britannica*, 1990 ed., s.v. "Mulberry."

23. Oranges were plentiful in Morocco, too—so much so that Hay remarked that near Rabat oranges "were sometimes sold on the trees at the rate of about a shilling per thousand." *Journal*, p. 43. Jackson noted that the vicinity of "Tetuan produces the most delicious oranges in the world; also

If it is a hot, summery day, they put them outside in the open air; if it is cold, snowy, or rainy, they bring them in for fear of their withering. In Paris we saw many rooms having windows and a roof of glass, in which they were set out in perfect order. On a sunny day, the [rooms] are opened up to let the air in; on a cold day they are closed. These boxes are huge, as are the trees in them. The date on one box showed that [the tree] was more than four hundred years old. They bring the boxes in and out with much pushing and pulling, to which they are quite accustomed. We did not see oranges planted in the ground, except a few in the region of Toulon. They told us that they also grow on an island in the sea facing Toulon.[24] Pomegranate trees are quite rare, and we saw them too in the [glassed-in] rooms.

Most of their trees are of the poplar variety, which grows magnificently tall. They are useful for the shade they give on hot days, and for the wood of their limbs and trunk. Firewood is a matter of great concern among them. The seller of wood there is like the seller of gold, because the kindling of a fire in every room on a cold day is of the utmost importance. You will see large open spaces heaped with wood, all of it dry, clean, and cut into short lengths of about a cubit. Wood is sold by weight, not by the load. They do not have open woodlands for gathering firewood, but each one cuts wood from his own property, planting trees in his fields and gardens for that purpose. A forest is the property of its owner and is not open to everyone.

They have rules about the cutting of trees, one of them being that he who has a forest must divide it according to when the trees mature. If they reach maturity in ten years, then [the owner] divides it into ten sections, [planting] a section each year. If it takes thirty [years], then he makes thirty [sections], so that when he cuts the last

figs, grapes, melons, apricots, plums, strawberries, apples, pears, pomegranates, citrons, lemons, limes." *Account*, p. 11.

24. These are the small Îles d'Hyères, also known as the Îles d'Or, which face the port of Toulon.

section, he will find that what he cut first has once again reached maturity. Another [rule] is that he may not cut a tree until an inspector approves it. If the wood suits the state[25] for shipbuilding or the like, [the inspector] will stamp it with his stamp, claiming it when he wishes, but only after paying the price. But if the wood is not suited for that, then the owner is free to cut it for himself after paying a tax[26] on the trees. Although trees are found everywhere in their country, not a single piece of wood is unclaimed, not even a twig. They watch over all of it, large and small, and do not permit it to leave their hands except at a price.

Another of their rules, and a basic tenet of their legal code,[27] is that the whole of France is inviolable, and no one is allowed to trespass on the property of another.[28] Whoever does so is punished with a penalty that is known to all. And there is no way of pleading or

25. Aṣ-Ṣaffār uses the Turkish word *beylik*, translated here as "state." *Makhzan*, meaning "government," was specific to Morocco. *Beylik* may have been suggested by interpreters who had spent time in Algeria; it was used also to denote the government ʿAbd al-Qādir had set up in Oran. Azan, *L'èmir Abd el Kader*, p. 133.

26. Arabic *kharāj*, the tax on land. Originally imposed on non-Muslims, it was later paid also by Muslims. According to Maliki law, the *kharāj* was not a tax but "rent" paid for use of the land, which was the property of the community. Established in Morocco around the thirteenth century, it was paid thereafter with some regularity, often under the name of *nāʾiba*. E. Michaux-Bellaire, "Le droit de propriété au Maroc," *RMM* 7 (1909): 365–78; and, by the same author, "L'impôt de la naïba et la loi musulmane au Maroc," *RMM* 11 (1910): 396–404.

27. *Sharīʿa*, the revealed law of Islam. Aṣ-Ṣaffār, like aṭ-Ṭahṭāwī, uses the term to denote the secular French legal code. *Takhlīṣ*, p. 94; *L'or*, p. 133. He also uses the word *qānūn*, meaning specific "rules," rather than a legal "code." Islamic legists made a distinction between the two: *sharīʿa* is the immutable law of God, while *qānūn* refers to regulations made by men to fit changing needs. The two are not incompatible, although derived from different sources. A. Hourani, "Aspects of Islamic Culture: Introduction," in Naff and Owen, *Studies*, pp. 266–67.

28. In France, aṣ-Ṣaffār did not find commons where people could cut fodder or graze their animals, as was the practice in rural Morocco.

paying one's way out of it. Along the road we saw low hedges separating the [public] way from private land. One of our [French] companions told us that he who steps over the line with one foot is imprisoned for five years, and he who stands completely inside [is jailed] for fifteen. So you do not see anyone, man or beast, wandering about on the property of another, even if it is an open field. The owner alone uses his land, not sharing it with others; even his animals are allowed to graze on it only rarely. The mainstay [for the animals] is cut forage. Each person plants on his own land whatever he harvests for food or forage during the year, using it himself or selling it to others. We did not see any pastureland where forage grew [untended], as we have here in Morocco.

Another benefit of the trees mentioned above is the huge timbers which help in building and other tasks, and the boards from which they make doors, boxes, and things of wood such as ships, boats, masts, and the like. They train a tree from an early age to grow straight as a shaft, so that it is suitable for masts and so on. Their need for wood in building is great because the partitions between rooms are painted wood. One realizes this only after a close inspection. Only the exterior walls are built of stone.

In planting trees, they align them in a way that is marvelous to the point of perfection. They make the rows equal and the lines parallel, so that not a single tree protrudes out from the next. You see long alleys between the rows of trees with no undulations; all the rows appear to be connected and absolutely straight. They put them in lines and sections according to their various kinds. Because of this arrangement in planting, the rest of the land is left free for plowing. Usually they do not leave cropland entirely bare, but grow trees at the edges, which does not prevent them from working the middle.

They have a great concern, one might even say an obsession, for the cultivation of the grape. Their vineyards are even more numerous than their croplands because of their passion for wine, which is one of their necessities of life. If you spilled out all their wine, it would fill up the sea. As for the arable land, it is sufficient when well tended. In the region of Paris there is much good land, and the flour of Paris is extremely white and pure.

Another of their rules of planting is that the state gives a prize to whoever excels over others in farming, thereby encouraging each one to work hard and harvest more than the rest. Another of their rules is that if their land produces sufficient grain, they are not allowed to import grain from outside. Even if it comes in only to be milled and leaves again, its entry and exit will be by weight, lest some of it stay behind and ruin the market for the grain grown in their own country. Otherwise they might become lax in planting, and in the future run short. However, if their yield is insufficient, they are permitted to buy it from other lands, and they exempt it from taxes[29] to encourage its coming from afar. Most of their land is not fertile and verdant like the land of Morocco. The soil is not flattened down by constant walking, yet once the crops have been harvested, it stays heavy, hard, and coarse, despite the constant digging, working, and manuring. They get out of it what they can. We did not see any of the green grass or new growth that we have here in winter.

On our way we saw many rivers and streams, all of them navigated by large and small boats, and even steamers. Their riverboats are long and flat-bottomed, since the rivers are not deep like the ocean; but what they take off from their depth, they add to their length. Boats are found in small rivers as well as large ones, for if the river is too shallow, they dig it out, widening its course until the boat can pass. Nor do they limit themselves to rivers that open up to others naturally, but make it happen by excavating in between. If two rivers run parallel with no connection, they make a channel allowing boats to pass from one to the other. You will not see a river

29. The Arabic is *ʿushr*, the "tenth part" of annual income, levied on all Muslims according to Koranic law. In Morocco, where revenue was measured chiefly in flocks and harvests, the *ʿushr* was equal to one-tenth of the annual grain harvest. *SEI*, s.v. " ʿUshr."

with its banks silted up, or one deviating from its course, or other results of neglect. Instead, they keep them in perfect condition. Most of the riverbanks are solidly built up.

If there is a road running alongside, they often build up its edge as part of the riverbank, shoring it with heavy stone posts. Then they stretch long pieces of wood along the tops of the posts, nailing them in place. This keeps the road from being ruined and the carts from tipping over; it also prevents the barrier from sliding down the slope.

There are many rivers in that country. Among the largest and most renowned that we passed is a river called the Rhône, which appears in the outskirts of the city of Lyon, where it meets another called the Saône. It leaves Lyon heading east and ends in the Small Sea west of Marseille.[30] On its way it meets other rivers, which add to it and increase its waters so that in some places it seems like a sea, with large steamers traveling on it. And they call all of it the Rhône. Along its banks between Lyon and Marseille are many towns and huge bridges of different types, and forests and vineyards. It swells with a plentitude of rain, and diminishes with a lack of it, but its trees and embankments are not affected by floods because their construction is solid.

A river called the Loire flows between Lyon and Paris and then westward until it empties into the Great Sea. We saw it first on our way to Paris in the city of Roanne, and we never left it until we passed Orléans, which is on the last stage of the route to Paris. It too has towns and farmland along its banks; large boats travel on it. It connects with [lesser] streams, but all of it is called the Loire. It passes through many villages, and in some places it is crossed by marvelous bridges of different shapes, even in the midst of towns, about which I shall say more later. Another river, called the Seine, flows through the city of Paris, as I mentioned, heading west until it reaches the Great Sea. These are the largest rivers we saw, but

30. The Rhône actually flows south from Lyon.

there are many small ones and almost all flow into one another; and if not, it is made to happen, as I have said.

Most of the goods transported on river boats are heavy, such as stone, wood, coal, building materials, vegetables, fruits, and the like. Most of the road [between Marseille and Paris] is flat and level. We did not see any towering peaks such as we have[31] except in the region of Lyon, where there are hills and even mountains. But they outwit the sharp incline by making the road turn with it, so that one does not feel the strain. If it is a small mountain they cut the road through it so that the carriages move along easily. Between Lyon and Paris the country is hilly, but close to Paris it is all valleys and lowlands, with no mountains at all. The most difficult [terrain] was between Aix and Toulon, where exhausting hills and steep rises made the carriage move slowly.

The whole way is settled, especially between Marseille and Lyon, with towns crowded close together, even more so than between Lyon and Paris, where the land is often empty; yet even there you are always in sight of towns or villages. The houses are found alongside the road, either singly or in groups, with no vacant places between. You will not pass anywhere without seeing a building, a village, a house, or a cluster of houses, either close by or within view. Even in each vineyard there is a dwelling place for its attendant and his family.

Everything along the road belongs to the town. Often the road passes through its midst, opening a way between its markets and shops. Either within the town or just beyond are all the crafts necessary to the wayfarer, such as carriage and cart makers, or blacksmiths who shoe horses and make tools. If the traveler needs to make repairs, he can find a place for it close at hand. Also along the

31. The High Atlas Mountains in the south of Morocco have a covering of snow throughout the year; Jabal Tubkal (4,165 m) is the highest peak in North Africa. J. Martin et al., *Géographie du Maroc* (Paris, 1967), pp. 130–42.

way are taverns[32] for travelers, and many posthouses to rent horses for the carriages and wagons. Whatever the traveler needs will be found nearby.

As for the towns and cities we passed on our way, the first was Marseille, where we disembarked. It is a large city, one of the centers of civilization[33] of France. It has no wall on the side facing the sea, but its port is fortified with cannon on all sides. It has a narrow entryway with huge beacons to guide [ships] at night. There are many cafés in the port; they are of the finest and richest decoration. The port forms a deep inlet next to the town, and lies between it and a small mountain. Its quays are built like those of Port-Vendres. In the port there are boxes anchored in place with many large holes. Whoever wishes to enter the port ties a rope to [one of the boxes] and hauls on it to pull the ship in, because there is no wind inside the port.

It is not a port for corsairs[34] or ships of war, but rather for ships of trade. We found so many ships loaded with goods there, we could not find a way between them. They said there were more than a thousand, for this is a city of commerce. Merchants from every clime come here, and goods and manufactures from all over France. Goods that are not French are rare, except those things they import because of their scarcity or absence in their own country. If goods are brought in and they [already] have them, they make the tax[35] on them excessive, so that the demand for them will not be

32. Literally "houses of winesellers."

33. Arabic *ḥāḍira*, a word used by medieval geographers to denote a large and populous urban center, as opposed to the *bādiya*, the underpopulated rural areas. *Muqaddimah* 1:lxxx; Dozy 1:299.

34. *Qurṣāl*, from the Italian *corsale*, a corsair or privateer. Since privateering was no longer practiced in the Mediterranean, the word here means simply a type of warship. It is sometimes written as *qurṣān*. Brunot, *La mer*, pp. 337–44.

35. Arabic *ʿushr* (see note 29) could also mean an export duty, collected as goods were leaving a town. In 1845, a tax levied in Fes on all goods

greater than for their own. In this way they protect their own crafts, lest they be abandoned for lack of a market.

In this city are lofty houses and imposing buildings, exquisite shops with all kinds of goods, and very elegant people. The shops in the port are next to the quays, and large and small ships come right up to them; the wall is built of huge rocks with only a roadway separating it from the shops. The streets are wide, with room on each side for those on foot; the middle is kept for carriages and carts. Something exceedingly disgusting is the filth and refuse flowing everywhere down the middle of the street, urine and even excrement; but they do not seem to mind it, and it is sold at a price. People charged with the task go about collecting it in large buckets, drying it for fertilizer.

All of their streets open onto one another, with no blind alleyways. There are wide open places lined with trees, where people come on days of heat to promenade under their shade. One of the most famous neighborhoods is known as Borély,[36] a place of trees and fountains where most of the houses of the notables and people of wealth are located.

This city is the seat of one of the provinces[37] of France, and it governs over the surrounding district. In the whole of France there are eighty-five or eighty-six provinces, each containing a large city and the smaller towns around. Each province has two governors,

---

destined for Algeria was called the *ʿushr funduq an-najjārīn*, "the duty of the carpenters' inn," from the place where it was collected. See E. Michaux-Bellaire, "Les impôts marocains," *AM* 1 (1904): 65.

36. The Château Borély, built by a wealthy merchant of Marseille in the late eighteenth century, surrounded by an expansive park. Aṭ-Ṭahṭāwī stayed there before his departure for Paris in 1831. *L'or*, p. 94 note 70.

37. *Iyāla*, an Arabic word that became an Ottoman administrative term (*eyalet*, or "province") and was adopted in Morocco during the Saʿadian period. Ibn Zaydān, *ʿIzz*, 1, glossary, p. 399. At the end of the eighteenth century, the huge provinces of pre-Revolutionary France were broken up and replaced by 86 *départements*, translated here as "province" to stay close to the Arabic original.

one for the army and the other for the common folk. The governor of the people is equal to a *qā'id al-bilād* in our own land, but the rank of governor of the army is higher.[38] Their seat is the [main] city of the province they govern, and each of them has deputies under his authority. The province of Marseille and its district includes Toulon and the city of Aix, which I shall mention later.

The outskirts of [Marseille] are crowded and bustling with life, with buildings one right after another. You go beyond it for a distance, yet you still seem to be in the midst of the town. The people of Marseille wanted to bring water from a river about three days away, near the city of Avignon, and they paid a great sum of money for this. But the water still has not come, although they are making a great effort, digging deep channels under the mountains and building enormous aqueducts between them. They are digging with the help of steam engines that take mountains of dirt out of the bowels of the earth.[39] They also are hard at work building a new port, for the old one is silted up with filth and waste from the town, its waters black and putrid. They want to make an improved one north of the present one, using the same well-made entryway we mentioned above.[40]

After our departure from Marseille we went on to a city called Aix, which is smaller than Marseille and part of its district. Here are

38. The "governor of the people" was the *préfet*, the highest civil official of the *département*. The "governor of the army" was a general in charge of a local garrison, serving under orders from the Ministry of War. *Grande encyclopédie Larousse*, 1882 ed., s.v. "Département."

39. An aqueduct from the river Durance to Marseille, a distance of 83 kilometers, was begun in 1839 and completed in 1847. More than 21 kilometers of its length was underground. *L'Illustration*, 6 September 1845.

40. The conquest of Algeria stimulated commercial activity in Marseille, creating the need for a larger port; the depth of the old port was too shallow to allow ships of heavy tonnage to enter. In 1844, just before aṣ-Ṣaffār's visit, a law was passed authorizing the construction of a new dock just north of the old quays. *Guide Michelin: Provence*, 1976 ed., p. 95.

shops, markets, hotels, and a military garrison.[41] It is especially renowned among the French because of its scholarship in the law. Whoever in the district of Marseille is convicted of murder will be executed in this town, because it is here that judgment takes place.[42]

In Aix we saw a huge cross made of wood standing on one side of the town square. At its top was a smaller bit of wood made into the likeness of a crucified man, naked except for a cloth covering his maleness. What a sight it was! We were terrified to see it and thought that he was a criminal they had hung there, for without a doubt, whoever saw it [would think it] was a crucified man. I asked about this and they told me that it was the deity and the crucifix which they worshipped. They claim he is Jesus, that is to say, a likeness of him crucified. And there is no doubt that they believe in his divinity just as the Koran tells us, and there is no doubt about the untruth of their claim and the falsity of their belief. "*For they have no knowledge of it, and only follow conjecture.*"[43] Those are the words of their mouths, which is [false] like the speech of those who become infidels just before they die. My God how they lie! This is the cross set up in their churches to worship and glorify, and which Jesus, may peace be unto him, will break upon his return, refuting the falsehood of their belief and the wrongheadedness of the Christian religion.

[A Hadith:] Al-Qasṭallānī[44] in his commentary on the *Ṣaḥīḥ* mentions the tradition about breaking the cross as follows: It is said

41. *Qishla*, a Turkish word meaning "barracks." Dozy 2:351.

42. The court of appeal for the *département* of Marseille had its seat in Aix. *Guide Michelin: Provence*, 1976 ed., p. 46.

43. Koran 4:157.

44. An Egyptian authority on Hadith who died in 923/1517. Muslim belief is that Jesus, revered as a prophet, was not crucified, but another "who bore his likeness" died in his place, thus disassociating Jesus from the idolatrous symbol of the cross. The passage quoted by aṣ-Ṣaffār comes from al-Qasṭallānī's commentary on the *Ṣaḥīḥ* of al-Bukhārī, entitled *Irshād as-sārī fī sharḥ al-Bukhārī*. *SEI*, s.vv. " ʿĪsā" and "al-Ḳasṭallānī."

that its origin is that a group of Jews insulted Jesus and his mother, peace be unto them, and God called upon the [Jews] and changed them into pigs and monkeys. Then the Jews decided to kill [Jesus]. God warned him and said he would raise him to heaven. Then [Jesus] said to his companions, "Which of you wishes to take on my likeness, be killed and crucified, and so enter the Garden of Eden?" One of them got up and God cast upon him the likeness [of Jesus], so that it would be he who was killed and crucified. And then people said, perhaps this man is a dissembler, and tried to prove it by entering the house of Jesus, but Jesus had already left and his likeness was cast on the other. So that when the Jews entered, they killed [the dissembler], claiming he was Jesus. Then they disagreed and some said that he was God and could not be killed; and others said that a dissembler had been killed and crucified; and others said that if it was Jesus, then where was his companion; and if it was his companion, then where was Jesus? And some said he was raised to heaven, and others said his face is the face of Jesus, and his body the body of the companion. Then the Jews oppressed the companions of Jesus, peace be unto him, by killing and crucifying and jailing [them], until the matter came before the Master of Rome.[45] He was told that the Jews were oppressing the companions of Jesus, because he said he was the Messenger of God, he was giving life to the dead, he was healing the dumb and the leprous, and working miracles, and that the Jews had killed him and crucified him. And [the Master of Rome] sent for the crucified body, which was taken down from the wooden pieces. The pieces of wood on which he was crucified were brought to the Master of Rome, who began to worship them. From them they made many crosses and from that day on Christians have worshipped the cross. The end.

The cross of the crucifixion appears there in different guises, but always in the same form. Sometimes it is large, at other times it is small. It may be of wood, stone, metal, brass, or gold, or in a picture. Sometimes the form of the crucified Jesus is on it, sometimes

45. *Ṣāḥib ar-Rūm*, or Pontius Pilate.

it is the cross alone, as was mentioned by al-Qasṭallānī. Many are sold in the shops. The figure of Jesus is portrayed in various ways: as a grown man, or a small boy in the lap or arms of Mary. In the church they pray to them both. If you ask one of them about this likeness, he will explain to you that it is God, or His son, or His mother if Mary is there. May [God] preserve them from that, and may He be raised high above what the sinners say. The proof of our eyes only increased our insight into their unbelief, the falsity of their creed, and the stupidity of their reasoning. Thanks be to God who guided us to the true religion. We ask God, praise be unto Him, to keep us in the true faith until death. Amen. With the help of our faithful prophet, may prayers and the purest peace be upon him until the Day of Judgment.

We left [Marseille], the place of our first night's rest, for Avignon, a large city surrounded by a wall and gates bearing the marks of antiquity. It was like other places with respect to its markets and garrison and so on. They say that thirty-three thousand souls live there. Alongside it flows the river Rhône. Enormous bridges span it at that place and there are many large and small boats there. Vast amounts of wood, boards, firewood, and charcoal are transported on the river. It is one of the centers of civilization in their land. The surrounding countryside is flat, fertile, and cultivated. Along the whole way we did not see any place greener than this. Nearby is another river called the Durance, spanned by a wooden bridge in which we counted about fifty arches.

After that we passed many towns, one called [?], and another Sorgues. The river Ouvèze flows nearby, crossed by a small bridge. Then comes Orange, an old town with an arched gate more than a thousand years old, according to the date upon it.[46] After that come

46. The *Arc de Triomphe* of Orange was built by Caesar in 49 B.C. to celebrate his victories over the Gauls. *Guide Michelin: Provence*, 1976 ed., p. 112.

Mornas, Lapalud, Montélimar, then Loriol, followed by the river Drôme, which is crossed by a small bridge where it meets the Rhône; then a town called La Paillasse. All these are small towns which look alike and are close together. We spent the second night in the town of Valence, a large place that bore the signs of civilization. It has a citadel[47] surrounded by an ancient wall with cannons in it. This town is skilled in the science of artillery, and they come here from other parts to study it.[48]

The night of our stay, there was a heavy snowfall which covered the earth, the rooftops, and the branches of the trees with whiteness. Carts which passed the night on the road or in the open fields had a covering of snow to the depth of a finger or more. This was the first time we saw snow there, and we were to see it again in even greater quantity.

After Valence there is a small river, the Isère, which has a new bridge over it. Whoever crosses over it must pay a set sum at a house to one side. No one passes over without paying, until they collect in full what was spent on [building] it. Then we passed a town called Tain on the banks of the Rhône; then another called St.-Vallier; then another called the village of Roussillon; then Vienne, which is ancient and known for its cathedral of St. Maurice. Workshops for making wool[49] are found in this village and it is famous for it. The whole day's journey was along the banks of the Rhône, and we spent the third night in the city of Lyon.[50]

47. *Qaṣba*; in Morocco, a walled section of the imperial town housing troops belonging to the Sultan.

48. The Ecole d'Artillerie, where the cadet Napoleon Bonaparte perfected his skills in gunnery in 1785. *Guide Michelin: Vallée du Rhône*, 1985 ed., p. 156.

49. *Mlūf*, a fine wool cloth used for outer clothing, originally from the Italian city of Amalfi. Harrell, p. 81; Dozy 2:61; *IB* 2:44 note 124; Ibn Zaydān, *'Izz*, 1, glossary, p. 418.

50. The text gives precise directions on pronunciation: "With a *hamza* at the beginning, a *sukūn* on the *lām*, and a long *yā*."

Lyon

This is a large city, one of the centers of civilization in France, larger than Marseille, situated between the mountains and surrounded by fortified walls. It is the center for silkmaking in France, and damask[51] and other fine silks are made here. They say that there are many thousands of silkworkers. Two rivers meet there, the Rhône and the Saône, and continue as one great river. They say that the Rhône is like a man and the Saône is like a woman: just as a man meets a woman, the two [rivers] are coupled there. There are countless small boats and steamers on the river at that place, and marketplaces and fancy shops filled with splendid goods, butcher shops and bakeries, fruit sellers and greengrocers. There is an enormous bridge at the entrance to the city built of huge pillars and arches, lined with rows of lanterns of clear glass which illuminate the way in the darkness. The streets and the shops have a wondrous appearance at night.

There are many soldiers here, for it is the seat of one of the provinces of France governing over [its surroundings]. A general (*jilnār*) of the army, whom they call in their language *le préfet*, just as in Marseille, is the most important man in the region. Many workshops called *fabriques*[52] are found there, and the walls [of the city] are black with their smoke. Women are usually employed in the workshops both here and elsewhere, for they are the mainstay of the crafts.

The people [of Lyon] are very industrious about increasing its size, and it is quite filled up with buildings; there are also new bridges and iron roads[53] that join it with other places. Travelers and goods are drawn to it because it is one of the centers of the land of France, specializing in crafts and manufactures not found in other

51. *Thawb al-mushajjar,* "flowered cloth," meaning damask, a richly patterned silk cloth made originally in Damascus. Dozy 1:730.

52. In Arabic, *al-fabrīkāt.*

53. *Ṭuruq al-ḥadīd,* cf. French *chemin de fer*: the railroad, to be described in detail later.

places. Its buildings are better constructed than those of Marseille. Its outskirts are so densely settled they seemed to be part of the city. We did not see as much of this place as we did of others along our way, for we only passed through and did not linger; therefore our description of it is brief.

We left by a winding road that went between the mountains and up to their summits, yet the coaches climbed with ease. You felt as if you were on the plain with the mountain rising in front of you, but suddenly you found yourself at the pinnacle. That is because of the smoothness of the road. They build it up where it is low, and take away from it where it is high, so that all of it is level and you do not feel the incline except in a very few places. Along the route, water ran in rivulets among the orchards, and there were gardens with all kinds of plantings set out in neat rows. We finally reached a town called Tarare, a small place with many sources of water, where they make a type of white cloth.[54] In the late afternoon a heavy snow fell, continuing on into the darkness of night. We could not tell the earth from the sky, because of the whiteness of the snow. As for the cold, do not ask how bitter it was! But we did not suffer from it, thanks be to God, because we were inside the coach. The windows were shut tight and our breath collected inside its closeness. The cozy warmth stayed with us and we felt no discomfort until we went outside.

We spent that night in the town of Roanne, a medium-sized place surrounded by villages scattered about on rolling hills. Before entering it we passed over the river Loire, mentioned before. Between this town and the city of Lyon is one of the roads of iron for the locomotive,[55] according to the description which follows.

We left this town and went on to a place called Lapalisse, a small village. [We passed] many villages after that until we reached the town of Moulins, a middle- to large-sized town where we spent the

54. Tarare was famous for the manufacture of *mousseline*, a fine cotton fabric originally made in Mosul, Iraq. *Guide Michelin: Vallée du Rhône*, 1985 ed., p. 149.

55. In Arabic, *bābūr al-barr*; that is, "a steam engine [that travels] by land."

night. Then we continued on to a village called Imphy,[56] then to one of their principal cities, Nevers, on the banks of the river Nièvre, which is small but has all kinds of vessels on it. We then passed Pouilly on the Loire, and spent the night in Cosne. After this came Briare, which is crossed by a small river branching off from the Loire; then the city of Gien, a big town on the banks of the Loire. Here there is a large bridge on twelve arches which we took on our way to Paris, heading north. That night, the seventh since our departure from Marseille, we stayed in Orléans, a large city said to have thirty-five thousand inhabitants, where there is a church of marvelous workmanship.[57] They claim there is none other like it in France, for it is built of marble. This city is on the banks of the Loire, and at the entry to it is a bridge fifty paces long and the width of three carts side by side.

In one of the squares of that city, next to the church I mentioned, is the likeness of a pious woman who they claim lived among them long ago.[58] When another race of Christians invaded their land, she met them at the head of an army and drove them out. All this happened about three hundred years ago. We saw the likeness of this holy woman in many places. Between this city and the city of Paris we still had ninety miles, which we covered by the iron road.

An Explanation of the Iron Road and the Means of Travel on it

First they laid out a road, making it firm and level. Then they stretched across its width crosspieces of heavy wood placed a cubit or two apart. On top of them on both sides, to the right and the

56. In the text, it is written *Fīnī*.

57. The Cathedral of Ste. Croix, built in the thirteenth century in the Gothic style. *Michelin Guide: Châteaux of the Loire* (English ed.), 1988, p. 149.

58. Jeanne d'Arc, the "Maid of Orleans" (1412–31). Aṣ-Ṣaffār refers to her as a *rāhiba*, a "holy woman."

left, they laid iron bars going the length of the road, securing them to the crosspieces with iron rings nailed into them from below so that the bars would not move from their place; and so it is from the beginning of the road until its end.

Then they laid down sand or earth, so that only the two rails stand out. They constructed a small engine, not the same as the steamer of the ocean, but having in it the force to turn the wheels and nothing else. Three men ride inside, driving it. They made carriages, similar to but finer and larger than those drawn by horses, adding to them wheels that go along the iron road. The wheels of the carriages are just like the wheels on each side of the engine and the distance between the wheels crosswise is the same as the width of the road, so that the edge of the wheel comes down on the protruding iron bar. The outside rim of the wheel is hollowed out, strengthening its bond with the iron bar, so that it does not deviate to the right or the left. And the wheels of all the carriages are like that.

These carriages are connected to one another with couplings and heavy chains of iron, making one long line with the steam engine in the lead. The people ride inside. Each carriage has two or more separate compartments, with benches facing each other for people to sit on. There are windows of clear glass on both sides which may be opened or closed, permitting full light and view. Moreover, if travelers have loaded carts, they may take them along on a conveyance having wheels like the [other] carriages.

When we were about to depart, the chief (*ra'īs*) started the engine, and it carried along whatever was joined to it at a speed we had never experienced, almost like a bird flying through the air. We covered the distance between Orléans and Paris in two and a half hours. When we looked at the sides of the road, we could not see what was there; it looked like an endless ribbon moving along with us, and we could not distinguish the rocks or anything. We tried as hard as we could to read the signs at the side of the road that measured off the miles—even though they were marked on white rocks in heavy black letters the height of a finger—but we were unable to fix our eyes on them because of our speed. They claim that if this road of iron extended from Marseille to Paris, it would take only a day and a night to cover the [entire] distance.

Many engines come and go on this and other iron roads, but each one has an appointed time of departure, lest two of them meet head on at the same place and prevent the other from passing. Generally, they make tracks for two on a single way, and each goes on its own track; if the two draw alongside one another, one will be going and the other coming, so that when they meet they will not ram into one another because each is in its own place. Perhaps they could even make room for three.

This roadway is reserved for the steam engine, and neither walking nor [horseback] riding on it is permitted. It is guarded carefully, for fear that the engine will collide with something. If someone walks there heedlessly, it is impossible to warn him before the engine reaches him, because of its great speed. For that reason they give the engines whistles, which they blow from afar to warn whoever might be unmindful of its coming; also, if there is another engine heading toward it, they will be aware of its approach. If the chief wants to stop the engine in the middle of the road he may do so. At times he is obliged to stop, to change the water whose steam drives the wheels. Along the way they have made certain places on the iron rails where he may turn off if the need arises.

Another thing about that road is that it must be level and smooth, with no bumps or dips. When it comes to a mountain, the slope rises gradually for some distance so that the hill is done away with. If they cannot do that and are obliged to pass that way, they cut the road through the belly of the mountain under the earth, boring through completely to the other side. Then with great skill and exactitude they build a domelike structure over [the roadway], and the engines pass through. We rode on another iron road from Paris to one of their gardens.[59] On the way we passed beneath the moun-

59. This was the railroad line between Paris and Versailles, the scene of a terrible rail disaster in 1842. Schivelbusch, *Railway Journey*, p. 131.

tains in many places, finding ourselves in such heavy darkness that we had to light the lamps although it was daytime. We traveled for half a mile under the earth. When we emerged we [looked back and] saw that trees, buildings, and farmlands had been above us as we passed beneath.

There are two kinds of iron roads. One type is built by the state, that is to say, what we call the "state treasury."[60] The other type, which is the more common, is built by [private] businessmen and is a form of commerce there. They get together a group who are in agreement about doing it, and then estimate how much it will cost. If they say it will be a million [francs], for example, they then divide that million among ten people, each one giving a hundred thousand. Then they write out ten papers, specifying the agreement in writing, so that it is known that whoever holds one of these papers has paid for building such-and-such road. Likewise, he will draw from its profits in proportion to what he has paid in, such as a tenth in this case. After they write out the papers they sell them for a hundred thousand [francs] each, until all the papers are sold. The million is then collected, and they pay it out bit by bit, for the workers and for whatever else is needed in the way of materials and so on. When it is completed and people begin to travel on it, they must pay a fee. Whatever profit comes from it is divided among the payers of the capital, each receiving an amount in proportion to what he paid in. This is only after the Sultan, or whoever is responsible, gives them permission to do this and sets a limit on the amount to be paid by the travelers and the length of time it may be collected. When the time is expired, the road returns to the state, which then takes the profits or allows people to use it for free.[61]

60. The *bayt al-māl*, the depository for the Sultan's wealth. In precolonial Morocco the treasury was located in three places—Fes, Meknes, and Marrakesh. *ʿIzz*, 1, glossary, p. 401.

61. On financing French railroads, see F. Braudel and E. Labrousse, eds., *Histoire économique et sociale de la France*, vol. 3: *L'avènement de l'ère industrielle (1789–1880)*, part 1 (Paris, 1976), pp. 257–62; Pinkney, *Decisive Years*, pp. 36–37, 45–46.

If someone owning a paper wishes to sell it, he may do so. If it yielded much profit and interest it will be much coveted, so that he may resell it for more than he paid; or the opposite may be true. The buyer then takes the place of the seller and receives the profit. They also do this with the building of bridges; all the new bridges we saw, the traveler had to pay a toll when crossing. This kind of commerce goes on until the time expires and the [investors] remove their hands from it and people begin to use the bridge without paying, as they do with the old bridges. They also do the same thing with mining ventures. Nor is [the buying of shares] limited only to the rich; sometimes they make many papers and reduce the price of each, to make it easy for people to buy. Then each person buys what he can pay for, even if it is only one percent.

Our travel by the iron road came to an end with our arrival in a great high room that was within the walls of the city of Paris. This is the place where the engines of steam arrive and depart—that is, their home port—just like the one from which they set out in the city of Orléans. We entered Paris at midday Sunday, the twenty-eighth day of the month of Dhū al-Ḥijja al-Ḥarām, the end of the year 1261, corresponding to the 28th of December, the end of the year 1845 since the birth of Jesus, peace be unto him, according to the calendar of Rūm. Our trip from Marseille to Paris took seven days, and from Tetuan to Paris, fifteen days.

On our return,[62] after leaving the carriages [pulled by] the steam engine we went by coach, taking a different route. One of the cities we visited was Toulon; we did not mention it before because we visited it only on our return from Paris. When we reached Aix, we left the road to Marseille and went instead in the direction of Toulon by a route that was difficult and exhausting because of the steep mountains. The way was sparsely settled, being mostly vineyards and olive groves, with a few orange trees at the approach to it.

62. Aṣ-Ṣaffār interjects here his narrative of "the return," so that his report on Paris, which follows, is set apart as the high point of the journey.

Toulon is home port for their marines and their ships of war. Although the port is small, it is heavily fortified with double walls, and in front is a deep, wide trench. The gate to the city is on the other side of the trench, and [to reach it] one must cross over a bridge which is raised at night and lowered by day. The town is encircled by fortifications bristling with cannon. There is no commerce there, and only a small market, for its main purpose is as a naval base. The port itself is very large and is situated in an inlet between the mountains, which shelter it from the wind. It is well protected by fortifications, and its shore is built up on all sides. Near the port are storehouses and a repair shop for ships and their equipment, which they call an *arsenal.*[63] These are very tall, huge rooms which a warship can enter in its entirety. Once it is inside the room, they raise it up on wooden posts to repair it. It is drawn out of the water by a moving force and lifted onto a wooden cradle, which they pull into the room. When the work is completed, it is returned to the water in the same way.

On our arrival the chief of a ship, whom they call *amiral,*[64] insisted that we visit some of the ships in the port. We had to comply, and they chose for us some of their best launches. We rode in one up to a steam-powered warship[65] and boarded. We saw its artillery pieces and cannon and the rest of its equipage, the fitness of its soldiers, the setting of everything in its proper place, the speed and

63. In Arabic, *ṭarsana*. This word came originally from Arabic, *dār ṣanʿa*, a "house of craft," but in the special sense of "an establishment for the construction and equipment of warships." It then passed into European languages (Italian *arsenale*, French *arsenal*) and later returned to Arabic in a new form. Dozy 1:420; *EI* 2, s.v. "Dār al-Ṣināʿa."

64. *Al-mirānḍ*, from the French *amiral*; another word borrowed from Arabic (*amīr al-*, "commander of") which later returned to it in another form. *Muqaddimah* 2:37.

65. *Bābūr qurṣāl*. This vessel was the *Descartes*, described as "a fine steamship of 540 horses" by Pourcet, who added that the Moroccans "examined every part in detail, asking for explanations about everything." AAE/CPM 16/35–37, Pourcet to Guizot, 2 March 1846.

obedience with which they followed the captain's orders, the energy, discipline, and precision of the men, which goes along with their enormous power, their singleness of purpose, and their readiness for any eventuality.

Before leaving this ship we saw one of the strangest things we found there. They were sweetening the seawater until it became drinkable. They did this by bringing it up from the sea by some means and putting it in a vessel inside an oven to boil. I saw what they did with it after that; it came out of another spigot cold and sweet. It might take the place of fresh water, but it was not the same in sweetness, although one could make do with it if necessary. We asked their chief about it and he told us this: they let the water drip until its saltiness rises to the top and its sweetness stays below—or perhaps it is the opposite—but I could not verify it at the time because of the lack of a fluent interpreter. He also told us that rainwater rises from the sea with its saltiness removed by the sun's heat. Here the heat of the fire replaces the heat of the sun. This is what he said, but he did not convince us of the truth of how it was done, although he tried. Indeed, one's own experience is the best measure of truth.

We went up on that ship to the sound of music and drums; and afterward, when we returned to our launch, they raised the flag of our Sultan to the top of the mast above their own. And they fired cannons of rejoicing more than a hundred and thirty times. Then we went to another, a huge man-of-war[66] with a hundred and two guns, so immense and well-equipped that it is difficult to imagine. All in all, this ship is a fortified city at sea, and we found there musicians and soldiers in great number. After we came aboard, they raised our flag above theirs and asked us to tour the ship to see what was there, for it is their nature to delight in showing off what they have, and they never leave a thing, whether significant or otherwise,

66. *Nābyūs*, probably from Spanish *navio*, "ship." This was the *Jemmapes*, which had participated in the bombardment of Tangier two years before. See Introduction, note 61.

without pointing it out. As for our reception on that huge ship, on the surface they manifest nothing but pleasure, but inside they fear us as well as delight in us. Praise be to God that we have no fear of them, for it is only God that we fear.

They showed us the manner in which they fire the guns on this ship. If they wish to do battle, each man has his special task and appointed place, either sitting or standing, and if another is in it, he is remiss. When the captain comes around, they stand at attention and then each goes about his work: the one in charge of gunpowder busies himself with setting the charge in the gun to which he is assigned, and not another; likewise the one who aims the gun, and the one who pulls and pushes it [back into place]. As soon as they find their posts they get to work, and so it is with each cannon and its crew. The upshot of this is that each one has his assigned task and does nothing else, each crew has its own gun and works only that one. If their captain comes around they do not stand before him and say, "What should I do?", nor do two of them undertake the work of one, nor do they all gather around one gun and leave another unused, for that is idleness. At the very moment when their chief bellows at them, they pull the cannon from its slot and fire it in an instant, as if they were a single man. They repeat this in a flash, so that one does not hear the sound of a single cannon but a continuous thundering roar. They fire, and then fire again, in the shortest time possible and with the greatest precision, exactitude, and attention. They have no special strength in their bodies that others do not have; perhaps they are even weaker than others. But they have a concern for organization and an aptitude for putting everything in its place. They construct all things on the firmest basis possible, and anticipate things before they happen. Only he who witnessed all this [with his own eyes] would accept the truth of it.

When they tired of this we returned to our boats and circled around the port amongst the ships. Whenever we drew alongside a ship its troops would line up on deck and greet us with music. Over fifty warships were there, for the French have no [naval] port on the

Small Sea other than this, although they have other ports on the coast of the Great Sea, for the land of France extends along two seas. Our stay in Toulon was one whole day, not counting the day we arrived and the day we left. We left it for Marseille, which we reached in six hours. Praise be to God the Provider of good fortune and the Guide to the straight path.

3

THE CITY OF PARIS

And everything about it. What we saw with our own eyes or learned by hearsay, including some words on the manners and customs of the French and the state of their affairs.

You should know that this city is the seat of government of the land of the French, the mother of its cities, the throne of its kingdom, the abode of its great men, the source of its laws, the home of its learning and sciences. The [French] glory in its name and aspire to live there, while imitating its inhabitants in their behavior, refined manners, and cultured way of life.

It is an enormous city, one of the greatest cities in those parts, just as Constantinople is for the Muslims, to which it may be compared; some say its distance around is forty-eight miles. Others among its inhabitants told me it takes twenty-seven hours to cross it on foot, and someone else told me that its circumference is twenty-one miles. Rifāʿa Effendi says in his voyage that its circumference is seven parasangs, and he stayed there about five years.[1] It

1. Seven parasangs is about twenty-one miles (see note 5 below). "Rifāʿa Effendi" is Rifāʿa Rāfiʿ aṭ-Ṭahṭāwī (see Introduction, note 132). References to his *Takhlīṣ* are taken from M. ʿAmāra, ed., *Al-aʿmāl al-kāmila li-Rifāʿa Rāfiʿ aṭ-Ṭahṭāwī*, part 2 (Beirut, 1973), pp. 9–266, and from

is situated at forty-nine degrees and fifty minutes in the northern direction [from the equator] and is therefore very cold.[2] Places shielded by walls that face south never see the sun in winter. The clouds are endless in that season and the sun is a rarity, coming out perhaps one day a month.

It is a city overflowing with people. Compared to the other cities of France, it is like a market day in our country compared with days on which there is no market.[3] Alongside it, you would consider other places empty, even though they may be filled with people. We heard from the lips of more than one of them that it has a million [inhabitants], and that accounting does not seem strange to one who has been there.[4] Anyone who is born or dies there, or comes there or departs, is recorded in a register—a ceaseless and perpetual task that is practiced everywhere in the land of Rūm.

Paris has a fortified wall of recent origin, for it did not have one

---

the abridged French translation by Anouar Louca, *L'or de Paris: Relation de voyage, 1826–1831* (Paris, 1988).

2. According to Ibn Khaldūn, Paris was in the second section of the inhospitable sixth zone. *Muqaddimah* 1:159. André Miquel says that most medieval Muslim accounts of Europe were based on the writings of a Jewish traveler, Ibrāhīm b. Ya'qūb (10th c.), whose own work has been lost. "L'Europe occidentale dans la relation arabe d'Ibrāhīm b. Ya'qūb (Xe s.)," *Annales: Economies, Sociétés, Civilisations* 21, 5 (September–October 1966): 1051. Mas'ūdī (d. 345/956) speaks of Paris (*al-Bawīra*) as a "huge city, . . . the home of the [Frankish] kingdom." *Les prairies d'or*, trans. C. Barbier de Meynard and Pavet de Courteille, 3 vols. (Paris, 1864), 3:67. Al-Idrīsī (12th c.) also mentions Paris (*Ibārīz*) as "a city of some importance, endowed with vineyards and orchards, situated on an island in the Seine." Charles Pellat, "La France dans la géographie d'al-Idrīsī," *Studi maghrebini* 10 (1978): 62. On the "Franks" in general, see Miquel, *Géographie humaine*, vol. 2, *Géographie arabe et représentation du monde: La terre et l'étranger*, pp. 354–59.

3. On *sūq* days, rural Moroccan towns become the scene of bustling activity, as country folk crowd in to buy and sell goods and livestock.

4. Aṭ-Ṭahṭāwī said the population of Paris was "about a million people." *Takhlīṣ*, p. 74; *L'or*, p. 117.

in the old days.[5] It can be seen from the outside but not from within, where it is completely covered up with earth and rubble. It is surrounded by a very deep and wide trench, and at its top are places for cannon. The wall is at some distance from the dwellings, leaving an open space between for more building so that the city can grow. There are [openings but] no gates in the wall, as there are in other cities. If you enter within the walls and reach the place where the houses begin, you will find iron gates flanked on both sides by railings;[6] no one can enter except through such a gate. Soldiers and guards are posted there, inspecting everyone who comes or goes, making sure that they pay the taxes imposed by the city on certain goods as they enter or leave. Opposite this gate is a bureau (*dīwān*) for the tax collectors, found at every entrance to the city.[7] I was not able to verify which goods are taxed and which are not, except that flour was exempt but meat was not, for slaughtering is done outside the city. The highest taxes are paid on wine. There is even a separate customs bureau for it, with storerooms set aside for keeping the barrels, for wine is a necessity of life there.

The taxes which they collect on goods entering the city do not go into the coffers of the state, but are destined for municipal im-

5. In 1840, a new fortified wall was built around Paris some distance from the eighteenth-century customs wall, which was now part of a densely inhabited area. Completed in 1843, its circumference was about twenty-one miles. Built into it were bastions for cannons, and it was protected outside by a wide ditch. Sixteen new forts were built surrounding the city, at the distance of a "cannon-shot" away. The purpose was to give Paris the appearance of a well-fortified camp. P. Lavedan, *Histoire de Paris*, series "Que sais-je?" no. 34 (Paris, 1960), pp. 78–79.

6. *Ḍarābīz*. In Dozy, *darābīz*; 1:430.

7. These are the old customs gates to Paris, known as *barrières*, manned by customs officers responsible for collecting the gate taxes. Jacques-Louis Ménétra, *Journal of My Life* (New York, 1986), p. 134 and note 167. In Morocco, *dīwān* meant both the tax rolls themselves and the place where taxes were collected, hence "bureau." Dozy 1:478–79.

provements such as repairing the roadways and lighting the street-lamps, which are found in every town but most of all in Paris, where it is said there are more than a hundred thousand of them. They are set up on tall wooden posts in orderly rows of equal height. Standing at the end of a row and looking down it, you see an endless line stretched out as far as the eye can see, not one out of place or taller than the next; and if you stand in an open place on a dark, cloudless night, especially near the river, they look just like the stars, a truly marvelous sight. Taxes also support the hospitals[8] for the sick, schools for the children of the poor, and other good works.

Surrounding Paris and a short distance away are heavily fortified strongholds built to protect the city, garrisoned by soldiers and bristling with cannon.[9] The artillerymen[10] live there in many small houses with their weapons and personal belongings. There are also storerooms of every size for weaponry such as swords, muskets, bayonets, helmets and armor, and the like, all clean and in the best condition, neatly stored in rows and heaps and straight lines, each according to its own type. Also within these fortresses are stables for the horses which pull the cannons and their equipment. Each stable has many workers who attend to taking care of them. The horses are tied up by their heads, not by their feet; each has a bridle made of leather, with two chains on each side of the head ending in a wooden ball. They slip the chains through a ring pounded into the wall facing the horse, and that ball restrains him. They lay down

8. Arabic *asbīṭār*, perhaps from the Spanish *hospital*. The classical word is *bīmāristān* (from Persian *bīmār* "sick" + *istān* "place"), often shortened to *māristān*, but in Morocco this word has the special meaning of "asylum." *EI* 2, s.v. "Bīmāristān"; W. Marçais, *Textes arabes de Tanger* (Paris, 1911), p. 465.

9. Aṣ-Ṣaffār visited the fortress of St. Cloud, southwest of Paris, on 5 February 1846. AAE/ADM Voyage, Beaumier to de Chasteau, 8 February 1846.

10. *Ṭubjiya*, from the Turkish. Dozy 2:20.

straw for each horse, but if he urinates or drops dung on it just two or three times, they change it for clean. At the entrance to the stable is a board on which the rules of conduct for the horses and the quantity of fodder [to be given them] are written, along with other matters relating to their upkeep. Every horse has its own special name, which is written on a small board affixed to the front [of the stall]. They separate one horse from another with a heavy piece of wood hanging down inside. If the horse kicks it, it moves; for if it were fixed to the ground, it would splinter with the blow.

Inside this stronghold are wagons and mountings for pulling cannons, and all the materials needed for them, such as gunpowder and balls and so on. There are many types of cannon, both large and small, arranged according to their size and type of shot. All of it is pleasing to the eye because of the brightness and neat arrangement; they looked as if they had just come from the foundry. There is also a storeroom for weapons, as I mentioned, and the workers are diligent in keeping them well oiled and in working order. A larger storeroom contained equipment for the horses, such as saddles, reins, ropes, chains, and so on. It went on as far as the eye could see. Each fortress is surrounded by a huge wall, like the wall of a city, and in front is a ditch crossed by a drawbridge; indeed, each fortress is like a city in itself.

The city of Paris is divided in two by a large river called the Seine, which flows through it from east to west. Crossing it are seventeen bridges of various types. Some are built with stone arches, and these are the majority, while others are made of iron arches, and between the arches and the flat part of the bridge are huge circles made up of large and small [pieces] of iron on which the flat part rests. Yet another type, which is truly amazing, hangs from above and is not resting on arches, like the others, but rests on the sides of the river. They build a solid structure [on each bank of the river] like a pillar with an arch in its middle to allow passage through it; and sometimes; if the river is exceptionally wide, they add another in the middle. The roadway is made of sturdy wooden boards resting on iron bars. Those bars are held in place by iron rods standing along the sides of the bridge. The rods enter the sides [of the bridge] as far as the lower edge of those boards, reaching the iron bars which support them, and are then nailed to them. Those standing iron rods are held from above by other huge rods stretching along the edges of the bridge from beginning to end, joining it with the structures already mentioned at the sides; and that is how the bridge is held together. When you cross over this kind of bridge you feel it tremble, because it is not resting on anything below.

Another type of bridge is made entirely of wood but has iron railings along the sides to prevent passersby from falling into the river. One comes across [wooden bridges], but the other type [of stone or iron] are the majority. Carts and carriages are found on all the bridges, but on those of unusual design, which are the newer ones, they charge a toll until the costs of construction are fully recovered. After that they are free like the others. Before they built these new bridges, the distance between the old bridges was often great, and they would cross the river by ferry, paying the small price of two coppers or so of their money for those on foot, and two or three times that for carriages and wagons. These are the types of bridges we saw in that city, and not once during our stay there did we see anyone fording a river either on foot or on horseback.

In the middle of this river is an island which was the original Paris in ancient times, and they call it by a name that means "ancient Paris."[11] On it is a very old church, the largest and most ancient in Paris. The river is crowded with boats of all sizes, including many steamers. One also sees great houses made of wood, shaped like large boats, except that they are covered with a roof. Some of them are open on the side facing the river, and are anchored in one spot. They are for washing clothes, and they rise and fall with the river just like boats.

11. Ancient Lutetia, known today as La Cité, was the original settlement of Paris; it is the site of the cathedral of Notre Dame.

There is another kind of structure made of wood, which is their public bathhouse. Inside it are small rooms that are enclosed, each with a large tub that may be filled with hot or cold water, or both to make it tepid. Whoever wants to bathe enters there, for it is their *ḥammām*; they do not have a *ḥammām* like ours. Other large bathhouses are found in the residential quarters and in the marketplaces.

The tub inside the bathing room may be of copper, but usually it is of marble and large enough to permit a person to more or less stretch out in it, legs and all. Two pipes lead into it, one for cold and the other for hot, and each has a spigot that may be opened or shut. In the bottom of the tub is an outlet for the water, which also opens and shuts. When the bather is ready to enter, they open the two spigots for him until the tub is filled, and the water is to his liking. Then he enters and undresses, and hangs his clothes on a hook. After locking the door, he gets into the tub and lies down in it. If the water is tepid, that is fine; but if it is burning hot, he may add cold, or if cold, then hot. When the water gets dirty, he may change it by opening the outlet at the bottom and letting it run out. After rinsing the tub, he closes the outlet and opens the two spigots again; and so on until he is fully satisfied, and gets out.

This room is lit by a large glass window covered on the inside by a thin curtain, which lets in the light while keeping out unwanted observers. Moreover, if you wish to take a bath in your own room, you may do so. They bring the tub along with containers of hot water and towels for drying, and one can wash in one's own room. But in this case it is not possible to change the bathwater when it is dirty, because there is no outlet at the bottom, and in their rooms they have no drains or holes for throwing out water. In fact, it was difficult for us to perform our ritual ablutions for that very reason.[12]

12. In Muslim practice, the ritual ablution (*wuḍūʾ*) is performed each time prayers are recited. It consists of washing the face, hands, forearms, and feet. The water used is considered unclean and must be discarded. In

We had to use two vessels, one for the [clean] water, and the other for the unclean. All of this was done with much difficulty and great contortions, due to the small size of the vessels and because of the rugs on the floor, which would have been spoiled if water had dripped on them. Indeed, they have no need for pouring out water [on the floor] and are ill-equipped for it.

Whatever is collected in the room in the way of dirty water or urine or the like, they carry off in containers. Urine is removed in receptacles intended for it, and performing one's bodily functions is also done into a vessel. As for urinating, it is done in something like a little milking jug, while the other is done into a container found inside a covered box. On top of it is another clean container, with a hole at its bottom that opens and shuts by itself. If you put something in the upper vessel, it immediately drops through the opening into the lower one, and the hole closes again. A small amount of water from the box enters the upper vessel with sufficient force to clean it. When you are finished, you close the whole thing up, thus preventing foul odors from escaping even when it is full. The servants then take it out, clean it, and return it to its place.

Along its entire length within the city, the banks of the river are built from large hewn rocks reaching up to the level of the road, about half the height of a man. Along its banks are wide streets bordered by shops and houses, whose windows overlook the river. The streets of Paris are paved with rough stones in the middle and smooth ones at the sides. The middle is for carts and wagons and the sides are for pedestrians. Its roadways are very wide and open to the sky, without any overhanging balconies or coverings. The houses are lit by the windows, which face onto the streets and squares. If the streets were covered over, the houses would be dark.

---

the courtyard of the mosque large fountains are used for washing, and drains in the floor carry the waste water away. *SEI*, s.v. "Wuḍū'."

There is a vast number of carts and carriages in this city. They say that there are 13,000 of them, with 8,000 for hire and the rest privately owned.[13] Indeed, the number of horses that draw them is reputed to be about 48,000. All of these carriages are very clean, shining, and well built, so that one would think that all of them are brand-new. For that matter, all the horses of this city are well fed, with glistening coats, sturdy bodies, and fine shapes. We did not see carriages or horses like those [of Paris] in any other place. To sum up, in comparison with the rest of what we saw of the land of the French, Paris is like a center of civilization compared with the countryside, and other cities seem rustic beside her.

People of wealth and importance do not walk on foot, but are almost always in carriages. This is for two reasons: first, their natural haughtiness and love of display keeps them from walking except as a means of relaxation and taking in the sights;[14] and second, the enormous size of the city makes traveling from one place to another there like going on a journey. For these two reasons you will see long wagons carrying many people, with "This one goes to such-and-such quarter" written on it, so that whoever wants to go there may ride, even if he is a servant or the like. Along the way, some get off while others get on.[15] The uproar of the carriages and the wagons does not cease day or night. The glass in the windows is perpetually rattling and shaking from the terrible din. For days sleep eluded us because of the frightful roar that never stopped. It felt as though we were standing at the seashore or next to a turning grindstone.

13. Aṣ-Ṣaffār's figure is far too low. *L'Illustration* reported on 15 November 1845 that Paris had 28,520 vehicles just for carrying people.

14. Compare with aṭ-Ṭahṭāwī, *Takhlīṣ*, p. 76; *L'or*, pp. 120–21.

15. The "Entreprise des Omnibus," founded in 1828, was the first public transportation company in Paris. Soon other private companies began carrying paying passengers, and in aṣ-Ṣaffār's day omnibuses with colorful names such as Josephine, Gazelle, and Hirondelle traversed the city. *Guide Michelin: Paris*, 1988 ed., p. 4.

All of the marketplaces and passageways are filled with carts for hire. As for the marketplaces, they are so numerous that you could say the whole city is a *sūq*, because all their markets are inside shops.[16] It is their custom when building to make the ground floor into shops, with dwellings above. In most places you will find shops right next to one another, but occasionally one will stand alone. It is seldom that you enter into a narrow lane and do not find a few shops. All of them are of a single design with respect to their decoration, doors, and windows; those which sell silk and jewelry appear the same as those selling groceries and vegetables. All of them are close to the street, not raised above it as ours are. They decorate them by lining the walls with bright mirrors that reflect everything in the shop, so that you have no idea where the shop begins or ends, or whether it is small or large. Nor does a marketplace specialize in one certain thing. You will find a butcher shop or a fish market next door to a clothing store or a jeweler's shop. Each of them is of equal cleanliness. In the butcher shops there are no bones or blood or disgusting odors, and the meat can stay there for days without spoiling or smelling rotten.

One of their most renowned markets, where very expensive goods are sold, is called the "Royal."[17] It is formed by two squares

16. Aṣ-Ṣaffār's notion of a great marketplace was the *qaysāriya* of Fes. People shopped there in the day, but at night its gates were closed and its streets empty. Selling was from open stalls raised above the street, and the same goods were often found in shops located side by side. Basic items were also sold in residential quarters, but these shopkeepers were petty tradesmen compared to the grand merchants of the *qaysāriya*. R. Le Tourneau, *La vie quotidienne à Fes en 1900* (Paris, 1965), pp. 121–24; al-Qadiri (trans. Cigar), *Nashr*, p. 221 and note 6; *EI* 2, s.v. "Ḳaysāriyya."

17. The Palais Royal, built in the sixteenth century. By the eighteenth century, boutiques, gambling houses, and other amusements filled its galleries. Halet Effendi, a Turkish traveler of the early nineteenth century, noted that the rooms above were used as brothels, and that "to go to that place by night is shameful, but . . . there is no harm in going there by day." Lewis, *Muslim Discovery*, p. 291. By aṣ-Ṣaffār's time, the more bawdy

around which there are more than four hundred shops. In the middle are trees and a large fountain; above the shops is a palace of the same name, which they say belongs to the present Sultan. The very finest things are sold here, such as jewelry, precious stones, gold, silver, and silken cloth, and there are cafés here too.

Another market is called the "Boulevard."[18] Everything is sold here, and it is very long. It took us more than an hour to travel its length in a carriage. Another market nearby is called the "Rue Montmartre," where there is a gathering place for businessmen called "the Bourse." The largest shop in Paris is located there—it is a [whole] marketplace in itself.[19] All kinds of silk, wool, and cotton clothing are sold there, along with other kinds of cloth, both sewn and unsewn. It has one hundred forty employees. The owner of the shop stands by the door to welcome customers and find out what they are looking for. Then he leads the customer to the right place, and the employees assist him in finding what he needs.

Everything has a price written on it, and there is no need to bargain or haggle. When the customer decides on something, the employee accompanies him with the article to the door of the shop. There four clerks keep the accounts and receive payment. The employee leaves the buyer with the clerks, who show him the account,

---

forms of entertainment had been closed down. *Guide Michelin: Paris*, 1988 ed., pp. 113–15.

18. The *Grands Boulevards* were built where the medieval fortifications of Paris once stood. In the 1840s, their sidewalks were lined with dance halls, *spectacles*, and restaurants.

19. This was the "Ville de France," the first large *magasin de nouveautés* in Paris and the forerunner of the modern department store, which opened in 1843. The shop was a novelty for Parisians too, for unlike other shops, it sold a variety of goods, had fixed prices, and made its profit on a rapid turnover. Michael Miller, *The Bon Marche: Bourgeois Culture and the Department Store, 1869–1920* (Princeton, 1981), pp. 21–25.

take his money, and make the correct change. We went there more than once and always found these clerks overwhelmed with doing the accounts and taking money from customers. They say that every day about 12,000 *riyāls* worth [of goods] are sold there.[20] It has many sections, each with its own type of goods, and at night one hundred seventy lamps are needed to illuminate it.

Goods in this city are very expensive because of the wealth of its inhabitants and the high quality of the merchandise. The franc there is equal to one-fifth of a *riyāl* of our money, and is like copper money is for us. Their five-franc piece is like our *dirhām*.[21] These two coins form the major part of their coinage. Most accounts there are in francs, as accounts with us are in *mithqāls*, and if they do it in something else, like *riyāls*, they go over it twice. For gold coins they

20. About 60,000 francs a day in trade. A franc was worth about twenty cents.

21. When aṣ-Ṣaffār says "their five-franc piece is like our *dirhām*," he is not referring to the specific value of the *dirhām*, which was about one-tenth the value of the 5-franc piece, but rather means that the 5-franc piece was the basic unit of French coinage, as the *dirhām* was in Morocco.

French goods seemed expensive because of the diminishing demand for Moroccan currency relative to foreign specie. The French 5-franc piece, weighing 25 grams, was used in Morocco and called the *riyāl*. In the eighteenth century, the principal Moroccan coins were local ones: the *mithqāl*, a silver coin of 29 grams; the *dirhām*, a silver coin of 2.9 grams, or one-tenth of a *mithqāl*; and the *ūqiya*, a bronze coin equal to one *dirhām*. In the nineteenth century, the heavier silver *mithqāl* was replaced on the local market by European coins of inferior value, such as the 5-franc piece, now called the *riyāl*. The Makhzan permitted this in order to maintain a desired nominal ratio between bronze and silver coinage; by the 1840s the old rate of 10 *ūqiyas* = 1 *mithqāl* had changed to a new rate of 16 *ūqiyas* = 1 *riyāl*. I am grateful to Thomas Park for this information. See his "Inflation and Economic Policy in 19th Century Morocco: The Compromise Solution," *Maghreb Review* 10, 2–3 (1985): 51–56; ʿUmar Afā, *Mas'alat an-nuqūd fī tārīkh al-Maghrib fī qarn at-tāsiʿ ʿashr: Sūs 1822–1906* (Casablanca, 1988), pp. 203–14; and G. Ayache, "Aspects de la crise financière au Maroc après l'expédition espagnole de 1860," in *Études d'histoire marocaine* (Rabat, 1983), pp. 97–138.

have small *dīnārs*,[22] each one equal to four of their *riyāls*. Their small money is copper; there are twenty in a franc, and they are called *sols*.[23]

Precious objects like pearls and gems are usually bought in shops that specialize in them. Another indication of their eagerness to sell their goods is that merchants write out papers mentioning their goods and their virtues, praising them so that people will want them. The price and the place are also mentioned. Then they affix these papers to walls where people pass by, or on the numerous little kiosks where they relieve themselves, or at the gates to the city so that whoever enters will see them, and in every place where people gather. They do not have secondhand shops (*jūṭiyāt*) where a middleman (*simsār*) does the selling, as we have.[24]

As for the types of houses found there, they are quite different from ours, for they do not have a courtyard, a ground floor, and upper stories, with large rooms and small ones, such as we have; rather, their courtyard is outside the house, where the carts and draft animals stand. As soon as you enter the gate, you climb the steps and see the rooms laid out story upon story until you reach the top. The rooms are called *salons*, and have very large windows which look out onto the street, the shops, and the squares. You will see one [window] shaped like an arch, clear like the others, but with an iron grating in front of it that is marvelously wrought. Behind the house there is usually a garden, and even if it is very small it will have water and plantings of some sort. In their gardens you never see fruit trees, grapevines, sweet-smelling flowers, or herbs like mint, basil, or marjoram, such as we have.

22. The *louis d'or*, which equaled 20 francs. The *dīnār* (from the Latin *denarius*) was an Islamic gold coin weighing about 4.25 grams. *IB* 2:444 note 111; *EI* 2, s.v. "Dīnār."

23. In Arabic, *ṣuld*; a copper coin equal to five *centimes*.

24. The *jūṭiya* is a secondhand market, or flea market. R. Le Tourneau, *Fes avant le Protectorat* (Casablanca, 1949), p. 242; *simsārs* were brokers dealing in new and used goods. Ibid., p. 378.

Throughout the city in the shopping places are kiosks in the shape of round enclosures intended for urination. In the doorway is an iron plate with two outcroppings above the ground [to stand on] so that the user will not stain his clothes. They also urinate at the base of walls and in alleyways, which is not disgraceful in their opinion. However, they are diligent in cleaning the streets by sweeping them and sprinkling them with water.

In Paris there are places where people take walks, which is one of their forms of entertainment. A fellow takes the arm of his friend, man or woman, and together they go to one of the spots known for it. They stroll along, chatting and taking in the sights. Their idea of an outing is not eating or drinking, and certainly not sitting. One of their favorite promenades is a place called the Champs-Élysées, which is close by the Seine on the same bank as the royal palace; our lodgings were here too. Along its length are even rows of trees, and between them straight pathways. When the foliage appears, and the birds twitter in the lattice of branches above, it is a sight to behold. Here too are many cafés and places for spectacles such as the theater, and huge fountains with statues of human forms with water gushing from their mouths.[25] They claim that these are the gods of water; they are holding fishes which also spurt out water. The water is in constant motion, and rises up in a single column. It is emptied out in cold weather because it would freeze.

Not far from here is the garden of the Sultan, where people also go to promenade.[26] This garden is walled and its gates are guarded,

25. These two large fountains, still to be seen in the Place de la Concorde, were installed by Louis-Philippe to change the public image of the place where the guillotine of the Revolution had once stood. *Guide Michelin: Paris*, 1988 ed., p. 47.

26. The Jardin des Tuileries borders the right bank of the Seine; at one end was the royal residence, the Palace of the Tuileries, and at the other the Place de la Concorde. The palace was destroyed during the Paris Commune of May 1871.

but no one is kept from entering. A small section near the palace is reserved for the Sultan alone. In this garden there are many huge trees, planted as they do for shade, with open spots and chairs for resting surrounded by lush greenery. Whoever is wearied by walking may sit, but they are usually women or old people. Here too are large fountains and cafés.

Another of their diversions is the Sultan's park, where wild animals of land and sea are found, both living and dead.[27] They play tricks with the dead ones, making them look as if they were alive, so that you see a fish and there is no doubt in your mind that it has just emerged from the sea. The way they do this is by skinning it in one piece and then stuffing it with straw or the like, so that it looks like a fish, flesh and all. Then they lacquer it in such a way that the body is preserved. We saw innumerable creatures kept in this manner, everything from the tiniest to the biggest fish, from the smallest turtle to the most enormous crocodile, from the Sea of Rūm, the Indian Ocean, the Great Sea, and the Nile.

There were several kinds of crocodiles, those from the Indian Ocean being larger and more dreadful than those of the Nile. There was also a huge fish with a long toothed bill with two rows of teeth like a saw coming out of his mouth, and another which they claim was the kind that swallowed up Jonah, peace be upon him. Another had huge claws—I don't know its name—and was suspended from the ceiling by an iron strap. The tiny fishes were so numerous that they could not be counted. So, too, the birds, gathered from every clime, many of them gorgeous and strange in appearance. One kind had bills on its wings, like those on its head. Each one was in its own room, even the tiny butterfly. There were also huge and awful

27. The Jardin des Plantes, founded in 1626 to provide a living laboratory for scientists and researchers in natural history. In 1640 it was opened to the public, and French naturalists enriched its collections with specimens gathered from all over the world. The menagerie was added during the Revolution, when the royal zoo was moved there from Versailles. *Guide Michelin: Paris*, 1988 ed., p. 205. For aṭ-Ṭahṭāwī's impressions, see *Takhlīṣ*, p. 164; *L'or*, pp. 190–92.

serpents and vipers coiled around pieces of wood, terrifying to look at, some at least as thick as the thigh of a man. Some of the living animals were creatures that came from western lands, such as the animals of America (*bilād mirīka*) and India, whose names I do not know.

Among the stuffed ones were the elephant—there were live ones too—and the rhinoceros, which is a huge animal, smaller than an elephant, having a single great horn on its nose. Because of its weight the head is always lowered. They say that it can fight an elephant with its horn and overcome it. One of its characteristics, so they say, is that when the female is close to giving birth, the newborn sticks its head out from her opening and begins to graze on the tips of the foliage; when it is satisfied, it puts its head back into her belly. They say that no other animal will stay within a hundred parasangs of it in any direction, such is their dread of it. The wild ox, also stuffed, is there. It resembles the horse, except that its legs are covered with thick hair, and the bear, which is an animal capable of great speed. They have both kinds [of bears], the white and the black, and they claim that the white one is found on the frozen water in the Sea of Darkness.[28] Also there were many lions and tigers, hyenas, wildcats, foxes, gazelles, horses,[29] and so on, all of them dead, but looking exactly as if they were alive.

Among the live animals were the elephant, which is an enormous creature with a long trunk having its mouth at the base. With this trunk he grasps things and tosses them into his mouth. Despite the huge size of his body he has an understanding and gentleness toward his master. He was inside a huge iron cage, and behind him was another cage made of wood with a door. His master spoke to him, saying, "Open the door," and he did so by turning the handle with his trunk. Then his master told him to close it, and he did that too. One of the other spectators told me that in the theater there are two

28. The Arctic Ocean.

29. Arabic *arwā*, a word denoting the mounts in the Sultan's stables. See Ibn Zaydān, *'Izz* 1:47.

elephants that play together, understand each other, and respond to whoever calls to them. If something is given to them, they will return it by grasping it in that trunk.

They also have the giraffe there.[30] It is an animal with a wondrous shape. His forelegs are longer than his hind legs, and if you place something on the ground for him to eat, he will seize it with his forelegs. He is gentle and has a handsome appearance: his neck is long, like a camel's, but even longer; his head is elongated, like a horse's, but even narrower; on his forehead are two short hornlike things, except that they are of flesh and hair, like cut-off ears. His tail begins like the tail of a cow, but becomes hairy at the end. His coat is beautiful; it is not one color, but spotted both white and red. The giraffe is clean—you will not see the marks of dung on its hind parts—and its nature is tender, kind, and affectionate. A person can feed it by hand and it will come up close to eat, and if he turns his back, it will not kick or harm him. They say that it is the offspring of three animals: the wild she-camel, the wild cow, and the hyena. The hyena mated with the she-camel, producing a male, and this male mated with the cow, which produced a giraffe. But the truth

30. *Zarāfa*, a word of Arabic origin. The giraffe had arrived at the Jardin des Plantes only a few years before, and was a novelty even for Parisians. Louca, *Voyageurs et écrivains*, pp. 40, 254–55. This passage bears a striking resemblance to the *ʿAjāʾib al-makhlūqāt wa-gharāʾ ib al-mawjūdāt*, by Zakariya b. Muḥammad b. Maḥmūd Abū Yaḥyā, known as al-Qazwīnī (d. 682/1283), still a standard Muslim reference on natural science in aṣ-Ṣaffār's day. Part Two of this work contains descriptions of the animal kingdom. The entry under "giraffe" reads: "Its head is like the head of a camel, and its horns like the horns of a cow. Its skin is like the skin of a leopard, and its hoofs like those of an ox. Its neck is extremely long, its forelegs long, and its hind legs short. It is shaped like a camel. . . . They say that a giraffe is born from an Abyssinian she-camel, a wild cow, and a hyena in the land of Ethiopia." See Kamāl ad-Dīn ad-Damīrī, *Ḥayāt al-ḥayawān al-kubrā*, 2 vols. (Cairo, 1306/1888–89), vol. 2; al-Qazwīnī's text is in the margin on p. 177. Also *EI* 2, s.v. "al-Ḳazwīnī, Zakariyyāʾ b. Muḥammad b. Maḥmūd Abū Yaḥyā." For an illuminated manuscript copy, see E. Atil, *Art of the Arab World* (Washington, D.C., 1975), pp. 128–29.

is that this is a completely separate creature, having both male and female, like all other living things.

There are buffalo here too, and the Bactrian camel, and the deer, which is an animal capable of great speed having two horns, each horn with tiny horns coming out of it, so that it looks like the branches of a tree. They say that the deer adds two small horns every year. There were donkeys from India of a handsome red color. They have violent natures and attack whoever comes near. They also had one of our donkeys there, claiming it was both male and female.[31] We inquired further, but they were mindful of the presence of the ladies. The many gazelles, lions, and leopards there were familiar to us, but they also had another type whose skin was striped. They said it was a tiger from the land of America. We also saw wolves, larger than the wolves of our country, which were violent and aggressive toward whoever approached them; many kinds of monkeys; and a large number of animals that resembled closely the rabbit, the hare, the weasel, and the rat. Also a huge cage filled with all kinds of birds, made of fine wire which let in the light but kept them from flying away.

A large pavilion in this garden had many small rooms in which there were countless stones and rare minerals. In the first room we entered, we saw a lump of congealed mud and bones; they claimed it was a remnant of the Flood. Also a huge chunk of pure gold whose like, they said, could be found in mines. There were innumerable samples of rocks containing gold and silver, copper, lead, and iron, and a great boulder of iron which they claim fell from the sky. Also many kinds of uncut emeralds, diamonds, and other [stones] whose names I do not know, although every type had written on it its name and description.

There were also varieties of crystal, both clear and colored, and dead bones which they claim were left over from the Flood; indeed,

31. Aṣ-Ṣaffār says it is *khunthā*, meaning "hermaphrodite." Perhaps the French interpreter provided this word. The identity of the ladies is unknown.

they have compared them to the forms of animals still living and cannot find their like.[32] Also you will see there the skin of a salamander, and all kinds of cereals that grow in their country, some whole and others displayed with their grains [under] glass.

In this garden there are various types of exotic plants. Some are planted outside, each planting having a bit of wood next to it with a paper telling its name and characteristics. Unusual [plants] which cannot endure the cold of that country are placed in rooms enclosed by walls and a roof of glass framed in wood that can be opened and shut. In the floor of the room are iron pipes flowing with water heated by a fire outside the room. The floor itself is made of an iron grating, and the plants are set on it in boxes and containers. The temperature of the room agrees with the plants in it. If the plants are from the desert, such as the date palm, they heat it like the Sahara so they will flourish; if the plant is from America, they heat it like America, and so forth. If it is the season of clouds and cold, they close the room on all sides and grow the plants by that heat alone; but if it is sunny and mild, they open it up partly to let in the air. In the summertime they take the plants out-of-doors altogether.

Among the plants we saw here were the date palm, the banana, the trees of coffee and tea, both of which are quite small, and a fruit called the pineapple,[33] which they get from the land of America. It is the size of a large orange with leaves coming out of its head, but graduated like the cone of a pine tree. They adore it even though a single one costs five *riyāl*s or more. They cut it up into small pieces and eat it with sugar, and sometimes they cook it. Its taste is both sweet and sour at once, and for that reason they pass sugar with it.

The expanse of this garden outside of the buildings includes huge trees [planted] in even rows, sources of water, sitting places of every

32. The "Flood" was the interpreter's means of describing prehistory to aṣ-Ṣaffār, who of course had no notion of history that did not presume God's creation.

33. *Anana*, in Arabic, from the French *ananas*. The botanical name is *ananas comosus*.

shape, and houses for servants and staff and the soldiers who guard it. It is one of the most renowned places in Paris. The purpose of putting all these animals, plants, and minerals in one place is so that whoever is engaged in the study of science and sees a name in a book can come here and observe the object in reality.[34] Anyone who wishes to learn by firsthand observation is free to come, although parts of it may be closed to the public except on certain days, such as Sunday.

The Theater

Among their spectacles are the "theater," the "comedy," and the "opera,"[35] where they put on plays that may be bizarre, humorous, fantastic, or heroic. It is seriousness in the form of levity, for the play may be a lesson in proper conduct, or a story rare and marvel-

34. Botanical classification was not unknown in Morocco. A sixteenth-century scholar from Fes, Qāsim b. Muḥammad al-Wazīr al-Ghassānī, wrote a treatise classifying 379 medicinal plants found locally. But the classification of plants having no practical use was new to aṣ-Ṣaffār. See H. P. J. Renaud, "Un essai de classification botanique dans l'oeuvre d'un médecin marocain du XVIe siècle," *Mémorial Henri Basset: Nouvelles études nord-africaines et orientales*, 2 vols. (Paris, 1928), 2:197–206.

35. *At-tayātrū, al-kūmathiya, al-awbra.* Public performances of a theatrical nature were not part of Sunni Muslim culture, and theater-going was a novel experience for most visitors to the West. Aṭ-Ṭahṭāwī stressed the utility of the theater in teaching public morality (*Takhlīṣ*, p. 119; *L'or*, p. 154), and Khayr ad-Dīn at-Tūnisī described it as "a poetical form suitable to be recited at meetings and intended for the polishing of manners." At-Tūnisī, *The Surest Path: The Political Treatise of a Nineteenth-century Muslim Statesman*, trans. L. C. Brown (Cambridge, Mass., 1967), p. 140. The Moroccans enjoyed the Parisian theater and went often. In one week (1–7 February 1846) they saw three different theatrical events: an opera, a play, and a performance by the celebrated Mlle Rachel. AAE/ADM/Voyage, Beaumier to de Chasteau, 8 February 1846.

ous, or a dilemma of a special sort that leads them to a more perfect knowledge of things.

The description of this place and the manner of playing is [as follows]: it is a huge domed place, and at its sides are little rooms, story upon story, that overlook the place of the play. Its floor is inclined and covered with chairs, row upon row, on which the spectators sit. The purpose of the slope is so that the person in front will not prevent the person behind from having his full share of viewing. Outside the domed part is a large open space for the play; its front is covered with a curtain that can be raised and lowered. The spectators sit in the little rooms at the sides, or on the [chairs] on the floor, each according to what he has paid. The players gather on the open space and the musicians next to it. It takes place only at night, when a huge chandelier is lit in the center of the dome, with smaller ones at the sides.

At the front of the open place is a single row of lamps, of the kind lit by "spirits"[36] which flow through pipes. They are remarkable in that they do not go out, even if they are puffed on with all the puffing in the world. They have no wick or candle, but a tongue of flame comes out of a small tube inside. There is a handle which may be turned to close off the flow to the tube, thus extinguishing the glow. But if it is turned in the opposite direction, [the flame] returns. All the lighting in their shops and marketplaces and in their streetlamps is of this type. Whoever desires [such lighting] can make a contract to receive it for a set period of time, such as an hour or two. When the time is past, the glow is extinguished because the sender has cut off the flow. This is one of their extraordinary ways of doing things.

To return to the theater. When the hour of the play comes, people gather together before the curtain, which is then raised, reveal-

36. *Asbīriṭū*, in aṣ-Ṣaffār's Arabic. Gas lamps first appeared in Paris in the second decade of the nineteenth century, and were called *bec de gaz*. *Asbīriṭū* in the Moroccan dialect means denatured alcohol, a fuel which looks like gaslight when lit.

ing marvelous scenes and strange forms on the open stage. They show cities and forests, land and sea, the sun, moon, and stars. All of it is drawn on paper, but to those who see it, there is no doubt that it is real. They represent the light of day, the night, and the dawn; they [even] can show the light of the moon behind the clouds. There are always beautiful young courtesans (*jawārī*), gorgeously bejeweled and costumed, and a king and his men wearing armor and bearing arms such as spears, swords, or muskets. They put on four or five plays each night, ending each with the lowering of the curtain and the changing of the scenery.[37]

Their plays are well known and faithfully preserved, not invented on the spot. The [title of] the play they will perform is written out beforehand on sheets of paper, announcing that such-and-such a play will be performed at such-and-such a place, thus making it known to all. The subject matter of their plays is the recitation of verses and the singing of songs in their language, especially between lovers. They make one of them the lover and the other the beloved, and the two of them come forward on the stage reciting and singing to one another. Sometimes the beloved is pleased with her lover, and draws near to him; at other times she loathes him and turns away from him, all the while reciting the proper words. Those who understand what they are saying to each other take pleasure in the talking and versifying. They enjoy that even more than the scenery and the other curiosities, because the talk is refined, well mannered, informative about unusual subjects and difficult problems, satisfying in its responses, and comical in its phrasing.

For example, when they want to depict a story of war, they show the Sultan and his army, horse, and weaponry as they were in that time and country where the war took place. Once we went to a play that told the story of a war in Seville, and they showed Seville and its minaret, gates, and famous places, so that someone who knew Seville said it was just like that. They dressed the Sultan and his men

37. Understanding neither language nor plot, aṣ-Ṣaffār thought each scenery change was the start of a new play.

as they were in that time, and the women too. They fought until they entered the city.

They told a story about monks carousing and drinking, but when the monks saw other people, and especially women, they showed humility and abstinence in their sight. They showed the church and everything in it and the vessels for wine. When [they] saw someone looking, they quickly hid [the wine] and returned to praying. And when a woman came to seek their blessing, they paid no attention to her.

They told the story of Pharaoh and Moses, peace be unto him, showing the sea and crocodiles just as if they were real. [The sea] split open to allow Moses and his companions to pass through, but closed upon Pharaoh and his troop. Another time they depicted Paradise, with castles and trees and rivers, a lovely sight, and they showed the angels flying about in the air on white wings. The way they did this was by taking young girls and tying to each a fine rope which you could see only after much looking, holding them from above without revealing themselves. They also showed the dead rising from the grave, and someone swallowed up by the earth who later reappeared in Paradise. And they also showed the Flood and Noah's Ark.

One time we went to a place there called the "Diorama."[38] We entered during the day, and went up a flight of stairs to find ourselves in total darkness, except for a light let in through a tiny window. The room was shaped like a theater. They lowered the curtain and began to furnish the place behind it. Then they raised the cur-

38. The Diorama, invented by Louis-Jacques-Mandé Daguerre (1787–1851), was a major Parisian attraction of the day. It consisted of a realistic backdrop with foreground figures painted in miniature, viewed through a small opening. The lighting was such that the scene looked lifelike. Dolf Sternberger, *Panorama of the Nineteenth Century*, trans. Joachim Neugroschel (New York, 1977), pp. 188–89; *Grande encyclopédie Larousse*, 1973 ed., s.v. "Daguerre, Louis Jacques Mandé." Aṣ-Ṣaffār saw a representation of the change of the seasons, and a scene of the interior of the Church of St. Mark in Venice. *L'Illustration*, 7 February 1846.

tain, revealing a church with domes and pillars and niches lit up with a light made to look like the light of day. Then they lowered it again to resemble the light of evening with the sun setting in the west, until the light was entirely gone and darkness reigned. Then a tiny light hitherto hidden became apparent, and grew and spread until a huge chandelier appeared, and below it a church with many people praying. Then the curtain came down and they changed the scene, and a great city appeared, with solid buildings and towering fortifications. Flowing out of the city was a river crossed by a bridge, above it were mountains, and surrounding it were forests and fields. They made snow fall; we saw it piling up and heard it fall on the roof above us. Whoever did not know that this was a play would have had no doubt it was actually snow. It continued to fall until everything was covered with white.

Another scene showed a different city, with ancient buildings and a fortress, and people in the streets. It looked as if the sky were overcast, and then the clouds increased and darkness descended, and a violent wind began to blow, rain fell in torrents, and the sound of thunder came from above. Then a light like the dawn appeared on the horizon and rose until it shone everywhere. They made it look as if the rain were falling in the mountains, and from there ran down to a sea behind the city. A river began to gush forth [out of the mountains], looking as if it would deluge the place. And then the curtain came down. All this took place within a quarter of an hour.

Sometimes their plays include women dancing. They clasp each other by the hands and begin a marvelous dance, intertwining their limbs and bending their joints until their mouths nearly touch their heels, then leaping on one leg and weaving in and out until it seems they are not human. At other times one of the men takes hold of a woman and the two dance together.

The theater is not a place for riffraff or men of the lowest classes. On the contrary, their leaders and the people of virtue among them go there. Moreover, a man and his wife and daughters, or a fellow and his friends, may also attend. Even the Sultan has it in his house,

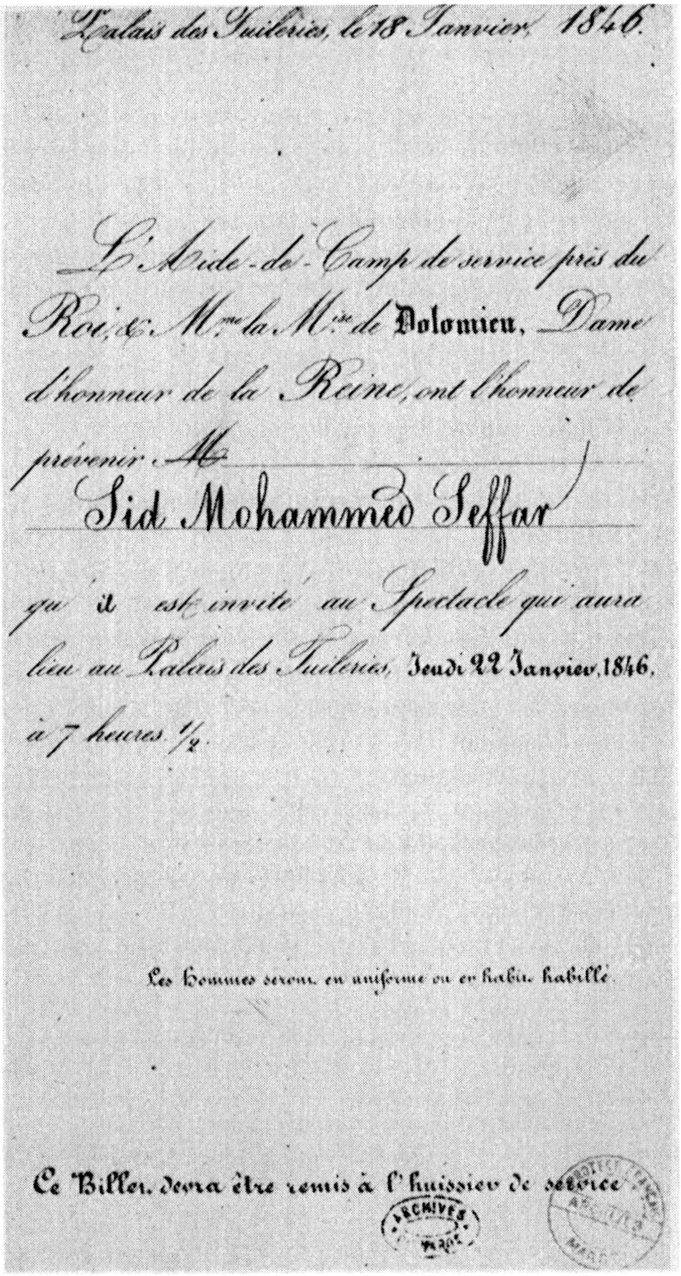
Palais des Tuileries, le 18 Janvier 1846.

L'Aide-de-Camp de service près du Roi, & Mme la Mise de Dolomieu, Dame d'honneur de la Reine, ont l'honneur de prévenir M.

Sid Mohammed Seffar

qu'il est invité au Spectacle qui aura lieu au Palais des Tuileries, Jeudi 22 Janvier, 1846, à 7 heures 1/2.

Les hommes seront en uniforme ou en habit habillé.

Ce Billet devra être remis à l'huissier de service

Plate 8. An invitation to a *spectacle* at the Royal Palace.
AAE/ADM/"Voyage de Sidi Aschasch, Pacha de Tetouan."

where there is a special place for it. He invites the players and spectators, and sits with his children and womenfolk, his ministers and entourage, while the actors perform their dancing and lovemaking. They watch and take delight in it. In fact, they claim that it is edifying for the spirit, instructive in morals, and restful for the body and soul, so that one may return to one's accustomed work with joy and determination.

> Nourish your spirit exhausted by work with rest,
> Mending and healing it with a bit of humor.

[A Hadith:][39] One day ash-Shaʿabī was asked, "Did the Companions of the Prophet, peace be unto him, make merry?" And he answered, "Yes, for belief was in their hearts like an immobile mountain." Of all the Companions of the Prophet, Nuʿīmān was most given to mirth, and he was in the battle of Badr.[40] It is said that he told the Prophet, peace be unto him, that he would like to make even more fun and laughter; and the Prophet replied, "He will enter Paradise laughing." One of the jokes that he told was about when he gave the Messenger of God[41] a jar of honey which he bought from a Bedouin for a *dīnār*. He came with the Bedouin to the door of the Prophet and said to [the Bedouin], "Get the money from him." And when the Prophet heard that, he asked Nuʿīmān, "Why did you do that?" And Nuʿīmān answered, "I wanted to buy you a gift, but I had no money." And the Prophet laughed and gave the Bedouin the money.

39. From Ibn Ḥajar al-ʿAsqalānī (d. 852/1449), *Al-iṣāba fī tamyīz aṣ-ṣaḥāba* (Calcutta, 1856–93), 3:569–70. *EI* 2, s.v. "Ibn Ḥadjar al-ʿAsḳalānī." My thanks to A. Mahdavi-Damghani for this reference. Ash-Shaʿabī is ʿAmr b. Sharāḥil ash-Shaʿabī, a noted scholar of the eighth century.

40. The first decisive military victory of Islam took place in 624 at Badr, not far from Medina. Hitti, *History of the Arabs*, pp. 116–17.

41. The Prophet Muḥammad.

[Another Hadith:] One day, Nuʿīmān was passing Makhrama Ibn Nawfal az-Zuhrī, a blind man, who said to him, "Take me along, because I have to urinate." And Nuʿīmān took him by the hand and led him to the mosque. The people started shouting at him, "You are in the mosque!" And he said, "Who brought me here?" And they told him it was Nuʿīmān. And he said, "By God, I am going to beat him with my stick if I find him." And Nuʿīmān heard about it and came to him and said, "O Abū Miswar,[42] do you want Nuʿīmān?" And he said, yes. And Nuʿīmān said, "He is over there praying." And he took the [blind man] by the hand and led him to ʿUthmān Ibn ʿAffān,[43] who was praying, and said, "This is Nuʿīmān." And the blind man was about to raise his stick over him when the people cried out, "It is the Commander of the Faithful!" Ibn Nawfal said, "Who led me here?", and they told him it was Nuʿīmān. And he said, "May God not harm him after all." ʿAṭṭā' Ibn as-Sā'ib, may God be pleased with him, said, "It was Saʿīd Ibn Jubayr who told this story, and he made us laugh until we cried."[44] [Ibn Jubayr] did not leave [people] until he had made them laugh and lifted their spirits.

Another joke [Ibn Jubayr] told was that once, after leaving an appointment, he heard the people quoting [a passage] incorrectly.[45] He said, "I did not know [the passage] and decided to inform myself, so I went to the street of the scribes and bought the book, and

42. Literally "father of Miswar," another name for the blind man.

43. The Caliph ʿUthmān (d. 35/655), third in succession after the Prophet, was a rich merchant of Mecca known for his piety, elegance, and good taste. He was murdered in Medina by mutinous troops from Egypt while reading the Koran. *SEI*, s.v. " ʿUthmān b. ʿAffān."

44. These two were Companions (*ṣaḥāba*) of the Prophet Muḥammad. See Muḥammad Ibn Saʿd, *Kitāb aṭ-ṭabaqāt al-Kubrā*, ed. Eduard Sachau, 9 vols. (Leiden, 1909), 6:178, 235.

45. *Taṣḥīf*, or the misplacing of diacritical marks, can completely change the meaning and pronunciation of a word in Arabic, and is the source of many jokes.

the first thing I saw in it was *sakbāj* distorted as *nīk tāj*, and I swore never to look at it again."[46] The people laughed at his words until they nearly fainted.

The Gazettes

The people of Paris, like all the French—indeed, like all of Rūm—are eager to know the latest news and events that are taking place in other parts. For this purpose they have the gazette.[47] These are papers in which they write all the news that has reached them that day about events in their own country and in other lands both near and far.

This is the way it is done. The owner of a newspaper dispatches his people to collect everything they see or hear in the way of important events or unusual happenings. Among the places where they collect the news are the two Chambers, the Great and the Small, where they come together to make their laws. When the members of the Chamber meet to deliberate, the men of the gazette sit nearby and write down everything that is said, for all debating and ratifying of laws is matter for the gazette and is known to everyone. No one can prevent them from doing this. However, if their words are about a disgraceful subject, they must conceal them from the public, and are not allowed [to write them].

46. *Sakbāj* is a kind of meat soup; *nīk tāj* is a woman's name. Except for the diacritical marks, the written form of the two words is almost identical.

47. In Arabic, *gāzīṭa* (unvocalized in aṣ-Ṣaffār's text). Al-Ghassānī first described the "gazette" (*kāsīṭa*) in his seventeenth-century *riḥla*, saying that it often "exaggerated and told lies to arouse people's curiosity." *Iftikāk*, p. 67. Aṣ-Ṣaffār's description of the press owes much to aṭ-Ṭahṭāwī. *Takhlīṣ*, pp. 104, 171; *L'or*, pp. 138, 200–201. Newspapers did not appear regularly in Morocco until the 1880s, in Tangier. In aṣ-Ṣaffār's day, official news was transmitted by courier (*raqqāṣ*), usually in the form of a letter from the Sultan to the local governor. Aubin, *Morocco*, pp. 68, 324; Ibn Zaydān, *'Izz*, I, glossary, p. 407.

They also have correspondents and reporters in other lands, who know what is happening there. You will find that the newspaper people are advised about unusual events before anyone else. [They] spend their day collecting news, handing in at night what they have gathered during the day. The owner of the newspaper then prints it, making numerous sheets by means of the printing press, which will be explained later. Then it is distributed to everyone who takes it, each receiving a set. All the leaders of France, and especially in Paris, make a contract with the owner of the newspaper to receive a new gazette each day, in return for a fixed sum paid annually. Likewise, all the cafés receive numerous gazettes each day from many places. When someone enters a café, first the waiter brings him a newspaper so he may learn what is new, and then he serves him his coffee. The newspapers are handed back and kept there. Whoever wishes to know what has happened in the past can hunt around in the café for a gazette from that time, and read about it.

On the front of the gazette is written its price each year. Every day during our stay in Paris, a new gazette with the most correct news arrived at our house. Written at the top was its price—sixteen *riyals* per year. One makes a contract with the owner [of the newspaper] and receives it for a short or long period, but never less than a month. They say that about fifteen thousand copies are printed daily.[48] Each [sheet] is a piece of paper about two cubits long, written on both sides. In it you will find the news from Paris and the rest of the land of the French; from all the lands of the Christians; from the lands of the East and the West; in fact, from everywhere. Some copies even travel to other countries. Whenever you enter another part of France you will find the gazette of Paris, just as in Paris you find gazettes from the provinces.

For this reason they are well acquainted with all the news,

48. For the particular newspaper aṣ-Ṣaffār received, 15,000 may have been correct; but the two most popular dailies of the 1840s, *La Presse* and *La Siècle*, together had a circulation of over 50,000. Pinkney, *Decisive Years*, p. 60.

whether it is local or foreign. Nor is it all necessarily true; it may be that the lies in it are more numerous than the truths, because it includes news that human nature loves to hear. But there are benefits in it too, such as learning what is new. Moreover, if someone has an idea about a subject but he is not a member of the press, he may write about it in the gazette and make it known to others, so that the leaders of opinion learn about it. If the idea is worthy they may follow it, and if its author was out of favor it may bring him recognition. As the poet says:

> Don't reject an idea if it is suitable,
> Or Truth even if it comes from error.
> Pearls are precious to acquire,
> But it is not the diver who decides their worth.[49]

Among the many laws which their Sultan Louis XVIII has made for them and they are obliged to follow is that no person in France is prohibited from expressing his opinion or from writing it and printing it, on condition that he does not violate the law. If he does, it is erased. One of the reasons they were so hostile to their King Charles X, who preceded the present king, and a cause for their overthrow of his rule, is that he proclaimed a ban on anyone expressing ideas, or writing them, or printing them in the newspapers, unless one of the men of state had read it [first]. Therefore nothing appeared except what he wanted to appear.[50]

In the newspapers they write rejoinders to the men of the two Chambers about the laws they are making. If their Sultan demands gifts from the notables or goes against the law in any way, they write about that too, saying that he is a tyrant and in the wrong. He cannot confront them or cause them harm. Also, if someone be-

49. *Takhlīṣ*, p. 104; *L'or*, p. 138.

50. The source is aṭ-Ṭahṭāwī, who witnessed the Revolution of 1830 at first hand and devoted a large section of the *Takhlīṣ* to it. *Takhlīṣ*, pp. 201–24; *L'or*, pp. 237–63.

haves out of the ordinary, they write about that too, making it common knowledge among people of every rank. If his deeds were admirable, they praise and delight in him, lauding his example; but if he behaved badly, they revile him to discourage the like.

Moreover, if someone is being oppressed by another, they write about that too, so that everyone will know the story from both sides just as it happened, until it is decided in court.[51] One can also read in it what their courts have decided. Whoever wishes to advertise his wares can write about them in the newspaper, praising them and mentioning their location and price in the hope of selling them; and whoever wishes to sell a house or property can publish it in the gazette to inform people. All in all, the gazette is of such importance that one of them would do without food or drink sooner than do without reading the newspaper.

The people of Paris, men and women alike, are tireless in their pursuit of wealth.[52] They are never idle or lazy. The women are like the men in that regard, or perhaps even more so. You will never see one of them at loose ends. Even though they have all kinds of amusements and spectacles of the most marvelous kinds, they are not distracted from their work, and give every moment its due. Indeed, the spectacles help them by providing rest for the soul, allowing them to return to their labors refreshed. Nor do they excuse someone for being poor, for indeed death is easier for them than poverty, and the poor man there is seen as vile and contemptible. As it is said:

> Let me get rich quickly,
> For I have seen people whose tragedy is to be poor.
> They are scorned and derided

51. *Maḥall al-ḥukm*, literally "place of judgment."

52. See aṭ-Ṭahṭāwī's chapter entitled "Profit and Proficiency in Business in Paris." *Takhlīṣ*, pp. 149–53; *L'or*, pp. 173–75.

Even though they are from a good family.
Their relatives keep away from them,
Belittle their wives and heap insults on their children.
If you meet a rich man, he has dignity,
While his [poor] friend has lost his senses.[53]

It is said that poverty is a tragedy and a motive for people's hatred. Whoever is poor is stripped of his manhood and humiliated. When poverty descends on a person, he has no choice but to feel shame. It is said, whoever guards his religion guards two most precious things—his honor and his faith. And as the poet says:

Do not reproach me because I have [ornate] serving dishes,
For they are the vessels of my dignity.

Luqmān[54] said to his son, "I have eaten the bitter apple and tasted the prickly pear, but I have never seen anything more bitter than poverty. If I ever become poor, do not tell others. They say that the rich man is fresher than water, higher than the sky, sweeter than the honeycomb, and more fragrant than the rose; his errors are truths, his sins are virtues, his words are accepted in councils and his speech is never boring, even though the fool may be falser than a shimmering mirage and heavier than lead; even though no one says hello to him when he arrives, or asks about him when he leaves; even though his hands violate the ritual ablutions and his recitations disrupt the prayers."

Someone else said: "I have noticed what brings down the mighty and breaks them; and I have seen nothing more humbling or destructive than poverty." As the poet said:

53. Compare with the verses of the Tāzā poet Ibn Shujāʿ cited by Ibn Khaldūn. *Muqaddimah* 3:469.

54. A legendary figure from pre-Islamic times, known for his wise sayings, stories, and pithy proverbs. *SEI*, s.v. "Luḳmān."

When the poor wretch asks for something,
People take him for a criminal.
My cousins used to say "Welcome,"
But when they saw me destitute, the greetings died.

And another said:

The wounds of time have no physician,
Nor do people benefit from privation.
You see how a poor man
Is taken as a fool by his own kind, though he may be wise.

And another said:

By your life, money makes the man
Honorable, while poverty wears him down.
Nothing lifts the humble spirit like wealth,
And nothing debases the noble spirit like penury.

As some wise men said: "Liveliness is a blessing, idleness is a waste, and laziness an evil; a walking dog is preferable to a sleeping lion. Poverty comes from weakness and indolence." And the poet said:

Idleness married his daughter to indolence,
Bestowing upon her at the marriage a dowry
And a soft bed. Then he said to her, "Lie back and be dutiful,
For surely you two will give birth to poverty."

Most of the wealth of this people is from commerce and crafts. In commerce they have gone beyond buying and selling and have something called a "bank." A man deposits a sum of money with someone who keeps it safe, and the holder of the deposit pays him interest each year at a rate known to all. If the owner of the money wants his capital back, he may take it. There are two sorts of banks, the state bank and the commercial bank. The interest from a commercial bank is greater than the interest from a bank of the Sultan, but the bank of the Sultan is more secure because the state is always there and cannot fail, unlike [private] businessmen.[55]

There is also an association whose name means "partners in guaranty," known there as the *secours*,[56] who are obligated to whoever pays them a set sum each year. If his house, or shop, or their contents are lost through unforeseen circumstances, a fire or a collapse, or if his ship goes down at sea or is damaged in a collision, they recompense him for everything he has lost. There is also something called a *compagnie*,[57] which is an association of businessmen. Each pays in an amount of money according to his means, and all together they open a mine, improve the roads, build bridges, or put ships on the rivers, having raised all [the money] required. Whatever profit they gain is divided up according to the amount of capital each put in. They also pay to the state treasury a fixed amount enabling them to do this, and the whole business returns to the state treasury after a certain period of time. Another of their laws is that

55. The "state bank" (*bankat ad-dawla*) or "bank of the Sultan" is in fact the Bank of France. Drawing a parallel with his Moroccan experience, aṣ-Ṣaffār saw no difference between the wealth of the King and the treasury of the State. While the Bank of France was the government's fiscal agent, it was privately owned and under only minimal government control. Pinkney, *Decisive Years*, p. 17; on the word *dawla*, see H. A. R. Gibb, "The Evolution of Government in Early Islam," in *Studies on the Civilization of Islam*, ed. S. Shaw and W. Polk (Boston, 1962), p. 46 note 1. For aṭ-Ṭahṭāwī's comments, which influenced aṣ-Ṣaffār, see *Takhlīṣ*, p. 149; *L'or*, pp. 173–74.

56. An insurance company. Aṣ-Ṣaffār learned about this from the *Takhlīṣ*, pp. 149–50; *L'or*, p. 174.

57. Aṣ-Ṣaffār's explanation of the joint stock company follows aṭ-Ṭahṭāwī's. On its role in the industrialization of France, see Pinkney, *Decisive Years*, pp. 36–39.

no one can begin doing business without first paying a set sum to the state treasury and getting a license[58] indicating he has permission to do so.

The science of commerce is one of the sciences they teach and write down in books, and there are schools and libraries for it. The women are skilled in commerce just like the men, or even more so. The majority of people running the shops are women. Another aspect of their desire for wealth is that you will never see a poor person who is capable of work begging from others. They do not allow this, considering that giving charity to an able person is a cause for laziness.

The people of Paris can be described as intelligent, perceptive, and quick-witted.[59] They are not content with knowing things by tradition, but study the roots of a matter [before] drawing conclusions. Only then do they decide whether to accept or reject it. All of them know how to read and write, and they write down everything in books. Even their artisans must read and write in order to practice their craft and be inventive in it. If a craftsman does something [new], his prestige and reputation are increased. Then the state rewards him, praises him, and makes much of him. In that way the desire for progress is cultivated among them.

Everything exists there in surplus, which allows them to give the closest scrutiny and attention to discovering and bringing to light the fine points of life. They have schools and libraries for the sciences of cooking, planting, building, farming, caring for plants, and producing livestock. Whatever they hear, see, invent, or learn from others they record in registers and keep forever.

By nature they are gay and frivolous. Whenever they get to-

58. Arabic *nīshān*. Letters written by clerks in the Ottoman imperial court and approved by the Sultan were sealed with the imperial stamp, called the *nīshān*. At-Tamgrūtī, *En-nafkhat*, p. 62.

59. This section is based on the discussion in aṭ-Ṭahṭāwī's chapter entitled "Some Words about the People of Paris," *Takhlīṣ*, pp. 75–91; *L'or*, pp. 118–31.

gether they never settle down, but rather move about among one another like ripples at the seashore, only sitting down when it is time to eat. As soon as they finish they get up again, for to them sitting is considered ill-mannered and only the women do it, even if it means standing up the entire evening, which is the case when they gather for merrymaking or dancing. If one of them wishes to sit down and rest, he may go out to another room empty of people, except for those who have gone there for the same reason. We never saw men sitting during an evening's entertainment except at the theater during a play, but as soon as the play ended they stood.

During their leisure time you will see them promenading on the streets and boulevards. One of them takes his friend, male or female, by the hand and they set out on a stroll, going back and forth with purposefulness as if they had a goal in mind, but their only intention is talk and relaxation. Sometimes one even does it by oneself. They say it is useful for reflection, for revealing hidden thoughts, and for discovering new ways of doing things; and I tried it and it was true.

It is also their nature to be enamored of those who are light on their feet, cheerful in their visage, and a source of merriment. They are full of statements and inquiries on matters about which they want to know more, such as getting information about strange places, the conditions in [other] lands, and the customs of their people. They incline very much to those who have this quality and render them every affection, even if they have no prior acquaintance and their conversation together is by means of an interpreter. They find onerous those who are of a contrary nature, avoiding them by instinct.

Another of their characteristics is a hot-tempered and stubborn arrogance, and they challenge each other to a duel at the slightest provocation. If one of them slanders or insults another, the challenged one has no choice but to respond, lest he be branded a despicable coward for the rest of his life. Then they decide the conditions of the combat—what weapons they will fight with, how it will be done, and the place—and no one in authority interferes with them. [Yet] they have a generous share of culture, gentility, and refinement in worldly matters. They are mindful of good manners in their conversation, and you will rarely hear something improper from them. They do not regard Muslims or strangers to their religion with ill will, nor do their children jeer at them or do them harm, as is said about others of the Christian peoples. All their studying and reading and writing of books has made them superior. They stand apart from the rest of the Christian peoples because of their culture, civilization, and virtue in matters of this world, so much so that the notables of [other] nations send their sons [there] to learn the manners and ways of the French, and to Paris in particular, because it is the seat of their kingdom and the most civilized place in that land.

Among their qualities is honesty in trade and in the rest of their business and daily affairs. You will not find a swindler among them, as one finds among the Jews,[60] or anyone straying from the right path. Nor are they sinful except in their religion. A clean appearance in their houses, streets, and shops and in their bodies and clothing is of the utmost importance to them. You will not see anyone wearing soiled or stained clothing, and in fact their garments are mostly new. In their residential quarters and their marketplaces people sit on chairs holding brushes; if someone sees that his clothes or shoes are dusty, he has them brushed until they look like new, and he pays something for that.

They do not neglect for a single day to shake out their beds, and after two or three days they change the linens and coverings for clean ones. Likewise, the little cloths you put on your knees at mealtime must always be clean. If a bit of grease or food drips on it, or you wipe your hands with it, they will not return it to you until it is washed. In their streets you do not see any refuse or garbage.

60. Jews were the only sizable non-Muslim minority in premodern Morocco, and stereotyped views of them abounded in the popular literature.

Every day they sweep and water them if there has been no rain. But the most shameful thing they do is urinate at the bottom of the walls, and the water mixed with urine flows on the ground. However, the width of the street lessens its bad effect, for it stays to one side and does not bother the passerby. All the doors of their shops and houses, the bars of their windows, and the streetlamps in the marketplaces are wiped clean and shining as if they were put there that very day.

Their women are exceedingly beautiful, with white skin and voluptuous bodies. Blackening their eyes and eyebrows is either rare or not done at all, for it is not their custom. Their women dress in black, which becomes them more than other colors.

> I saw you in black and said, it is the moon
> Rising in the gloom of a pitch-dark night.
> I saw you in black and said, it is the sun
> Eclipsing with its radiance the light of the stars.

[A story:] They tell about the rich merchant who arrived in a town carrying veils from Iraq. He sold all of them except the black ones, and told his problem to an ascetic who was pious and observant. The ascetic composed two couplets and asked that they be sung in the town, and they were:

> Ask the beauty in the black veil,
> What do you want from the pious ascetic?
> He was preparing his shawl for prayers
> When you met him at the gate to the mosque.

And word spread in the town that the ascetic had abandoned his simple ways and was courting a woman in a black veil. There was not one beautiful woman left in town who did not buy a black veil. When nothing remained of the merchant's goods, the ascetic returned to his old habits, putting on his tattered garments once again.

Flirtation, romance, and courtship for them take place only with women, for they are not inclined to boys[61] or young men. Rather, that is extremely disgraceful for them and punishable by law, even if the two are desirous of it. By contrast, love of women and intercourse with them takes place when she is willing, and no one will raise objections to it. Nor are they obligated in any way. But going with prostitutes, and especially female ones, is considered a corruption of morality and a defect in one's honor; no one pays heed to them and people of virtue avoid speaking to them or greeting them, even for some other purpose. For if that were freely permitted, then everyone would indulge in it.

As for the chaste women among them, if you enter a man's house and a woman is present, you are not considered gracious or well-mannered unless you approach her with greetings and friendly speeches in a tone of modest gentility. Her husband will delight in that and his esteem and love for you will increase. After that you greet the husband and the others present. When you wish to conclude your business with the man, you go again to the wife. This is how their custom has established it, and God is my witness.

61. Arabic *ghulām*, a young man "whose mustache is growing forth"; sometimes, a "male slave." E. W. Lane, *Arabic-English Lexicon*, 1877 ed., 6:2286–87. See also at-Tamgrūtī, *En-nafkhat*, p. 55.

4

THEIR FOOD AND CUSTOMS AT THE TABLE

Concerning their habits in regard to dining, and a description of the kinds of food found there.[1]

You should know that among the customs of these people is that they sit only on chairs,[2] and they know nothing about sitting directly on the floor. During our stay in their country, not once did we see one of them sitting on the ground.

Another of their customs is that they do not touch food with their hands, nor do they gather around a single platter.[3] At meal-

1. Aṣ-Ṣaffār's discourse on French cooking and eating habits is much longer and more detailed than the comparable section in aṭ-Ṭahṭāwī. See *Takhlīṣ*, pp. 113–15; *L'or*, pp. 148–50.

2. Arabic *shilya*, from the Spanish *silla*. Dozy 1:783.

3. Jackson described the Moroccan meal as follows: "The Moors . . . wash their hands before every meal, which . . . they eat with their fingers: half a dozen persons sit round a large bowl . . . each person puts his hand to the bowl, and taking up the food, puts it by a dexterous jerk, into his mouth, without suffering his fingers to touch the lips. . . . They have no chairs or tables in their houses, but sit cross-legged on carpets and cushions; and at meals, the dish or bowl of provisions is placed on the floor." *Account*, p. 139.

times the servants make ready a wooden table standing on [tall] legs. These legs can be opened out or folded in; if they are opened out, then the whole table is made larger by adding a board in the middle; but if [the company] is small, the [original] table is sufficient. That is to say, they can make the size of the table match the number of diners: four, ten, or whatever. After that they cover it entirely with a spotless white cloth and put at each place a small empty dish, setting on it a little folded white towel for the knees. There is also a piece of bread, a silver spoon, a small knife, and a small fork with three teeth, also made of silver. In the center of the table they place bowls of fruit and sweets, and perhaps vases with flowers. They give each person a pitcher of water along with a glass for drinking. Two people may share one pitcher, but each has his own glass from which no one else may drink, for they regard that as the height of cleanliness. If it is one of their own people, they also give him a pitcher of wine and a glass. Every two or three places, they set down a holder with two small glass dishes, one containing salt and the other ground black pepper, which we call *libzār*, along with a delicate little spoon for serving it, for they do not cook with salt and each diner adds it according to his taste.

Then they bring on a basin made of bright brass with holes at the sides—it may be either round or rectangular—with a flat cover. Inside is a lighted candle. They place one of these at each end of the table and set the platters of food on top to keep them hot. The chairs are lined up at the sides of the table, and nearby they make ready great numbers of plates, spoons, knives, and forks. It takes the servants two hours or more to prepare the table.

When mealtime arrives, the diners enter and sit, while the servants stand at the head. They bring each person a little glass bowl of water for washing the hands and a second small towel for drying them. Then each [diner] takes the first towel and puts it on his knees, and takes up the spoon that is at his right hand. First they bring on the soup, known to us as *shurba*. They have many creative ways of making it. Sometimes they combine greens with meat broth, and at other times they make it with flour and thin noodles. It is drunk with the spoon. When it is finished, the servant removes the bowl with the spoon in it, replacing it with a clean one. Then he brings a large platter of meat, fish, or chicken, already cut into small pieces to make it easier to serve; there is also a large spoon for serving. It is offered to each diner in turn, and if he desires it, he takes it himself or asks the servant to serve him; or he may refuse it, saying "*merci,*" which means "thank you very much," for that is considered polite there, even with servants.

If the dish being served is meat, for example, he takes up the fork in his left hand and the knife in his right and thrusts the fork deeply into the meat, cutting it with his knife, then raising it to his mouth and not seizing it directly with his hand, for that is considered disgusting by them. If the food is tasteless because it lacks salt, he finds it nearby and adds the amount he desires, and the same with the pepper if it is needed. If he wants some bread he may break off a bit with his hand, but if he wants to soak it in sauce he must take it on his fork and sop it up; otherwise he may [eat it] from his hand. If the food needs oil and vinegar, they are found in two bottles sitting together in a little holder; the servant passes them if the food requires it. At the end of every course, the servant removes the dishes and other things, and brings fresh ones. The number of dishes piles up, because they change them at every course, and no dish is ever eaten from twice. This is due to their excessive concern for cleanliness.

Every meal has an established order. They begin with a type of broth of meat or the like, follow that with a roast of chicken or some other meat, and then finish off with fruits and sweets. They begin each meal with something easily digested and light on the stomach, put fish or chicken before the meat, and separate one course from the next by a little wait. The sign of the end of the soup and the beginning of the roast is that they serve a little glass with egg thickened with sugar, flour, and milk. It has been left on ice until it too is like ice. The sign that the fruit is about to be served is that the plate and utensils are changed for a beautifully fragile dish, with a fork and knife plated with gold. When the meal is over, the servants bring out water infused with something that adds an aroma to the food, such as thyme. Then they wash their hands and dry them, and get up.

If they are in the home of one of their own people, they do not rise until the mistress of the house rises, nor do they sit down in the first place until she has been seated. After rising they all go into another room, for the dining room is not a sitting room, and the sitting room must be kept spotless. The servants follow with coffee, which they drink while engaging in easy conversation. Then each leaves for his own affairs.

They linger at the table for more than two hours, because it is their custom to stretch out the talk during the meal so they can over-indulge in food. The Arabs say that perfect hospitality is friendliness at first sight and leisurely talk with one's table companions. But we detested the arrival of mealtimes because of the endless waiting, nor did we understand their conversation. Moreover, much of the food did not agree with us, and we got tired and irritated with the long sitting and waiting. This is everything that relates to their manner of eating.

As for their diet, it is mostly meat, fish, the large chickens known to us as turkeys,[4] wild game, goose, rice, noodles, and little balls made of flour which are moist in the middle and are fried like small fritters. They have green peas[5] all through the year because they plant them indoors, as we have already mentioned. Other greens are found year-round, [such as] spinach and green beans, which they cook with milk, and celery, both cooked and raw. Turnips,

4. *Dajāj al-hind*, literally "chickens from India."

5. Peas (*jilbāna*) is Moroccan dialect, as are mushrooms (*fuqqāʿ*) and cress (*karwīnash*); other vegetable names are in Classical Arabic. See H. P. J. Renaud and G. S. Colin, *Tuḥfat al-Aḥbāb: Glossaire de la matière médicale marocaine* (Paris, 1934), passim.

which they cook separately and not with meat as we do, are so sweet that some people are not able to eat them. They have various kinds of thick puddings, some from eggs, sugar, flour, and milk, others from coffee and the like. Other vegetables are the artichoke, both stem and cup, which are cooked separately, and also a variety of cauliflower which they cook without salt, but serve with salt, oil, and sugar.

The European potato is also found there, and it is rarely absent from a meal. They prepare it by itself or with other things. Also the truffle,[6] which is black; generally they add a bit of it to the cooking, or stuff a turkey with it, for it is exceedingly expensive there—someone told me that it is sold for twelve *riyāls*. Think what an exorbitant price that is! They have mushrooms like those which grow wild in Morocco; they make much of them, serving them by themselves or along with something else. They have apples cooked with sugar. Among their raw vegetables are celery, and the greens known to us as cress and lettuce. Small, delicious radishes and green olives are a must at the table. All these are served as salads, but separately, without mixing them together. They also have shallots with green peppers soaked in vinegar. As for onions, they do not care much for them and one sees them hardly at all.

Their meat is chiefly beef or lamb, all of which is extremely fat, especially the veal. They have a special occasion for fattening meat, which is an annual feast called *carnaval*.[7] It lasts for three days, during which they make merry by dressing up in costumes and dis-

6. In Morocco, truffles (Arabic *tarfās*) grow wild in the oak forests of the north, in the mountains of the Middle Atlas, and in the Sus. Jackson reported that they were in great demand when in season, and "sell at a much higher price than grapes, or any other fruit or vegetable." *Account*, p. 76; Dozy 1:145.

7. Carnival, from the Latin *carn* "meat" + *levare* "to raise." The festival of merrymaking before the season of Lent. Parisians of every social class would dress in costumes and carouse in the streets. Aṣ-Ṣaffār did not see Carnival at first hand, but may have read about it in aṭ-Ṭahṭāwī, or heard about it from his escorts. Compare with *Takhlīṣ*, p. 123; *L'or*, p. 159.

guising themselves with ugly masks having huge eyes or crooked mouths. During those three days they parade around the countryside in a great procession led by the fattest bull of all. Then the bull is slaughtered and its owner is given an amount of money equal to its fat. Therefore people fatten their calves, each hoping his calf will grow into the fattest and win the competition. For this reason you will not find lean meat there.

As for fish, they are extremely artful in its preparation. Sometimes they cook it in water and at serving time sprinkle vinegar, butter, and salt on it; other times they remove the bones and put breadcrumbs on each piece, one by one, making rolls of it and then baking or grilling it. They eat a certain kind of fish that may be large or small; its peculiarity is that in the water it is green, but when cooked it becomes red.[8] They give fish an important place in their diet and there is hardly a meal without it.

They are not creative in varying their menus with different things. Even if they have just eaten [something], they bring it on the next time. In general their food lacks flavor, and even salt and pepper. But he who has no choice can make do; of necessity, one can stay alive on it.

Their fruits and sweets, on the other hand, are delicious and good-tasting. Among the fruits we ate there were apples and pears, which are available all through the winter season. They are quite perfect and free of rot. Oranges are not abundant in their country, and they bring them in from abroad. Grapes grow year round but are not as plentiful as apples or pears, so they only serve a bunch or two of them. They eat apples and pears raw, or cook them and sprinkle them with sugar. Among their other common fruits are apricots, which they preserve in sugar, and plums, peaches, and green figs, which are also served with sugar. They also have dried ones. Sweet oranges and bitter oranges are found there too, as well as almonds, whose skin can be removed by rubbing them with the

8. Lobster and shrimp have a pigment in their shells that changes from blue to red when heated.

hands. Also hazelnuts and chestnuts are plentiful, but walnuts, currants, and dates are not, and have to be brought in from outside.

For sweets they have what is known to us as "biscuits,"[9] which they make in various ways, either with almonds or sesame seeds, or by filling them with egg whites mixed with sugar, or by sprinkling them with orange water. They are very good. They also make them with sugared almonds and chocolate,[10] which they know about and cook in the usual way. They make dry cakes from it. Another kind of sweet, made from almonds and honey, is in the shape of a dome or tower, or a large vase. They often use bitter almonds in making sweets. All their sweet syrups are made from sugar, for bees' honey is very scarce and used only for medicaments. They get it from other countries, because there is none in their own land due to the cold. They have many [kinds] of candies wrapped prettily in colored paper to make them more appealing to the eye, and [selling them] provides a living for the poorer ones among them.

Their drink at mealtimes is wine, generally mixed with water, for they never drink it alone, just as they do not drink water alone. They cannot do without it, and wash down their food with it at mealtimes. Many varieties exist, but two are used more than others, the well-known red and another they call *champagne*; if you pour it into a glass, large bubbles rise up and then sink back down. This is the finest of all their wines. They never overindulge in it to the point of drunkenness or keel over, for that is considered disgraceful. Whoever does that is not counted among the people of good breeding.[11]

These people do not make a practice of storing up foodstuffs.

9. *Bishkitū*. This word is not vocalized in aṣ-Ṣaffār's text, suggesting it may have been in common use. Al-Ghassānī, *Iftikāk*, p. 87, defines it as "bread kneaded with sugar and egg yolks," an adaptation of the Spanish *bizcocho*, according to Bustani. Aṣ-Ṣaffār uses it to mean pastries in general.

10. *Shaklāṭ*; also found in al-Ghassānī, *Iftikāk*, p. 87.

11. Al-Ghassānī noted the same decorum among the Spanish. *Iftikāk*, p. 37.

You will not find any in their houses except at mealtimes, even in the homes of the rich and notable. Nor do they make bread at home, as we do, but get it from the marketplace. At the start of the day the master of the house gives money to his servant, who goes out and buys everything needed for that particular day, such as bread, meat, chicken, fish, vegetables, and so on.

Chickens are sold killed and already plucked clean, for they do not slaughter them as we do. Likewise all their game meat, such as rabbits, birds, etc., is already dead, and is not killed by slitting the throat. They claim that by strangling it, the strength stays in it.[12] The servant brings the provisions home and roasts what needs to be roasted, grills what is to be grilled, treating each thing in its proper manner. This is their custom every day, and no one is burdened with buying grain, or grinding it, or storing it up.[13]

The important men of the marketplaces[14] are responsible for provisioning the city sufficiently so that nothing will run short during the year. You will not find people crowding around to buy what is there. Despite the huge size of the city and its vast population, everything is available in plentiful amounts, to the point where you would think there were no buyers because of the quantity you see in the shops and marketplaces. Moreover, none of it spoils and meat stands for days at a time without getting rotten.

Now a few words about what we learned about the butchering of meat in Paris. One day I saw in the gazette that in the month of January [1846], during which they observed the festival of the New

12. According to Islamic law, only animals killed by slitting the throat and draining out the blood are suitable for consumption. An animal strangled to death falls into the category of *mayta* ("carrion"), and the thought of consuming it is repugnant to the practicing Muslim. *SEI*, s.v. "Maita."

13. Moroccan households would stockpile certain types of foodstuffs, taking advantage of seasonal prices. Quantities of wheat would be bought at harvesttime, ground into flour, and then turned into couscous, the tiny grainlike pasta which is a staple of the Moroccan diet. The couscous would then be put in sacks and stored in the house for family use.

14. In Arabic, *arbāb al-aswāq*.

Year, they slaughtered 7,248 bulls, 1,839 cows, 7,228 calves, and 41,819 sheep. This month did not show a great increase over the previous month, the difference being only because of the holiday. [The difference was] 461 bulls, 289 calves, and 188 sheep.

Likewise a few words on what we learned about prices. First of all, you should know that their coinage [includes] the *riyāl*, which is known to us, since it circulates [in Morocco] now at the rate of sixteen *ūqiyas*. Also the *franc*, which is one fifth of it, and the *sol*, their smallest coin, twenty of which make a franc.[15]

The price of good bread is four *sols* a *raṭl*, for they do not sell it by the piece, as we do, but by weight. The loaf which is less than a *raṭl* costs two *sols*. A *raṭl* of meat is fifteen *sols*, with no difference between beef and mutton, except that veal is eighteen *sols* a *raṭl*. A small chicken costs a *riyāl*, a turkey eight francs, a single goose half a *riyāl*, and butter, depending on its quality and freshness, from twenty to forty *sols*. Eggs are two for a *sol*, and a rabbit is a *riyāl*. A *raṭl* of sugar is a franc, a *raṭl* of coffee two francs, and chocolate is half a *riyāl*. A *raṭl* of tea costs from twelve to fifteen francs, but it is not good—indeed, not even mediocre. It looks like dry grass and does not have the taste of the tea we know. If it were not for the milk, one could not drink it, nor do they care much for it [themselves].[16] The price of a live bull is 120 francs or more, and a prize bull that they parade at *carnaval*, such as we have mentioned, can cost as much as 3,000 francs. They say that these bulls sometimes weigh twenty-four *qinṭārs*.

I saw good olives, the sweet variety, for two francs a *raṭl*, and

15. See p. 134 note 21.

16. Introduced into Morocco in the eighteenth century, the consumption of tea was at first restricted to the Makhzan. Often it was included among the gifts of foreign ambassadors to the Sultan. By aṣ-Ṣaffār's day, tea-drinking was widespread, reaching as far as the Saharan oases. Moroccan tea is prepared with fresh mint and sugar, giving it a distinctive taste. See J.-L. Miège, "origine et développement de la consummation du thé au Maroc," *Bulletin économique et social du Maroc* 20, 71 (1956): 377–98.

other varieties for fifteen *sols*. A *raṭl* of candle wax costs thirty-five *sols*. Their candles are made from the fat of the cow, or perhaps from fish fat, which is extremely white, but the former is more usual. As for beeswax, it is extremely scarce there. They burn candles more often than oil, though their light is feeble. One candle of ours is equal to three or four of theirs. Wood is sold by weight, not by the load, a *qinṭār* of it costing about three francs.

This is what we learned on this subject, and God is my witness.

5

OUR STAY IN THIS CITY

Concerning what we saw, our audience with their Sultan, and other matters.

We have already noted that we arrived in Paris on Sunday, the 28th day of Dhū al-Ḥijja, and our departure took place on Monday, the 19th day of Ṣafar.[1] The length of our stay was fifty days. Not only was our visit brief but we rarely ventured out, leaving our place of residence only when invited somewhere special, such as to an evening in their hospitality, or to the theater. The reason for this was that we wished to preserve our reputation, our pride, and our dignity. Praise be to God, we were valued in their eyes and considered with respect. We could have been commonplace by coming and going frequently, but we were opposed to that. As Ardashīr[2]

1. The arrival was Sunday, 28 December 1845, and the departure Monday, 16 February 1846.

2. Founder (d. 242) of the Sassanid dynasty of pre-Islamic Persia, and the inspiration of an oral tradition on princely duty that passed into Arabic literature and was "cited whenever worldly wisdom and circumspect behaviour in politics or war were in question." C. E. Bosworth, "The Persian Impact on Arabic Literature," in A. F. L. Beeston et al., eds., *Arabic Literature to the End of the Umayyad Period* (Cambridge, 1983), p. 488; *EI* 2, s.v. "Ardashīr."

said to his son, "Don't let people gain power over your soul; the boldest one with the lion is he who sees him the most."

> Just as new clothes become threadbare through overuse,
> So do searching eyes wear out the man.

Moreover, we never ventured out by ourselves, because of our ignorance of the place and the language, but were always in the company of a guide. Therefore we should be excused for a lack of details about this city and its inhabitants.

When we arrived in Paris we were settled into a house prepared for us on the famous Champs-Elysées mentioned above, which means "garden of paradise" in their language. It is one of their favorite places for strolling, relaxation, and amusement, with its straight rows of splendid trees. It runs along the river, and extends from the Sultan's garden at one end to a lofty arch built by Bonaparte at the other.[3] Its length exceeds six thousand paces.[4] Despite its great length, it is so straight and level that if you stand at one end you will see the other directly opposite. They selected a house for us there because of its superb location. On a sunny day, and especially on Sunday, which is their day of leisure, everyone in the city comes there to promenade and relax with his companions. They arrive in carriages or on foot, but mostly in carriages; they leave their carriages waiting and continue on foot, walking to their heart's content. From time to time one sees young maidens there, giving intense pleasure and distraction to the eye.

When we entered the house we found that they had readied it with the very finest things for us. It was reserved for us alone, for it was not a hotel open to the public. They had installed the richest furnishings, the most priceless clocks, the brightest chandeliers, and the most willing servants to demonstrate their high esteem for us.

3. The Arc de Triomphe, begun under Napoleon in 1806, completed in 1836.

4. The pace (*khaṭwa*) is the length of a stride, about one yard.

They also assumed the costs for all our needs, food and otherwise, and even had carriages waiting for us whenever we went out. Each day our expenses for food and the rest came to about two hundred *riyāls*.[5] Twenty servants were provided to us, and each had a special duty. For our chief they set aside the best bedchamber with the finest appointments; we also had a salon where we all gathered. Every two or three of us had a separate chamber for resting and sleeping, and each had his own bed. Every chamber was equipped with writing instruments, [washing] vessels, and comfortable chairs.

The day of our arrival we rested. The next day, we received a summons from their Sultan to an audience at ten o'clock the following [morning], and we spent the whole day preparing for our meeting. In the morning his chief of protocol[6] arrived, accompanied by a general and four coaches. The largest one, for our chief, was drawn by ten horses and adorned with silks and rich brocades inside and out. Following it was another drawn by eight horses for other dignitaries, and then a third and a fourth for the different ranks of our party. Each of us rode in a coach, and each coach stood out because of its magnificence.

The [people] knew we were coming, and they thronged the streets and avenues, eager to catch sight of us. When we reached the palace, they honored us by having us pass beneath the arch reserved for the Sultan and his family; we entered a vast courtyard where we were met by soldiers standing at attention. They stood in groups,

5. Or 1,000 francs, a considerable sum. Beaumier said that the daily cost of food alone was about 600 francs. AAE/ADM/Voyage, Beaumier to "Mes chers amis," no date.

6. *Qā'id al-mashwar*. See Introduction, note 106. This event was reported home in a letter from Ashʿāsh to his brother in Tetuan, who in turn forwarded the news to the court. See, for example, DAR 17579, ʿAbd al-Qādir Ashʿāsh to his brother ʿAbd Allāh, dated 1 Muḥarram 1262/30 December 1845. In the handwriting of Muḥammad aṣ-Ṣaffār, this letter recounts the reception at the palace in language resembling that used here, suggesting that Ashʿāsh and aṣ-Ṣaffār worked together in composing at least some parts of the *riḥla*.

dressed in their finest uniforms and bearing arms. In front of each [group] stood an officer, who held an unsheathed sword. Hardly had we arrived when music broke out. We alighted from our carriages and entered the palace, where they had some light refreshments readied for us, and then we climbed the stairs.

This was an imposing palace of marvelous construction and unusual decor, with lofty domes and the finest furnishings, superb statues, exquisite vases, crystal-clear mirrors, and rich ornamentation. It was the palace of a king who knows no limit or constraint: [in it] was everything that gives pleasure in this life. "*Yearn not for that which We have provided some wedded couples to enjoy of the splendors of this world, that We may thereby try them.*"[7] We passed from one vast room to the next until we reached the chamber of the Sultan, which was the most splendid and ornate of all. We found him seated on the throne of his kingdom, surrounded by the great men of state. His throne had three steps and was encircled by a golden rail, and from above hung silken draperies fringed and corded with gold.[8] The dress[9] of the Sultan was like that of the others about him, not exceptional in any way. He wore a sword and a hat[10] while the others were bareheaded, which is their practice when standing before their superiors.

Their custom in greeting is that the envoy contrives[11] some

7. Koran 20:131. The rest of the verse reads: "The provision of thy Lord is better and longer lasting."

8. Ibn Khaldūn noted that one of the marks of kingship is a raised throne, symbolizing the superiority of the monarch over others. *Muqaddimah* 2:53.

9. *Kiswa*, literally "cloth"; especially, the richly embroidered cloth covering the Kaʿba, within the great mosque at Mecca; also, the cloth covering on the tomb of a saint. Dozy 2:469; *SEI*, s.v. "Kaʿba."

10. *Barnīṭa*, from the Italian *berretta*. In the Moroccan dialect, a European-style hat. Dozy 1:80.

11. The Arabic verb root is *z-w-r*. Used in the second form, it has the sense of "falsifying" or "forging," bearing out the motif of dissimulation that underlies this account of the meeting with the King. The Arabic text of Ashʿāsh's speech is found in AAE/MDM 4/135–36.

choice expressions, writes them down on a piece of paper, and recites them upon meeting the Sultan; the Sultan then responds in a like manner. Our chief prepared such a speech, writing it down on a piece of paper, which he took out and read in Arabic. His words were as follows: he praised and complimented the Commander of the Muslims,[12] may God grant him victory and think well of him, since it was he who sent [us] to this Sultan. He also complimented the [French] Sultan with appropriate words, and mentioned his subjects, lauding them for their civilized and proper conduct in worldly affairs, and the kindness and good intentions shown [us] since our arrival in his country, along with other topics required at such occasions. As they say, "Don't insult a host in his own house." The blessings of God upon him who said:

> He who fails to dissimulate in many matters
> Will be pierced by the eyetooth
> And flattened by the foot of destiny.

And another said:

> Greet with gladness if you are unable to engage in combat,
> Conquer thusly if you are unable to succeed by arms.
> Meet the enemy courteously during his happiness,
> Until his world is overturned.

And another said:

> God rewards the wise man
> Who takes fate in his stride,
> Who recompenses friends with good deeds
> And puts the enemy aside until the right time,

12. *Amīr al-muslimīn*, a title of the Moroccan Sultans. Compare with al-Ghassānī's account of his meeting with King Carlos II. *Iftikāk*, pp. 42–44.

Who clothes destiny in pleasing garb
And dances with the monkey in his house.

And another said:

If weaker than your enemy but in his house
Make merry if it is seemly;
For fire is put out by water,
But together they cook, though its nature is to burn.

Blame or reproach [were out of place] here. As it says in the Hadith: "Let us smile outwardly, while in our hearts [we] despise them."

After he had ended his speech and the interpreter translated it, the Sultan gave us his reply, saying, among other things, that he praised God for the renewal of the truce[13] and friendship between him and the state [*dawla*] of the Sultan of the Maghrib, and said he would not issue any order opposing the state of Marrakesh and the Maghrib. He spoke in his own language, and the interpreter translated it into Arabic. We then handed over the letter of our Sultan and he took it with great feeling. After that, we left him and were presented to his wife, his daughters, and his other female relations. They were very polite and spoke pleasantly with us until our departure.

When we arrived home, we found invitations to honor them with our presence at dinner. That evening we went to [the palace] and found the rooms lit by huge crystal chandeliers whose brilliant reflections captivated the eye. The walls were hung with great mirrors, taller than a man, which caught in the clarity of their glass the chandeliers and everything else, so that one imagined seeing a second room just like this one. All of his ministers and notables, their wives and daughters, and all his sons and their wives were there, about seventy people in all.

We entered the dining room and found a huge table, long enough

13. *Muhādana*, an armistice.

to accommodate that number; indeed, so long that you could not see from one end who was at the other. It was laden with fruits and sweets, vases of flowers, and a row of golden candelabras in the middle. From above hung crystal chandeliers aglow with candles, with smaller ones at the sides; in all, there were three hundred thirty candles lighting the room. All the serving dishes were of silver and gold, and the guests wore gold on their clothing and on their swords. The scene was one of magnificent splendor, with the flickering of the candles on the gleaming dishes and attire of the diners, the brilliant mirrors and chandeliers, the fine pearls and rare gems of the ladies. The glowing cheeks of the maidens were enough to make the hearts of young men ache. The splendid repast and the delectable fruits and sweets were plentiful and in perfect taste.

When we finished, first the Sultan, then the whole company, rose and went into another room where we remained standing, except for the women, which is their custom. The Sultan came to each of us and spoke in an easy and open manner, asking about our health and making friendly gestures. Also his wife, who is quite ancient; nevertheless she was bedecked with jewelry, pearls, and diamonds,[14] whose like you have never seen except there. His daughters too spoke with us, for women talking to men is not considered shameful or harmful to one's virtue. On the contrary, it is encouraged, as long as it is done with modesty and discretion, even if a woman is alone. Talk with women should be polite, gentle, and subdued, with questions about her children, their names, and so on. We stayed there for about an hour after dinner, and then we left.

The following day and the days after, there was not a single foreign ambassador[15] in Paris who did not call upon our ambassador

14. *Al-yāmand.* In al-Ghassānī, *yāmanṭ. Iftikāk*, p. 84.

15. *Bāshādūr*, from the Spanish *embajador*. Lévi-Provençal (*Les historiens*, p. 82 note 62) counted this among the "new words" found in az-Zayyānī's *At-tarjamāna al-kubrā* (late eighteenth century), but it already appears in the seventeenth century in al-Ghassānī's *Iftikāk*, p. 40.

to greet him and wish him well, following the example of the Sultan and his ministers.

On Thursday, two days after our reception, their New Year began—the year 1846 since the birth of Jesus, peace be unto him—the first day of January, which corresponds to the twentieth day of December according to our reckoning, for they are eleven days ahead of us in every one of [our] non-Arab months. The reason for that, according to what they told me, is that the sun is faster in movement than the days of the year by some minutes. They ignored this for some time until about six hundred years ago, when one of their authorities calculated that a number of days had already accumulated from those minutes. When it was the first day of January, according to the old calendar, they determined that [the date] should advance by eleven days made up from those minutes. And they have continued according to that reckoning ever since.[16]

It is their custom on the New Year that everyone of consequence in the city of Paris comes before the Sultan, it being one of their feast days. We had no choice but to do the same. We went at the time of the afternoon prayer. Entering the palace, we found all the great men of state and foreign ambassadors there in a multitude, all gorgeously arrayed and conversing in flattering tones. Among the Muslims we met there were seven Egyptians. Two were grandsons of Muḥammad ʿAlī, Pasha of Egypt, and two were the children of his stepson, Ibrāhīm Pasha. We also met another person from the inner circle of Muḥammad ʿAlī named Sāmī Pasha, along with two more from their retinue. In all, there were about sixty people sent there by Muḥammad ʿAlī to learn the sciences one finds only

16. The solar calendar followed in Morocco for agricultural purposes was the old Roman (Julian) calendar. However, that calendar was inaccurate, and had to be corrected in 1582 by Pope Gregory XIII. The new Gregorian calendar, eleven days ahead of the old, was not known in Morocco. While the gist of aṣ-Ṣaffār's explanation, probably provided by an interpreter, is correct, the details are inaccurate. See S. B. Burnaby, *Elements of the Jewish and Muhammadan Calendars* (London, 1901), pp. 512–15.

there.[17] These Muslims were not dressed like Christians, but wore long gowns covered with so much gold embroidery, pearls, and precious stones that the cloth beneath could hardly be seen. Their buttons were studded with gems, and the girdles from which they hung their swords were heavy with gold. Their splendor was indescribable; they were more handsome than the Christians by far. The ambassador of the Ottoman Sultan was also present.[18]

When we had all gathered, the Sultan appeared and greeted first the ambassador from Rome, which is the font of their religion and the seat of their Pope (*bābā al-kabīr*), who guides them in matters of faith. They claim that he is the deputy of Jesus, peace be unto him. First the ambassador from Rome spoke, reading from a paper, as is their custom. His words were as follows: "This blessed New Year we take joy in the well-being of you and your people. Praise be to God who has put you here and given you the strength to bear the burdens of your rank. Since the day you assumed the throne of France you have led firmly, reining in the wild horses, checking those who wished to deviate and go their own way. With reason and good sense you have brought them together, leading them down the straight path. The Sultan rules only with the permission of God. We see your work is guided by Him, and that His power protects you. And we ask Him to keep you as rudder[19] of this ship, that you may steer it according to your best judgment. May God

17. Muḥammad ʿAlī, governor and later khedive of Egypt, ruled from 1805 to 1848. Illiterate himself until the age of 47, he had a passionate belief in education, and sent student missions to study modern science in France. The first, in 1826, included aṭ-Ṭahṭāwī. In 1844, thirty more students arrived in Paris, among them four royal princes: two sons of Muḥammad ʿAlī, Ḥalīm and Ḥusayn, and two of his grandsons, the sons of his eldest son Ibrāhīm (incorrectly referred to here as his "stepson"). They were Aḥmad and Ismāʾīl, the future khedive. The two were attended by their Armenian governor, Stefan Bey. The Sāmī Pasha mentioned by aṣ-Ṣaffār is unidentified. Louca, *Voyageurs et écrivains*, pp. 75–83.

18. This comment was written later in the margin.

19. Arabic *dumān*. Dozy 1:463.

bless you and increase the number of your grandchildren in the year to come, so that your family tree will branch out in glorious profusion. May God preserve us both."

Then the Sultan answered him by saying: "God bless you and reward you for this speech and for your friendly wishes; for those are meant for you as well, and for the people who sent you here. Truly it is God who has placed me here, inspired me in this work, guided me on this path, and empowered me in what I do. All Sultans have a responsibility for which we are answerable only to God. We are shepherds who must protect our flock. I will remain on the path of goodness so long as I am called on to continue in the kingship. My whole purpose is to protect the [ties of] brotherhood among mankind. I do not prefer one nation over another, but wish for pure love to exist among all of us equally. May God protect you for your good wishes to me and those who will be born to us [in the coming year]. May God make our progeny follow the right path, granting us goodness." The end.

Then the Sultan greeted everyone until he had spoken to one and all, and we left.

On Tuesday, the 7th of Muḥarram, the Minister of Foreign Affairs, named Guizot, invited us to spend the evening with him.[20] He accompanied us into a very beautiful domed chamber, in whose center hung a huge chandelier of crystal. Set around the edges were plants and flowers, so arranged that their containers were invisible; it seemed as if they were growing there. Circling the dome on all sides were columns decorated with gold, and from each column

20. Tuesday was actually the 8th of Muḥarram, corresponding to 6 January 1846. F. P. G. Guizot (1787–1874), the Foreign Minister, is called *wazīr al-muwakkal bil-barrānī*, "Minister in charge of the Exterior." This soirée was reported in the *Journal des débats* of 8 January 1846: "The Minister of Foreign Affairs gave a grand dinner for Ben Aschache. . . . After dinner . . . the Concert Society and the students of the Conservatory, numbering about three hundred, performed pieces from Gluck, Beethoven, Weber, Rossini, and Handel with rare perfection. The ambassador appeared very pleased with the brilliant reception."

[hung] a cluster of candles. There were also many comfortable chairs set about. Leading from it was another domed room containing musical instruments, among them tall violins (*kamanjāt*) the height of a man, more bowed instruments (*rabābāt*), and other such things for making music.[21] Their custom in singing is that they recite it from pieces of paper. Chairs were set up in front, and placed on each were more papers written with music, so that each [singer] would have a book before him.

After getting up from dinner with the other guests, we entered the domed room, men and women together. A herald stood at the doorway, and when someone entered he announced him by saying, "So-and-so has arrived." Some men came with their wife or daughter, but there were also women alone. And so it went until the place was filled.

No one sat except for the women, who wore their finest frocks in a multitude of colors, white, red, and blue. Their clothing covered their breasts, which were hidden from view, but the rest of their bosom, face, and neck was bare and exposed. They cover their shoulders and upper arms in part with filmy, closefitting sleeves that do not reach the elbow. They bind in their waists beneath their dresses with tight girdles which give them a very narrow middle. It is said that they are trained into this [shape] from earliest childhood by means of a special mold. Indeed, you could make a circle around the waist with your fingers, it is so slender and fragile. Moreover, their clothes fit tightly over it, so that its exquisite delicacy is open to view. In the lower part they drape their clothing in such a way that the backside is greatly exaggerated, but perhaps this is due to something they put underneath. And it was just as the poet says:

> Women smooth of body, slender of waist,
> Yet luxuriant in the drapery enfolding them.

21. See H. G. Farmer, *A History of Arabian Music to the XIIIth Century* (London, 1929), p. 210.

Their dresses hang down to cover their ankles, and nothing of their lower part shows. If one of them is close by you, you are seized with the desire to grab her by the waist.

> The thinness of his waist appealed to me
> And I said, "The middle is the best of things."
> But he hid his backside from me with its heaviness
> And I said, "This excess is the cause of my impotence."[22]

As for her hair, she begins by combing it through, and then she divides it into two parts from the forehead, leaving a path like a glistening rivulet between. Then she braids the [parts] together, twisting them into one plait on her crown so that it forms a perfect shape like the tip of a pomegranate. Then she sets a comb of mother-of-pearl studded with diamonds in it, or perhaps intertwines a rope of jewels into the braid when she coils it around her head. Some adorn their heads with a fine silken veil bordered with pearls and precious stones, but only the old ones do this. The young women leave their heads bare, a lovely sight. By combing their hair away from the temples, the forehead is laid naked as the moon. Sometimes she will plait a sprig of flowers into her hair at the sides.

On their necks they wear necklaces of the finest pearls, perfect in their roundness, a single bead of which costs about sixty *riyāl*s. On their bosoms they wear a brooch studded with jewels, and on their wrists they hang bracelets of gold and gems, or strings of precious stones. Their jewels are the finest and clearest diamonds that dazzle the sight with their brilliance, for they do not use fake gems and only the roundest and purest pearls. This is their finery on occasions when they gather for a spectacle. However, on the streets they cover their entire body and even their hands, leaving only their faces exposed.

After everyone had gathered in the room, the musicians entered,

22. Erotic love poems in Arabic were sometimes phrased in the masculine gender.

and a row of young girls dressed in white seated themselves on chairs in front of the musicians, each holding a book in her hand. They began strumming and singing in their language. An old patriarch came forward with a baton in his hand and directed them to raise or lower their voices. They played their instruments for a short while and then fell silent in order to look at the pages before them. Then they returned to their playing, and so it went. All in all, their music and singing did not arouse in us the desire to either clap or sway. We stayed there for a short time and then left the company amidst their resounding applause.

> In a group, all about they laughed with joy
> Because it was marvelously strewn with blossoms.

And another [verse]:

> They say that Umm ʿUmar[23] is distant;
> Earth and sky are between us.
> Know that the closeness of a beloved or her distance
> Is all the same, if one cannot reach her.

The next evening they urged us to attend the theater, which we had never seen before and knew nothing about. I have already described it in detail.

On Friday, the 10th of Muḥarram, we were invited to visit one of their ministers, a respected man of great age named Soult.[24] At his house there was no singing or strumming, only the music of

23. The name of a woman; here, the beloved one.

24. Friday, 9 January 1846, was actually the 11th of Muḥarram. J. Mayr and B. Spuler, *Wüstenfeld-Mahler'sche Vergleichungs-Tabellen* (Wiesbaden, 1961), p. 27. Nicolas Jean de Dieu Soult was Minister of War, President of the Conseil d'État, and Marshal of France. A hero of the Revolution and the Napoleonic Wars, in 1846 he was 77 years old. *Dictionnaire d'histoire de France Perrin*, 1981 ed., s.v. "Soult."

trumpets and drums, for it is their custom to play music during the meal to increase their desire for food. Other ministers followed suit with their hospitality, but we only accepted invitations from the royal entourage or men of state.

On Wednesday, the fifteenth of the month, the Sultan invited us to a night of dancing at his palace, which they do every year. We arrived there and found the palace overflowing with the most beautiful daughters of Rūm, wearing jewels and gowns that defy description. Their bare necks and shoulders, dainty waists, ponderous backsides, and ample bosoms were lovely enough to make the sun and the moon blush. Their naked upper arms flashed like lightning. They dazzled the senses with their honeyed curls, graceful shapes, rosy cheeks, lithe limbs, and clinging folds. Men in even greater number were there too, but the women stayed apart from them. Some of the women were seated, while others stood. Only the daughters and wives of men of standing were there, such as the womenfolk of the Sultan and his close associates, and those of the ministers of state, or other notables. No whores or harlots were present.

After everyone gathered together, the music sounded and the men and women began to dance. A man would take the hand of a woman and the two would dance together delightfully, holding hands. Their best dance is when the man holds her by the waist, putting his arm around her and gently embracing her without squeezing her too hard, and then dancing. Their dancing is mostly in circles, with the feet indicating the direction. Sometimes the women and the men dance separately, and at other times two men may take hold of a woman and dance with her, for that is not considered shameful or indecent. A woman may even dance with a man other than her husband in his presence. It also happens that a man pursues a woman so that the one with her must release her, and the other who wishes to dance with her takes hold of her. She delights in this and makes much of him, for it is considered a compliment to her marvelous dancing. I even saw the Sultan himself, his daughters, his sons, and their wives all dancing together and with others. He was laughing and enjoying himself immensely.[25]

All in all, this was a great occasion for merrymaking and enjoyment that comes only once or twice a year. They continued dancing for an hour or so, then the music stopped and they rested; then they resumed dancing, and so it went until late at night. Whoever wished to rest a bit could go into another room set aside especially for sitting, for only the women sat in the place of entertainment. Servants were in attendance the entire night with drink, fruits, and sweets for those who wished them. If someone tired and lost interest in dancing, he could go to yet another room where tables of refreshments were set up just for the women. If he were interested, he could position himself high above that place and feast his eyes below.

They say that more than four thousand people attended that night, fifteen hundred of them women. The reception rooms of the palace, despite their great number and size, were so tightly packed with people that you could not pass through them. It was also said that the total sum spent by the Sultan that night was twenty thousand *riyāls*. As for the candles and lamps that were lit, they must have been in the thousands.

Their House of Books[26]

The next day we went to the Sultan's house of books, that is, his library (*khizāna*), which was a large building, four stories high, each

25. Compare with al-Ghassānī's comments on Spanish customs in dancing, *Iftikāk*, p. 30.

26. The Bibliothèque Royale, now part of the Bibliothèque Nationale. In Morocco, great libraries were attached to the mosque-universities, such as the Qarawiyīn, while private collections were found in the homes of wealthy individuals. G. Salmon, "Catalogue des manuscrits d'une bibliothèque privée de Tanger," *AM* 5 (1905): 134–46; R. Basset, "Les manuscrits arabes de deux bibliothèques de Fés," *Bulletin de correspondance africaine* 1, 7

floor having five or six great lofty rooms. Every wall was filled with books on wooden shelves from floor to ceiling, and in the middle was another row of shelves the length of the room. They were crammed with books newly bound in red leather, the title of each written on its spine.[27] All these rooms were spotlessly clean; no rubbish, dust, cobwebs, bookworms, or bugs were to be seen.

Custodians and workers tend the books and guard them. Their chief holds the key to the rooms and they allow whoever wishes to enter, but he must sit in a designated place at a table surrounded by chairs. He requests the books he wants from the custodian, who brings them and then stands on guard. You may read and copy from them to your heart's content; but no one is permitted to carry off a single book. The custodians are always there on duty, but they do not bother you. They know the name of every book. You may ask for whatever you want [by saying]: "Bring me such-and-such a book," and they will fetch it for you in an instant. Some of them know Arabic, and if an Arab goes there, he will find someone who comprehends his words.[28]

All kinds of books are found there, [such as] books in Arabic

(November–December 1883): 366–93; P. Maillard, "Bibliothèque de la Grande Mosquée de Tanger," *RMM* 35 (1917–18): 107–92.

27. In Muslim libraries books were usually stacked flat, with the title of the book written on the bottom edges of the leaves facing the observer, rather than on the spine. F. Rosenthal, *Technique and Approach*, p. 11 note 3.

28. Arabic was taught in Paris at the Ecole des Langues Vivantes from the late eighteenth century. Silvestre de Sacy (1758–1838) was the leading French Arabist of the period. In 1824 he became director of the new Ecole des Langues Orientales and trained a generation of disciples. Some worked in the Bibliothèque Royale, where de Sacy himself was named conservator of manuscripts in 1833; others became official interpreters, such as Alix Desgranges, who knew both Arabic and Turkish and accompanied the Moroccan delegation in Paris. De Sacy was also the inspector of Oriental type at the Imprimerie Royale. Henri Dehérain, *Orientalistes et antiquaires: Silvestre de Sacy, ses contemporains et ses disciples* (Paris, 1938), pp. iii, vi, xvii, 1–12.

from the Arab West and the Arab East; books written by hand or printed on a press; and non-Arabic books in Greek, Latin, Hindi, Turkish, Coptic, Ethiopic, and Persian. We asked for Arabic books and they brought us an enormous Koran in a single volume; two men had to carry it between them because of its size. It was in eastern script, and we had never seen anything approaching it in beauty, splendor, and perfection. The gold and ornamentation on it were beyond words. It should rightfully belong in the library of one of the kings of Islam, may God render them victorious and deliver it from the hands of the infidel![29] It is guarded extremely closely and no one may touch it except those of the front rank of learning. We asked them from whence it came, and they told us from Egypt, when they conquered it.[30]

They showed us other Korans, including one written on one long page inside of the Verse of the Throne; that is, they wrote the Verse of the Throne in large letters, and then the entire Koran from beginning to end in very tiny letters inside of it.[31] Then they brought us the *Muwaṭṭa'* of Imām Mālik,[32] written in Andalusian

29. Compare with Aḥmad b. Qāsim al-Ḥajarī al-Andalusī (known as Afūqay), *Nāṣir ad-dīn ʿalā al-qawm al-kāfirīn*, ed. Muḥammad Razūq (Casablanca, 1987): "I became incensed when I saw the Holy Book in the hands of an impure unbeliever (*kāfir najis*)" (p. 50).

30. Napoleon invaded Egypt in 1798 and brought with him a team of Orientalist scholars who "discovered" manuscripts and other treasures, later removing them to France. This giant Koran from Egypt is still in the collection of the Bibliothèque Nationale; it comes from the al-Azhar mosque in Cairo, where it was "saved from flames during the revolt of 30 vendémiaire VII (21 October 1798) and brought to France." Bibliothèque Nationale, *Catalogue des manuscrits arabes*, part 2, "Manuscrits musulmans," Tome 1, 2, "Les manuscrits du Coran," ed. F. Deroche (Paris, 1985), pp. 60–61.

31. The Verse of the Throne is Sura 2:255. This seventeenth-century Koran is still part of the collection of the Bibliothèque Nationale. See *Splendeur et majesté: Corans de la Bibliothèque Nationale* (Paris, 1987), p. 57, entry 26.

32. *The Leveled Path*, the earliest surviving book of Muslim law, written by Mālik b. Anas (d. 197/795), a jurist of Medina and founder of the Maliki school of jurisprudence. *SEI*, s.v. "Mālik b. Anas."

script on parchment; the *Sharḥ al-ʿAynī ʿalā al-jāmiʿ aṣ-ṣaḥīḥ*;[33] and a book entitled *Kashf aẓ-ẓunūn ʿan asāmī al-kutub wal-funūn*,[34] as well as other Arabic books. If our eyesight had allowed it, we would have whiled away the entire day there.

Then we visited the other rooms, and they told us about the books in them. They showed us samples of the earliest writing and how it changed, along with many old manuscripts. In addition to books, they have many things from the ancients, such as signet rings, princely armor, shields, swords, maces of iron, axes, and so forth; and everything that belonged to [the king]. If they have a thing that is rare or valuable, they guard it in their library as a relic for later generations. They do not lose it or let it get destroyed.

There were many ancient coins there, some of stone and iron, including coins of the kings of Andalus and the Maghrib. Each coinage was laid out in a small circle, and the name of its Sultan and its place [of origin] were indicated. They were displayed in rows of cases covered with glass to protect them. There were also many kinds of keys and other ancient objects, such as a golden bowl standing on tiny legs and encrusted with jewels and precious stones. They claimed it was sent to them by Hārūn ar-Rashīd as recompense for a Koran which their Sultan sent to him.[35] Also many artifacts from the Greeks, and necklaces of gold found buried in graves from the time of ignorance.[36]

33. A commentary by Abū Muḥammad Maḥmūd b. Aḥmad al-ʿAynī on the *Ṣaḥīḥ* of Bukhārī. The full title is *ʿUmdat al-qāri' fī sharḥ al-Bukhārī*. *GAL* 2:52–53; *S* 2:50–51.

34. A great bibliographical dictionary containing over 14,500 entries, written by the seventeenth-century Ottoman scholar Katib Çelebi, also known as Ḥajji Khalīfa (d. 1067/1657). *EI* 2, s.v. "Kātib Čelebi."

35. Hārūn ar-Rashīd, the fifth Abbasid Caliph (d. 193/809), made famous by the *Thousand and One Nights*. An exchange of embassies and gifts was said to have taken place between him and Charlemagne, but the incident goes unmentioned in the Arabic sources. Hitti, *History of the Arabs*, p. 298; *EI* 2, s.v. "Hārūn al-Rashīd."

36. *Al-jāhiliya*. The name given to the condition of the Arabs before the coming of Islam; hence, pre-Islamic times. *SEI*, s.v. "Djāhilīya."

The following day their Sultan summoned us to attend a review of the troops as an extravagant expression of his high esteem for us, for he does that only for those whom he holds in great favor. But for us it was more a gesture of spiteful mockery.[37] We came to a great building, where they put our chief and several of our cavalrymen on horseback, while the rest of us went up to a balcony overlooking a great long field filled with soldiers, cavalry to one side and infantry to the other. We were blinded by the flashing of their swords, the gleam of the horses' trappings, the shine of their helmets, and the radiance of the armor they wore both front and back. In the midst of the field stood their Sultan's eldest son and his brothers, along with our chief.

Then the cavalry moved back to the sides of the field, and the infantry began to march. At first they stood in close ranks, but then they separated into rows and columns. Then they divided again into ranks to pass in review. Then they split into six or seven sections, each section made up of twelve companies, each company with its own leader who held a naked sword. Then they formed into three lines of more than thirty men each, not counting the line of musicians. In the lead of each section, which they call a "troop" (*ṭarūnba*), was a row of thirteen men bearing muskets and carrying hatchets across their shoulders. They wore leather and tall black hats like inflated goatskins on their heads. They come first to remove any trees, brush, or fallen logs encountered on the march.

Then came two rows of musicians, led by a man carrying a baton. Behind him were two lines of drummers of eighteen men each, followed by one man with a large drum, and with him were two

37. This review took place on Saturday, 17 January 1846, on the Champ-de-Mars. Troops gathered from Paris and its environs in order to show the ambassador "the brilliant and varied uniforms of the French army." They moved "with a precision which completely astonished and aroused [his] admiration." *L'Illustration*, 31 January 1846. See illustration, p. 191.

Plate 9. The military review on the Champ-de-Mars. From *L'Illustration*, 31 January 1846.

others, each with a set of large copper cymbals[38] which he was banging together. Then came the woodwinds, and after them men carrying brass poles topped with tiny bells. When they struck the poles with their palms, the bells tinkled. That was all their music.

Following them were the companies of soldiers, moving their legs as one, each staying in line and not straying to the right or the left or leaving his place. When a row reached the corner of the field and was about to turn, the end toward the middle marched [in place] while the other end wheeled, so that the row stayed even. As they turned, their leader walked backwards and directed them with his baton, extending it outward to indicate who should advance and who should stay behind. When the musicians in the lead reached the center of the field, they continued playing until their troop had passed. Whenever a leader drew near to those at the center of the field, he pointed the tip of his sword to the ground in a salute, which they returned by raising their hats. The troops followed each other in rapid order, always keeping the same distance apart. Each troop had its own pennant carried by someone in the rear, for they do not carry them in front. Some were torn, for they had been in battle and were kept that way out of pride.

Some of the companies had a woman in military garb in the rear. She marched with them and carried a box with drink. There was also a doctor, his assistant, a female nurse, and a bearer for his medical instruments. Each soldier carried a sack on his back containing his food and other needs. At the top of the sack was a rolled-up cloth, perhaps his bedroll, and in his hand a musket. He also wore a sword and carried his powder, bullets, and other battle gear stuffed into his belt, so that if his leader ordered him to march, he would be ready in an instant.

After the foot soldiers came the cannoneers. There were twenty-four cannons of the twelve [pound] type, each shining on its mount-

38. Arabic *handaqa* [?]. Not found in any dictionary; the meaning is surmised from the context.

ing.[39] They were lined up in four rows of six cannons each, followed by a second row of caissons[40] that carried the supplies. Each cannon was mounted on a cart drawn by six horses, two by two, and accompanied by ten artillerymen. Three rode on the horses, while the rest rode on the cannon or the caissons. Hanging from every cannon were traces [connecting it] to the caisson behind, pulling it carefully lest anything be broken. In this way, everything is close at hand.

After the lines of cannon came the cavalry, who were also sectioned into troops and companies like the footsoldiers. First came the musicians, mounted on horses; they played only woodwinds (*ghayṭāt*) and had no drums. Then the cavalry, who were of different types: some had drawn swords and short muskets at their sides, while others had lances tipped with small, tricolored pennants, red, white, and blue. The fluttering and waving of the flags from afar is intended to increase the fear and astonishment [of the enemy], just as the glinting of swords and armor is calculated to strike terror into their hearts.[41] Still others wore helmets and armor like the infantry. Each group has a special task in the conduct of war, either taking part or standing in reserve, or putting out fires if they occur, and so on.

So it went until all had passed, leaving our hearts consumed with fire from what we had seen of their overwhelming power and mastery, their preparations and good training, their putting everything in its proper place. In comparison with the weakness of Islam, the

39. *Ṣiqāla*, from the Italian *scala*, meaning a staging or scaffolding. Dozy 1:839.

40. *Rabīʿa*, a box for holding ammunition. In Moroccan usage, a strongbox placed at a saint's tomb for the purpose of collecting donations. Harrell, p. 123.

41. Ibn Khaldūn noted the psychological effect of flags and music in battle, saying that "the display of banners and flags and the beating of drums and the blowing of trumpets and horns" were intended to arouse terror. Music causes "a kind of drunkenness" among one's own troops, making men willing to die, and this is why non-Arabs bring musicians into battle. *Muqaddimah* 2:48–49.

dissipation of its strength, and the disrupted condition of its people, how confident they are, how impressive their state of readiness, how competent they are in matters of state, how firm their laws, how capable in war and successful in vanquishing their enemies—not because of their courage, bravery, or religious zeal, but because of their marvelous organization, their uncanny mastery over affairs, and their strict adherence to the law.

Even when one of them commits a crime, they know what to do, for he is subject to their law, regardless of whether he is great or humble. If one of them shows excellence, they elevate him in standing. They do not fear that another will seize their property, nor do they covet what is not theirs. In battle they give their utmost, hurling themselves into the thick of it. If you could see their conduct and their laws [at work], you would be profoundly impressed with them, despite their infidelity (*kufruhum*) and the extinction of the light of religion from their hearts. [As it is said:] "Seeing is believing." May God return to Islam its strength and renew His support for [our] faith with the help of the Prophet, God bless him and grant him salvation.

The next day and the one after they took us to two palaces of their Sultan, one called the "Palais Royal" and the other called the "Louvre." Each was enormous and solidly built. The first contained furnishings of their kings no longer in use, yet preserved and kept in readiness at all times. It is empty and no one lives there. Here too are furnishings belonging to the present Sultan and portraits of his family, including some of him from an early age until he inherited the throne.

The palace of the Louvre is close by, and it too is uninhabited, but it is not furnished. Instead, it is filled with portraits and likenesses too numerous to count, along with bodies made of stone, and all kinds of drawings. Here you will find many likenesses of Mary and Jesus, so they claim; portraits of their former sultans; portraits of the Greeks, including Socrates and Plato, the two wise men; and likenesses of those who lived in the days of the Flood at the moment the waters overtook them and they clung to the trees; all of these images were hanging together.

This palace is solidly built. Among the things there are relics of the ancients, including bodies of the dead preserved by coating them with a kind of plaster. [The body] was wrapped in a striped cloth, and on the outside they put a face with two huge eyes and black eyebrows, just like a living person. They claim that these bodies were found in Egypt, and that these were the earliest people of that land. When someone died they treated him like that, and left him in his house. They are still found underground in Egypt. Someone there told me that he was present a year ago when they opened one that had been purchased in Egypt. After much preparation (for it was coated with tar), they opened it and found a woman. Some of them are stretched out on boxes in the midst of the room, while others are standing about.

I read a few words about them in one of their history books. It is said that the people of Egypt did this so that their dead would never leave them. Moreover, if one Egyptian borrowed money from another or bought on credit, he would give one of these bodies, such as his father or daughter, as security until he had repaid the debt; then it would be returned to him.[42]

There are many rooms in this place, story upon story. Here are pictures of all the ports of their country, their manner of construction, and their special features. Also, models of ships that were real, not pictures, but very small; such as a steamship, a huge warship, and a frigate (*firāgṭ*); also a locomotive (*bābūr al-barr*). [They showed] how ships were made from the earliest times. Each ship had all its equipment—masts, ropes, and chains—even though it was tiny. Ancient instruments of war are also found there, such as bows, shields, armor, lances, and the like, and likenesses of cannon of all

42. Priests in the necropolis where royal mummies were kept during the Ptolemaic period could hold an interest in mummies that "could be disposed of by will or contract, bought and sold." *Encyclopaedia Britannica*, 11th ed., s.v. "Mummy."

sizes that resembled the ships [in their detail]. Everything was pleasing to the eye. In short, this huge and well-built palace would have been nicely decorated were it not for the many portraits which disfigured its beauty.

The House of Physics

The next day we went to one of their institutions for learning called "the House of Physics,"[43] which is the name of one of their sciences and can be translated as "the science of natural things" or "the science of chemistry." Its subject matter is acquiring knowledge about the natural properties of things, such as the magnet's pull, the vibration of the air when sound passes through it, and other [things] whose names we do not know. In this place are many strange instruments and marvelous devices.[44]

43. *Dār al-Fizig.* The word *fizig* is aṣ-Ṣaffār's creation, from the French *physique.* He defines it as "the science of natural things," but in fact he uses the term in a wider sense, to mean "scientific experimentation." He witnessed experiments with static electricity, compression, sound waves, and magnification. Aṭ-Ṭahṭāwī offered little help on the subject, although he mentions chemistry among the sciences to be found in France, saying that its aim is "knowledge of the composition of things . . . not . . . finding the philosopher's stone, . . . for the Franks know nothing of this, nor do they believe in it." *Takhlīṣ,* p. 22; *L'or,* p. 57. The Tunisian Khayr ad-Din also used the word *fizik* to indicate the idea of scientific experimentation. At-Tūnisī (trans. Brown), *The Surest Path,* p. 109 note 112. The "House of Physics" was the Conservatoire des Arts et Métiers, now known as the Musée National des Techniques, where most of the instruments seen by aṣ-Ṣaffār were still on display as of June 1990. AAE/ADM/Voyage, "Visites dans Paris."

44. In aṣ-Ṣaffār's day, Maghribi science had not advanced much since the time of Ibn Khaldūn. The lack of innovation did not mean a disinterest in scientific matters, however, for students continued to study centuries-old texts, chiefly for the knowledge they contained on subjects relating to religious practice, such as astronomy (for calculating the correct times for prayer) and geometry (to fix the direction of prayer in the mosque). See H. P. J. Renaud, "L'enseignement des sciences exactes et l'édition d'ou-

The first thing we saw was a circle of brass spools standing on little legs, and connected with a moving force from above.[45] On its face was a large round piece of glass turning like a waterwheel, with a handle like the handle of a waterwheel. If a person put his hand near the spools while the glass turned, something like lightning in color and speed came out at him in brief flashes. His hand felt as if it had been struck, causing a sharp pain; but no trace of the pain remained afterward, as it would have from a real blow.

An amazing aspect of this was that when someone stood near the glass while it was turning, and held a brass ball connected with the spools, his hair stood on end, one hair after another. When he took the ball in his right hand and stretched out his left toward another person, lightning jumped from the outstretched hand, though the person holding the ball felt nothing. Nor can it be said that the one holding the ball was playing a trick, because one of us held the ball and we felt nothing either. Those spools are enclosed on all sides. They claim this is like lightning in the sky, which has its source in the compression of air, just as fire has its origin in the compression of the space between rocks and iron.

Then we went to another place where we saw a hollowed-out board; inside it was a moving force and coming out from its sides were two wires, vibrating like a metal thread; wound around them

---

vrages scientifiques au Maroc avant l'occupation européenne," *Hesp*. 14, 1 (1932): 78–89.

Aṣ-Ṣaffār himself was keenly interested in the "science of timekeeping" (*ʿilm at-tawqīt*), according to Dāwud, *TT* 7:93. Muḥammad al-Manūnī showed me a manuscript in aṣ-Ṣaffār's handwriting entitled: *Nuṣra baʿḍ al-mutaʾakhkhirīn li-miḥrāb masjid al-Qarawiyīn*, a treatise on the orientation of the *qibla* of the Qarawiyīn mosque in Fes. Ministry of Culture, Exposition 1973, no. 220.

45. Aṣ-Ṣaffār uses the word *ḥaraka*, which I have translated as "moving force," to denote the various new and mysterious forms of energy—electrical, steam, and mechanical—that made things work in France. "Spools" in Arabic = *qanūṭa*, from the Spanish *canete*. In popular speech in Tetuan, these are wooden bobbins around which thread is wound. Al-Khaṭṭābī, "Mushāhadāt," part 2, p. 43 note 17. Here aṣ-Ṣaffār is describing an experiment with static electricity.

were other threads made of silk. At the ends of these two wires were two spools of copper. If the force inside the board moved, the spools began to tremble. If someone touched the spools, the veins inside his hand would shake unbearably. They say the force continues the length of the wires, even to the other end of the country, and whoever touches them will feel their force, even at a great distance. The utility of it is in sending the news, as I will explain shortly.

Then one of them stood next to a board with a small tube at its center wrapped in a ring. Over its opening was a piece of glass shaped like a little bucket that opened and shut. A motion began inside the little tube and the glass came down tightly onto the board. Then the little tube opened up and filled with drafts of air; one saw steam coming out of the tube and circulating inside the glass. Then the tube closed but the air remained inside the glass. The glass stuck so firmly in place that no one could raise it. It may be that something other than the heaviness of the air inside made it expand and then rise up. For them, that is an example of how, when air is present and has no outlet, it makes whatever descends on it so heavy that it cannot be moved or lifted.

We went from that place to another, where a man brought a small sheet of copper with a spring in its center. He put some fine black sand on it and took a bow like that of a fiddle, drawing it over the edge of the metal so that it resounded sharply. The sand moved and took on shapes [that looked] as if they were made by hand with a precise instrument. Here is a drawing of it:

Figure 1. An experiment with sound waves.

That is all of it, although in reality it is better and more exact. They claim that the sound is what causes the shapes and circles; for them, that is an example of how the air moves in waves with sound, producing shapes that spread out in ripples like those in the sand. It is a demonstration of perception by the senses. Another example is when you throw stones in water and make ripples and circles that spread out as far as the eye can see. Their objective in this is to arrive at a knowledge of how long it takes for sound to travel from one place to another.

They have many instruments of different types there, but only they understand their effects. We saw instruments that increase [the size of] small bodies, making them look large to the eye. They did this by closing off a room and making it pitch-black. Then they brought out a lamp made of wood and metal, not of glass, with a tiny hole covered by a bit of glass the size of an ant. They lit a small candle inside it and closed it, and then placed the opening facing a wall. When they put something against the glass, even the smallest thing, it would reappear imprinted in light on the wall, but in a much greater size. The stinger of a bee looked [as large as] seven spans of the hand, almost like a broom. They put a louse in it and it looked like an eagle, and the eye of a fly looked like a huge sieve, full of tiny holes. They put the tongue of a frog in it and it appeared imprinted on the wall as large as could be; all the blood vessels could be seen, with the blood flowing back and forth like ants running from a ruined anthill. A bit of yeast that had been left standing until it spoiled was put in it, and we could see worms like huge snakes twisting and coiling around each other. When it is not in that [device], one sees nothing. They put in it a piece of meat, and we saw what happened when it spoiled.

Then they brought in a glass open at the sides and standing on iron rods. Resting on it from above were more rods, and where the two rods met was a piece of copper connected to a device [in which] there was a moving force. When the tips touched, a great light illuminated the room, even though it was pitch-black. They said that if they [could] put this thing high above Paris, it would light the whole city and make streetlamps unnecessary. Then they put a bit of silver between the heads of the two rods, and it melted in an instant; then another piece of metal (they claim that fire has nothing to do with it), and that melted too. If one of the two pieces of copper touches the other, fire comes out between them like lightning. One of them took it in his hand wet with saliva, and the veins of his hands shook so, he had to drop it. When they removed the pieces of copper from the device, [the shaking] stopped. This device was [made of] small metal dishes all joined together with bits of copper. I wonder if the explanation is in those dishes.

The most remarkable and strangest thing we saw here was a force that carries news from one place to another in an instant with complete clarity and accuracy, even if the two places are far apart, because it is done with writing.[46] The way they did it was with a disk of brass like the face of a clock, engraved with all the letters (and the vowels too, because the vowels are letters for them). This disk was firmly fixed to a stand, which had as many holes in its sides as there were letters, a hole under each letter. Across from it was another disk, lying flat, that was also marked with all the letters, with a pointer at its center. The two disks were connected by two wires that vibrated. If one person wished to talk with another, he would turn the first disk so that the needle lodged in the hole below the letter [desired]; the pointer on the second disk would stop at the same [place]. So it went until the words were complete and perfectly understood—all with the greatest speed. They claim that the force between these two disks can carry words instantly from one place to another. Even if there were thousands of hours of travel time between them, it would take just a second, that is, one-sixtieth of a minute.

This device completely staggers the senses, but one who has seen

46. At that time the electrical telegraph was still in its infancy. In 1844, the Chambers voted funds to establish the first telegraph line between Paris and Rouen, but it was not opened for public use until 1851. *Grande encyclopédie Larousse*, 1886 ed., s.v. "Télégraphe"; Pinkney, *Decisive Years*, pp. 58–59.

it with his own eyes will not doubt it. We tried it ourselves with a few words and could not move our eyes from one disk to the other before the pointer stood at the correct letter. They claim that they have set this up between Paris and Orléans, a distance of ninety miles, and also between the Chamber where they gather to make their laws and the palace of the Sultan, by means of a device hidden underground with an attendant at each end. They talk to the Sultan from the Chamber while he is in his palace, and he answers them, although they are a great distance apart. Here is an approximate drawing of all of it:

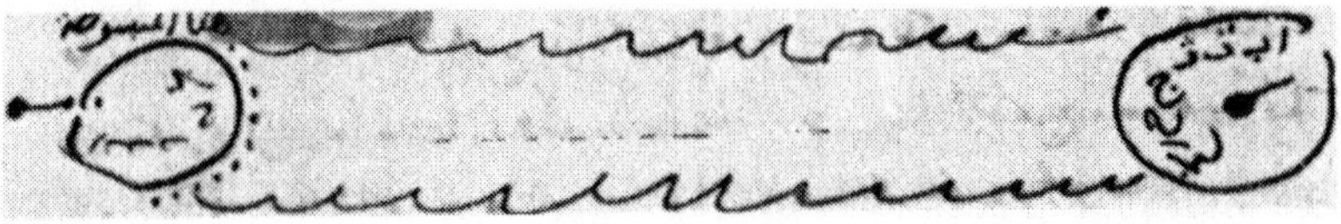

Figure 2. The telegraph.

This is everything we saw in that place.

The House of Printing

On Thursday, the twenty-third day of the month, we went to the house for printing books called the *aṣṭanbā*,[47] which is another of

47. The Imprimerie Royale. *Aṣṭanbā* comes from the French *estampe (Spanish estampa)*, or printing press. Secretary and man of letters, aṣ-Ṣaffār not surprisingly paid rapt attention to the mechanical printing press. The first Moroccan press was a lithograph workshop set up in Fes in 1864, where works of a primarily religious nature were printed. The first typographical press appeared in Tangier in 1880, but typography was not generally used for Arabic books until early in the twentieth century. For the history of printing in Morocco, see M. Al-Manūnī, *Maẓāhir* 1:201–51; G. Ayache, "L'apparition de l'imprimerie au Maroc," *H-T* 5 (1964): 143–61; and Fawzi A. Abdulrazak, *The Kingdom of the Book: The History of Print-*

their amazing crafts. First of all, you should know that the letters are cast in tin, thick at the bottom and narrow at the top. Some letters are single, and others are made of two letters joined together. [The printer] takes the letters he wants and puts them in a frame the size of the page to be printed, setting them in straight lines like writing. The letters are held tightly with a clamp that keeps them in order. Then they coat them with ink and lay a sheet of paper over them, pressing it down firmly by means of a vise. When the paper emerges, it is completely covered with writing. This is a general description of it. Now let me tell in detail about what we saw in this place.

First we entered a room with an oven where the workers cast the letters in copper molds the size of the type; the letter is engraved on the bottom of that mold, like the letter *sīn*, for example.[48] When the melted tin comes out, the letter at its head is reversed, but when they print with it, it comes out straight like any stamp. These workers cast letters in many types, both Arabic and non-Arabic. In the next room there were many workers, more than in the first; their task was to straighten and polish the letters, removing the bumps so that they would fit smoothly together in the frames. There were others who sorted the letters into compartments, one for each letter.

Next came the room of the typesetters.[49] Sitting before the book to be printed, the typesetter takes the frame and arranges the letters in it just as they are on the page. He sets down the first line on a metal rule and puts it in the frame, then he composes the second line, and so on until he fills [the frame]. Even if he does not understand the writing and cannot read it, he knows its equivalent in

ing as an Agency of Change in Morocco between 1865 and 1912 (Ph.D. dissertation, Boston University, 1990). A complete list of Fes lithographs is found in Fawzī ʿAbd ar-Razāq, *Maṭbūʿāt al-ḥajariya fil-Maghrib* (Rabat, 1989).

48. A little sketch of the Arabic letter *sīn* as it appeared on the mold is drawn in the text.

49. *Nassākh*; "copyist" or "scribe," but from the context, a typesetter.

type. We tested one of them by writing out a line [in Arabic], and he set it down exactly. We told him to break it up, which he did, and there were thirty-four letters. Then he returned each to its place swiftly and without a mistake. This completely astonished us.

Once the type is set in the frames, it goes into the hands of others. We entered a room in which there were large open tanks of water with bundles of paper resting on their edges. Here they soak the paper in water, four or five pages at a time, and set it on the edge of the tank to drip off. Then it goes into another room with machines and rollers worked by a fire you cannot see which dries the papers. Each machine is run by three women workers: one puts the [wet] paper into the rollers, another turns the rollers, and the third takes it out, completely dry from the heat of the fire inside.

Then the sheets of paper and the frames go to the printing room, where there are two types [of printing]: one is by hand, the other by rollers. The first requires three people. One worker takes the frame with the letters and sets it in place. The next has a piece of leather in his hand, folded over several times and coated with ink, which he passes over the letters to blacken them. Their ink is not liquid like ours but gives color nevertheless. The first worker then takes a blank sheet of paper, putting it on a second frame which is pressed down on the letters from above by means of a heavy iron device that moves with a turning motion. Then they open it up and out comes the printed sheet, which a third worker removes. With these letters they can print as many pages as they want, a hundred, a thousand, or ten thousand, all exactly alike. They do the same for every page, until they reach the last page of the book. The day a book is completed, it may come out in a thousand copies. If all the necessities are on hand, and no difficulty is encountered in the printing, two hundred or more pages can be printed in a single hour.

The other type of printing is with rollers, sometimes turned by hand, at other times turned by steam power or by running water like a mill. [A worker] takes the sheets and feeds them into the rollers, which swallow them up until they pass over the letters and emerge printed. The leather that takes up the ink and blackens the letters works by a moving force, not by hand. With the first turn, the paper comes down on the letters and is printed, and with the second, ink is put on [the letters] to blacken them [again]. Everything happens in one continuous movement. When the printing is completed, the letters in the frame are broken up and new letters are set to print a different page. However, they leave some books set in their entirety, so that when they want to print them again they do not have to bother with resetting the letters. We saw rooms with frames [containing] books set in type.

After a book is printed it must be bound, and that too is a craft there. They take it into other rooms where they trim the margins of the pages by means of steam power, which operates the knives. In another room they gather the papers in a bundle between two boards, and press them from below with an iron bar moved by water power. Yet another room is for binding. [In sum,] paper enters this place blank and comes out a bound book.

The most amazing writing machine we saw there was a special way of printing a book regardless of the writing, be it Arabic or non-Arabic, eastern or western [script], or whatever. They do this by taking a sheet written on with special ink that is reddish, like the dye from walnuts. Then they fasten it to a stone. When they open it up, the writing appears on the stone just as it was on the page. With this stone they print as many pages as they like; all of them emerge exactly like the original, without additions or subtractions, corruptions or alterations. I wrote a line with that ink on a piece of paper, which they then placed on a stone, and the writing became imprinted on it. Then they printed other pages from the stone, which came out exactly like the first page. [In this way] one can print an entire book in whatever handwriting one wishes.[50]

50. This is the lithographic process. Traditional scholars admired it because it avoided the step of typesetting, and so reduced the chance of errors entering the text; at the same time, it did not sacrifice the individuality of the scribal hand. ʿAbd ar-Razāq, *Maṭbūʿāt*, p. 8. Also see n.47 above.

The total number of workers employed in that establishment was eight hundred, and they work continually, without a stop. One wonders, where do all these books go? But everything there is recorded in books; no place is without them. They take down information and benefit from it, not depending on memory for fear of forgetting it. As it is said:

Knowledge is the prey, and the book its snare;
Tie down your quarry with a strong rope.
Ignorance is trapping a pigeon
And leaving it unfettered with maidens.

And something that is said about books:

When you sit with my companion, he relieves
Your heart of pain and suffering.
He gives you knowledge and adds to your wisdom.
Not jealous or given to hatred,
He keeps faithfully what is entrusted to him,
Not betraying his trust with the passage of time.

And another said:

While others sit in their houses
With limpid wine and women with lovely breasts,
And fate has been good to them,
Bringing noble friends and torrential rain,
I sit alone with my companions, books of knowledge,
And spend the night with my bride, daughter of a book.

And another said:

When I left my friends,
And my notebook was my sole companion,
I did not lack the finest poet,

A scholar who was devoted and faithful.
There was wisdom between its two covers,
And benefit for the seeker and thinker.
If at times my heart was constricted with happiness
I consigned my secret to it, keeping it unseen.
When poetry proclaimed the name of my love,
I was neither embarrassed nor speechless before it.
When I responded to anger with mockery
That provoked the Caliph, I was not afraid.
I need no other companion.
We are friends, until the Day of Judgment.

And another said:

I got used to solitude during my life,
With no friends in all the world.
I made my notebook my comrade and companion
At the table, instead of a friend.
I have no need for a horse or an unruly mule
When I voyage, for I have my feet.
My lap is my table, my pockets are my saddlebags,
My girdle and purse are always with me.
My abode is wherever the heavens shelter me,
And my family all have rare good sense.

This is everything relating to the printing press.

About two days later we went to a place they call the "Panthéon,"[51] a very tall building with a very lofty dome about four hundred cubits high from which all of Paris can be seen; from it people on the ground look like small children. Their great ones are buried

51. Built in the eighteenth century as a church, the Panthéon was rededicated during the Revolution to the ancient gods. The huge crypt beneath it became the resting place of many of France's great men.

there inside stone boxes in underground chambers, with the boxes sealed over them. On the side of the box is an urn containing the heart of the dead one; they remove it and coat it with something that preserves it, and then put it into the urn and hang a sign on it saying it was his heart. Here too are huge statues of humans, and one of them was carrying a crown. They claimed it was an image of Fate. When one of their kings dies, [Fate] removes his crown and places it on another; kings grow old and die, but [Fate] never dies. In the hand of another [statue] was a sword, and they claimed it was the Day of Judgment.

One of the stories they tell [about the Panthéon] goes like this: In one corner is a hole that opens into the crypt. If the custodian puts his mouth to it and calls out to the dead, an echo will answer from underground, saying, "How are you?" If he says, "Well," the echo will answer, "Well," as if the dead were answering him; but he is really answering himself by himself. If he drums on a piece of hide, a great noise like thunder is heard underground, as if the dead had cannon down there and were firing them.

Some days later they insisted that we go to two palaces of the Sultan outside of Paris, one of them in the village called Saint Cloud and the other in a village called Versailles. Both are close to Paris, and are strongly built palaces surrounded by enormous gardens with graceful trees, gushing streams, and fountains with statues spouting jets of water. In one of them we saw a table of marble they claimed was a piece of wood which stayed in the water until it became marble. That for them is a special kind of wood. They take great care with plantings, especially along the pathways, where they trim and prune the trees so that they are even with each other both above and below. They also set down benches and make open places [for sitting]; they have houses in the gardens where the plants stay during the cold weather. [These gardens] are of such vast extent you would think they went on forever.

Among the objects we saw in the palace of Versailles were paintings of wars from the beginning of time to the present; but they only show the wars in which they were victorious. [An anecdote:] They tell the story about a man who walked through the marketplace and saw people gathered around the picture of a man overwhelming a lion. He went on until he met a lion, and he told the lion what he had seen. The lion said to him: "If the lion knew how to draw, you would see what he would do; but since he does not know how, then each one draws what he pleases."

We saw likenesses of their notables and great men, their sultans, heroes, and priests; some were carved in stone and others were drawn. We saw painting[s] of their entry into the cities of Algiers and Constantine, and a picture of their victory over all those lands; a likeness of the Ottoman Sultan ʿAbd al-Majīd,[52] and one of Muḥammad ʿAlī, the Pasha of Egypt. This castle is built of the finest-colored marble. Some rooms there belonged to Louis XVI,[53] and when he died they remained exactly as they were, with his furnishings, bed, chairs, crown, and chapel preserved down to the very last detail.

The Chamber[s]

On the 14th of Ṣafar we went to the two Chambers, the Great and the Small.[54] The Chamber is the house where they gather to fashion

52. The reigning Ottoman Sultan. *EI* 2, s.v. "ʿAbd al-Madjīd I."

53. King of France who, together with his wife Marie-Antoinette, died on the guillotine of the Revolution. *Dictionnaire d'histoire de France Perrin*, 1981 ed., s.v. "Louis XVI."

54. Chamber is *qamra*. The Great was the Chamber of Peers, the Small the Chamber of Deputies. The former met in the Palais du Luxembourg, the latter in the Palais Bourbon; aṣ-Ṣaffār says he visited both. Most of this passage on the conduct of government is taken from aṭ-Ṭahṭāwī. *Takhlīṣ*, pp. 93–106; *L'or*, pp. 132–39; aṣ-Ṣaffār even adopts aṭ-Ṭahṭāwī's term *malik* ("king") instead of his usual *sulṭān*. The *charte constitutionale*, granted by King Louis XVIII in 1814 and revised in 1830 by Louis-Philippe, kept a

their laws and talk over their affairs. The place where they gather is domed and is built like the theater, with an inclined floor and rows of chairs. The reason for the slope is so that everyone can see what is in front of them. At one end there is a raised platform shaped like a *minbar*[55] except that its steps are at the side.

Whoever wishes to speak mounts this platform, looks out over those who are seated, and says his piece. Everyone seated has pen, ink, and paper. The speaker talks and they write it down. Then he sits down and they reflect on his words, either accepting them or rejecting them. If one of the listeners is opposed to the words of the speaker, he may rise from his chair and discuss it with him, but if the objection is a lengthy one, then he waits his turn, mounting the dais to speak. Behind the speaker are three people whose task is as follows: if the talk goes on too long, they may pass judgment and terminate the discussion.

According to a law recognized there, when it comes to choosing one of two sides [in a debate], the decision is in favor of the majority. That is, when ten people say such-and-such, and twenty are opposed, the decision is in favor of the twenty. This is true even if one side is greater by only a single person. This is the practice in the Small Chamber too.

The difference between the two [Chambers] is as follows: The Great Chamber protects the interests of the King and the great [men] of state. Among its tasks are the renewing of defunct laws and the continuation of existing laws. The Small Chamber stands for the people, champions its [causes], and asserts its rights when it is in conflict with the other. A member of the Great Chamber must be twenty-five years of age, but he does not have the right to speak until he has reached thirty, unless he is a relative of the king. In that case, he attends from a very young age, but without the right to

limited suffrage and favored the nobility and propertied classes. *Grande encyclopédie Larousse*, 1972 ed., s.v. "France."

55. The pulpit of the mosque and the place from which the Friday sermon is delivered.

speak until he reaches twenty-five. The majority of those in the Great Chamber are the important men of state, such as ministers, judges, governors, and other public figures.

The Small Chamber is made up of representatives of the people sent from all parts of the country, more than four hundred in all. Conditions are imposed on those who are selected to represent [the people], and they are: A person may not enter this assembly[56] or speak before it unless he is [at least] forty years old, and he must own property on which he has paid taxes to the state treasury in the amount of a thousand francs [or more]. Another condition is that those who elect them must be thirty years old and own property on which they had paid at least three hundred francs a year.

This assembly sits from the first of one year to the first of the next, and only by order of the Sultan. When he wishes to dissolve it he may do so on condition that another be called in its place within three months. Not a single law or resolution may be passed without the approval of both Chambers, the Sultan, and his ministers. As for the legal precedents and special cases,[57] they are recorded in books, and the Sultan cannot act on his own in making laws. However, no law is passed that does not suit his purposes, for he is the most powerful man in the state. It is he who has authority over the army on land and sea; it is he who declares war and makes peace; it is he who concludes alliances and commercial ties between his people and others. Moreover, he presides over important occasions, he initiates law and policies and sees that they are passed into law once they are approved, and he officiates when they are signed. This is everything that relates to their Chamber[s].

Two days later we went to a school attended by 1,125 students.[58]

56. *Dīwān*; in Ottoman usage, "a council of state containing the chief officers of the realm and presided over by the sultan or grand vizir." Naff and Owen, *Studies*, glossary, p. 409.

57. The Arabic is *nawāzil wa-juz'iyāt*.

58. Most likely the Ecole Polytechnique. Founded during the Revolution, it was run like a military academy for students aged sixteen to twenty;

Six hundred went back and forth from their homes to the school, while 525 lived there. There were forty teachers and forty supervisors. It was a large building, and those who stayed there had their own rooms and beds for sleeping. There was also a place for the sick, a doctor's room complete with instruments and medicaments, places for bathing and keeping their clothes, and a place for washing their faces in the morning. Everything was extremely neat and clean.

They study arithmetic, geometry, philosophy, languages, physics, chemistry, natural sciences, drawing, and anatomy. They also learn how to jump and climb walls, how to walk over narrow places, how to sail through the air holding on to a ring hung from above, how to vault over an outstretched rope raised up high, and so on. Some might consider this play, but for them it is one of their sciences. Here they study and learn everything from firsthand experience. One of their rules is that the students eat at midday. During the mealtime one of them stands on a dais and reads aloud to the others from a history book or the like, so that even this moment will not be wasted. After they finish eating, they are allowed to play, racing about and competing strenuously with one another for half an hour before returning to their work.

We visited another school for the education of young children. This place was for the children of the poor whose mothers and fathers had to work, leaving the children unattended. To keep them from wandering about the streets in a confused state, they brought them together here. A young woman teaches them something of good manners, their letters, and the fundamentals of reading. All this is done without payment. They also learn how to sit and stand, how to meet people and greet them properly, how to hold their slates and erase them, and how to walk in single file like soldiers. All are very young, about four years old, for after six the girls and boys do not remain together.

---

the two-year course prepared them for higher scientific and technical studies. *Grande encyclopédie Larousse,* 1973 ed., s.v. "Polytechnique, école."

We went to another [school] for young boys. First they learn one letter, then two, then three, until they learn them all; then two letters are joined, then three letters, then a whole word, then two words, and then a sentence of words, and so on.

Two days later, we left Paris and returned to whence we came, praise be to God, Master of the Universe.

6

EPILOGUE

An explanation of their revenues and means of taxation, and of their expenses, including an explanation of some of their rules and regulations.

You should know that one of their rules is that the two Chambers must meet every year to discuss new laws and to review existing ones. Among other things, they estimate the amount of taxes (*jibāyāt*) to be raised [that year], and how much will be spent from the state treasury, provided that the Sultan and the men of influence agree. As is their custom, they have made an assessment for the current year. Whatever they estimate as income and outlay is recorded in a book which is open to the public, a number of copies being printed for sale. At the moment we have in our hands the book for this year, which one of their interpreters has explained to us.[1]

Another of their rules is that [all] revenues are handed over to the Minister of the Treasury,[2] that is to say, the administrator (*amīn*) of their state treasury. Then each Minister is given what he needs to

1. The "book" is *Recueil des lois de finance et autres lois de la session de 1844* (Paris, Imprimerie Royale, 1846). AN/ADXIX/F–28/1844–46.
2. *Wazīr al-khazna.*

meet his expenses. The reason for this is that they saw that the Sultan alone could not take on the whole task of governing his flock. Therefore, they have relieved him of carrying the entire burden by appointing a number of people called "Ministers" and assigning each a special duty, while supervising them closely.[3]

There are nine Ministers, the first being the Minister of the Treasury, that is, their *bayt al-māl*. Into his hands go all the revenues of France, and out of them come all its expenditures. He pays every [other] Minister whatever he needs to spend, and it is said that he has fifteen hundred clerks [under him].

The second is the Minister of Foreign Affairs, whose task it is to oversee everything external to France and its provinces, such as setting up diplomatic missions (*qunṣuwāt*) in [foreign] lands and sending ambassadors to them. He is also in charge of conducting talks with other kingdoms and sending spies to gather information and observe events in distant parts. In his hands are all the monies relating to foreign affairs.

Third is the Minister of Internal Affairs, that is, within the dominion (*sulṭa*) of France. He oversees the appointment of the governors[4] throughout the land, and assures the well-being of all the towns and cities and the right conduct of the people's affairs, and everything else relating to internal matters. He has the rank of our *qā'id*, except that they put one of them in charge. He has deputies under him throughout the country.

3. In the 1840s, the uppermost level of the Makhzan consisted only of the Sultan and his First Minister (*wazīr al-awwal*), who served as an adviser and executor of the Sultan's orders. A small cadre of scribes (*kātibs*) maintained the correspondence. It was not until the reign of Muḥammad IV (1859–73) and his successor Ḥasan I (1873–95) that separate ministries were established with distinct functions. See Laroui, *Origines*, p. 88; Lahbabi, *Le gouvernement marocain*, pp. 131–39; al-Manūnī, *Maẓāhir*, pp. 29–30.

4. Arabic *ḥukkām*, literally "governors." Here he means the *préfets*, or heads of the local *départements*. See Ch. 2, note 38.

The fourth is the Minister of Religious Courts and the Law.[5] He oversees church affairs and the appointment of judges and notaries and other matters relating to their religion and holy law.

Fifth is the Minister of Schools,[6] who supervises the teaching of the learned sciences. He oversees all matters of education, including the organization of the schools and libraries, and the dispatching to distant parts of those who will teach the latest knowledge, including the planting of trees, for that too is one of their sciences. A learned man (*ʿālim*) there is someone who is able to invent new and useful [ideas] and demonstrate their fine points by presenting sound proofs to those who doubt or oppose his findings. The name *ʿālim* for them is not limited to someone who has studied the sources of the religion of the Christians and its various branches—they are called priests—for knowing that is rather undistinguished [in their view] as compared with knowing the other logical and precise sciences.[7]

The sixth is the Minister of Commerce and Agriculture, and his function is to supervise everything relating to them.

The seventh is the Minister of Buildings, Roads, and Bridges,[8] and what relates to them.

The eighth is the Minister of War, who has authority over everything connected with all of the ranks of the army, their organization, equipment, and preparedness. He is in charge of artillery, gunpowder, weapons, and all matters associated with war.

5. *Wazīr maḥkamat ad-dīn wash-sharʿ*; in French it is *Ministre de la Justice et des Cultes*.

6. *Wazīr al-madāris*, or *Ministre de l'Instruction Publique*.

7. Compare with *Takhlīṣ*, p. 161; *L'or*, pp. 187–88. Ibn Khaldūn's idea of the learned man was someone who had acquired knowledge by practice; according to the fourteenth-century philosopher, "scientific instruction" was a "craft" or "habit," learned through repetition to the point of perfection. *Muqaddimah* 2:426, 3:299–300.

8. *Ministre des Travaux Publiques*.

The ninth is the Minister of the Sea,[9] who supervises the ships, the teaching of naval sciences and crafts related to it, and other maritime matters.

All the money that they spend with the approval of the Sultan comes out of the hands of these Ministers, each one staying within the limits of his authority.[10] If his expenses are found to be correct, then the Minister is free and clear; but if not, he is fined and must pay [the fine] himself. As for the Sultan, he does not make any claims [against the Minister], even if he is in agreement with the paying [of the fine], because all their laws and statutes maintain that [private] property is to be respected (*muḥtaram*). That is, the Ministers are held responsible.[11]

The amount paid into the hands of the Minister of the Treasury by the bankers—for they are the ones who pay the money into the treasury, taking interest from it—is 281,500,000 and something [francs] each year. All the figures are in francs, which is one-fifth of a *riyāl*.

[Aṣ-Ṣaffār now copies out part of the French national budget for the year 1846, following the original very closely, stating expenditures and their purposes, with one important exception: the interpreter carefully edited out expenses relating to the war in Algeria. This portion of the text has been omitted.]

9. *Wazīr al-baḥr*. The French equivalent was *Ministre de la Marine et des Colonies*; the title, with its allusion to Algeria, was no doubt abbreviated by the interpreter.

10. The phrase "with the approval of the Sultan" was added later in the margin.

11. "Held responsible." The Arabic text says they are *kufalā'*, or "bondsmen." In Morocco, the Sultan would commonly "eat up" the wealth of officials found mishandling state funds. Not only was the guilty party fined, but often his property was confiscated (as in the case of Ashʿāsh; see p. 41). The *kāfil* (bondsman) in the Muslim court guarantees the appearance of one of the contending parties. *SEI*, s.v. "Kafāla."

The Revenues and Sources of Taxation in France

As for their revenues, they come from divers sources, one being the land. The tax on land (*kharāj*) yields 275,997,484 [francs]. The production from state-owned lands is valued at 129,000,610 [francs].[12] The tax on trees—for they pay for them—is 72,800,000 [francs]. The rent on state properties in different parts of the country is 5,660,000 [francs]. Another kind of tax is on doors and windows; whoever puts a door or window [in his house] must pay a tax on it. The yield from this tax was 91,488,930 [francs] in a single year. Another very important source of revenue is from appointments, which yielded them 57,737,310 [francs].

One of their laws is that whoever plans to open a shop for trade has to pay a fixed sum to the state, and that is a source from which they get 788,930 [francs]. Another law is that when someone is overdue in paying his taxes, he may be excused for fifteen days; if he still does not pay, then they write him a chit asking for it. Then he must pay a small fine in addition to his tax. From this they collected 788,930 [francs].[13]

There is also a law that whoever buys real estate must write his contract on a special paper bearing the stamp of the state in order for it to be valid. The price paid for this paper produces revenue in the amount of 235,328,000 [francs].[14]

12. Aṣ-Ṣaffār or his interpreter made several errors in transcribing the figures in the French budget. Income from state-owned lands was actually 1,029,610 francs; the revenue from the tax on trees should read 30,342,500 francs; the rent on state properties amounted to 5,606,000 francs; and the tax on doors and windows equalled 33,751,638 francs.

13. Aṣ-Ṣaffār assigns the amount of 788,930 francs to two different sources of revenue, one being taxes collected on the opening of shops, and the other being fines on late taxes. The French budget lists only one such amount, calling it a *taxe de premier avertissement*, meaning the collection of fines on late taxes.

14. The correct amount is 253,328,000 francs, according to the original.

Their Ministers and other high officials are given houses to live in, which belong to the state along with all their furnishings. The day he assumes office, the Minister moves in, and if he is removed from office, he leaves it as he found it. At the start of each year they inspect [the houses] and sell whatever is worn or soiled, replacing them with new things. The income from these sales is 100,835,000 [francs].[15] The nobility of the provinces pay a tax on their cultivated land in the amount of 1,600,000 [francs]. Duties on goods entering France other than sugar yielded 102,925,000 [francs], and for sugar specifically the sum is 50,252,000 [francs]. From duties on exports they get 1,244,000 [francs].

Another of their sources of revenue is that everyone who owns a boat at sea must pay something to the state, which amounts to 2,916,000 [francs]. From fines on those who deal in contraband[16] they earn 2,886,000 [francs].

There are three things over which the state has a monopoly of sale: tobacco, salt, and gunpowder. From tobacco they earn 107,156,000 [francs]; from salt, 71,488,000 [francs]; and from gunpowder, 5,296,000 [francs]. The gate tax on wine from outside France yields 98,233,000 [francs]. From the sugar factories within France they make 10,771,000 [francs]. In addition, they have other minor sources of income. Because of the large number of [tax]payers, they collect a great amount.

The sum total of income and expenditures, according to what the interpreter explained to me from those pages, is that income is 1,303,684,134 [francs], and their expenses are 1,300,077,889 [francs], with 3,606,245 [francs] left over.

They do not have a treasury where they store up their money, as we do; rather, they estimate the amount of income and expenditures and make them equal or have a little bit left over. If the revenue is less than the amount of expenditure, they create other sources of

15. The correct figure is 1,885,600 francs.

16. *Kutrabanḍū*. This detail came from the interpreter. The budget entry reads simply: *droits et produits divers de douanes*.

income until it is sufficient to meet their outlay. If it is greatly in excess of their expenses, then they cancel some of the sources of their income. We heard that this year they removed land taxes from small villages in the provinces because their revenues now meet their expenses.

The officials of the state are not able to conceal anything of this, or to add to it or subtract from it on their own, for the Small Chamber, which represents the people (*raʿīya*), begins [each year] by calling the state to account for its income and expenses during the past year. Another innovation of theirs is that everyone who takes up an official position, such as a soldier or the like, gives a small amount from his salary that will not burden him, such as one percent. This money is collected and redistributed to whoever is unable to work because of age or ill health. They give to each kind of worker the amount collected from the same kind [of worker]. If this amount is not enough, then the treasury adds to it and makes it sufficient.

They do not think the existence of money to be strange, and their wealth is great because of their appetite for acquiring it. Nothing is more important to them than money, and every source of income for them is very profitable, such as commerce, crafts, and agriculture. They manage their affairs with the closest attention, to the point where whoever invents a new design does not have to contend with others in his trade, and whoever shows excellence in his craft, business, or farming is given a generous reward.[17]

One of their innovations for increasing their wealth is that they issue papers printed with a special stamp from the Sultan, covered with writing and having the amount engraved on it, and use them like *dirhām* and *dīnār* coins. They have a paper for a thousand [francs] and another for five hundred, as well as smaller and larger ones. In one hour they can produce a million of these, which circulate there just like coins. Indeed, they are sought after even more than coins, especially for the traveler, because of their lightness and ease in car-

17. Compare with aṭ-Ṭahṭāwī, *Takhlīṣ*, p. 169; *L'or*, p. 197.

rying. They circulate everywhere in their domain; one can present these papers to the first moneychanger (*ṣayrafī*) one meets, and he will exchange them for the *riyāl* or other coins at the same rate as they were bought.

Most of their business dealings and their earnings are heavy with usury,[18] such as the bank, which is one of their greatest means of profitmaking. Another source [of profit] that businessmen use among themselves is [as follows]: One man buys goods from another at a certain price, but the purchaser does not pay the price and the seller does not [hand over] the goods. They decide on an appointed day and when it comes, they take a look [at the situation]. If the goods have increased in price, the seller pays the buyer the difference; if the price has dropped, the buyer pays [the difference]; but if it has stayed the same, neither one [pays]. Their wiles and stratagems are beyond calculation, and their inventiveness has no limits. They know well what is apparent in the life of this world, but are completely ignorant about the hereafter.

This is all that it is possible for this poor insignificant self to do, given his muddled brain and the pressures of other work. Were it not for the sake of helping him whose request is hereby answered—for obedience to him is an obligation—I would not have completed it. Nor could I have done it had my knowledge and learning been deficient in following the right path. But the blessing of obedience refilled the quiver of my thought and saved me from embarrassment, although I apologize for my shortcomings and acknowledge my weakness in composition.

18. *Ribā*. While the taking of interest was debated among the ulema, in practice Moroccan businessmen would lend money and receive capital plus interest in return. However, the interest was usually paid indirectly, "in the form of a fictional sale of goods at above market value . . . or by repayment in currency different from the one of the original loan." N. Cigar, "Socio-economic Structures," p. 56; Maxime Rodinson, *Islam and Capitalism* (New York, 1973), p. 18; *SEI*, s.v. "Ribā."

May God forgive me for what my hands have committed, for the repulsive abominations my eyes have witnessed; and for the abhorrent blasphemies and confused mutterings of the misguided that my ears have heard. I ask Him to lead me back to the path of the righteous, even though I am not their equal in good works, and to bring my days to a favorable conclusion, with the help and intercession of our Lord and Master Muḥammad, may God bless him and grant him salvation, and his family and friends, his wives and the progeny of his household, his relations and companions, and the people who share his belief and his law, may all of them keep to the right path. Amen.

(Our final invocation:) Praise be to God, Master of the Universe. Completed on the eleventh of Ramaḍān, in the year 1262.[19] May God grant us His blessings and keep us from harm. The end.

19. 2 September 1846.

SOURCES AND SELECTED BIBLIOGRAPHY

I. MANUSCRIPTS AND ARCHIVES

A. Morocco

1. Rabat

a. Bibliothèque Royale (BRR)

#113. *Majmūʿa* (collection). The second manuscript in the collection is "The Voyage of the Scholar Sid Muḥammad b. ʿAbd Allāh aṣ-Ṣaffār to France as Secretary to the Ambassador al-Ḥājj ʿAbd al-Qādir Ashʿāsh of Tetuan."

#12419. *Taqyīd fī tarjamat al-wazīr aṣ-Ṣaffār.* ("Anonymous Taqyīd") Aṣ-Ṣaffār's biography, author unknown, no date.

b. Direction des Archives Royales (DAR)

Documents relating to the Embassy of Ashʿāsh: Record numbers 10794, 10795, 17542, 17560–83.

c. Bibliothèque Générale (BGR)

#K2276. *Al-ḥusām al-Mashrafī li-qaṭʿ lisān as-sāb al-ʿajrafī, an-nāṭiq bi-khurafāt al-jaʿsūs, shayʾ aẓ-ẓann Akansūs*, by al-ʿArabī al-Mashrafī.

2. Tetuan

a. Bibliothèque Générale

ʿUmdat ar-rāwīn fī tārīkh Tiṭṭāwīn, by Aḥmad ar-Ruhhūnī. In 9 vols. The biography of Muḥammad aṣ-Ṣaffār is in 6:523–33.

b. Aṣ-Ṣaffār Family Archives: manuscripts, documents, poetry, family tree; also books that belonged to Muḥammad aṣ-Ṣaffār, and his will

B. France

1. *Paris*

a. Archives du Ministère des Affaires Etrangères (AAE)

Maroc: Correspondance politique (CPM)
Volumes 14–16: June 1845–June 1846.

Maroc: Mémoires et documents (MDM)
Volume 4: "Ambassade de Bin Achache," pp. 122–66.
Volume 9: "Correspondance entre le Ministre et les agens de la France au Maroc," pp. 332–430.

Maroc: Correspondance consulaire et commerciale (CCC)
Volume 32: 1843–48.

Dossiers personnels: Roches, Beaumier, de Chasteau, Desgranges

b. Archives Nationales (AN)

Archives du Ministère de la Marine (MM)
BB2/288 Ports 1845.
BB2/291 Ports 1846.
BB3/629 Toulon 1845.
BB3/635 Toulon 1846.
BB4/642 Correspondance du *Météore*.

Recueil des lois de finance et autres lois de la session de 1844. Paris, Imprimerie Royale, 1846. ADXIX/F–28/1844–46

c. Ministère de la Marine (MM)

Direction du personnel militaire et mouvements de la flotte, notes confidentielles, Dossier 390, Commandant Goeffroy

2. *Nantes*

a. Archives du Ministère des Affaires Étrangères (AAE) (Archives du Consulat-Général à Tanger)

Maroc: Affaires diverses (1845–52) (ADM), "Voyage de Sidi Aschasch, Pacha de Tetouan, 1845" (originally Tanger AGT Carton A 10/11 bis, "Ambassades marocaines en France")

3. *Toulon*

a. Archives du Port de Toulon (APT)
Météore: Rôle d'équipage, 1845–46, 1C2754.
Météore: Journaux de bord, 1846, 2C201.

II. PUBLISHED SOURCES IN ARABIC AND TRANSLATIONS FROM ARABIC INTO OTHER LANGUAGES
(*indicates a Moroccan *riḥla*)

ʿAbd ar-Razāq, Fawzī. *Maṭbūʿāt al-ḥajariya fil-Maghrib*. Rabat, 1989.

Abū Ḥāmid el Granadino y su relación de viaje por tierras eurasiáticas. Translated and edited by César Dubler. Madrid, 1953.

Afā, ʿUmar. *Masʾalat an-nuqūd fī tārīkh al-Maghrib fī qarn at-tāsiʿ ʿashr: Sūs 1822–1906*. Casablanca, 1988.

Akansūs, Muḥammad b. Aḥmad. *Al-jaysh al-ʿaramram al-ḥumāsi fī dawlat awlād mawlāna ʿAlī as-Sijilmāsi*. 2 vols. Fes, 1336/1918.

*al-ʿAmrāwī, Idrīs b. al-Wazīr b. Idrīs. *Tuḥfat al-malik al-ʿazīz bi-mamlakat Bārīz*. Translated and edited by Zakī Mubārak. Rabat, 1989.

ad-Damīrī, Kamāl ad-Dīn. *Ḥayāt al-ḥayawān al-kubrā*. 2 vols. Cairo, 1306/1888–89.

Dāwud, Muḥammad. *Tārīkh Tiṭwān*. 8 vols. Tetuan, 1959–79.

al-Fāsī, Muḥammad. "Ar-raḥḥāla al-maghāriba wa-āthāruhum." *Daʿwat al-ḥaqq* 2, 4 (January 1959): 22–25.

———. "Ar-riḥla as-safariya al-maghribiya." *Al-Bayyina* 1, 6 (October 1962): 11–24.

Gharrīṭ, Muḥammad. *Fawāṣil al-jumān fī anbāʾ wuzarāʾ wa-kuttāb az-zamān*. Fes, 1347/1928.

*al-Ghassānī, Abū ʿAbd Allāh Muḥammad b. ʿAbd al-Wahāb. *Riḥlat al-wazīr fī iftikāk al-asīr*. In Spanish: *El viaje del visir para la liberación de los cautivos*. Translated and edited by A. Bustani. Tangier, 1940.

*al-Ghazzāl, Aḥmad b. al-Mahdi. *Natījat al-ijtihād fil-muhādana wal-jihād*. Edited by Ismāʿīl al-ʿArabī. Beirut, 1980.

*al-Ḥajarī al-Andalusī, Aḥmad b. Qāsim. *Nāṣir ad-dīn ʿalā al-qawm al-kāfirīn*. Edited by Muḥammad Razūq. Casablanca, 1987.

Ibn Baṭṭūṭa: see *The Travels of Ibn Baṭṭūṭa*.

Ibn Khaldūn. *The Muqaddimah: An Introduction to History*. Translated and edited by Franz Rosenthal. 2nd ed. 3 vols. Princeton, 1967.

Ibn Saʿd, Muḥammad. *Kitāb aṭ-ṭabaqāt al-kubrā*. Edited by Eduard Sachau. 9 vols. Leiden, 1905–28.

Ibn Sūda, ʿAbd as-Salām. *Dalīl muʾarrikh al-Maghrib al-aqṣā*. 2 vols. Casablanca, 1960–65.

Ibn Zaydān, ʿAbd ar-Raḥmān. *Itḥāf aʿlām an-nās bi-jamāl akhbār ḥāḍirat Miknās*. 5 vols. Rabat, 1347–52/1929–33.

———. *Al-ʿizz waṣ-ṣawla fī maʿālim nuẓum ad-dawla*. 2 vols. Rabat, 1929–33.

*al-Kardūdī, Abū al-ʿAbbās Aḥmad b. Muḥammad. *At-tuḥfa as-saniya lil-ḥaḍra al-ḥasaniya bil-mamlaka al-iṣbanyūliya.* Edited by ʿAbd al-Wahāb Bin Manṣūr. Rabat, 1963.

al-Kattānī, Muḥammad b. Jaʿfar. *Salwat al-anfās wa-muḥādathāt al-akyās bi-man uqbir min al-ʿulamāʾ waṣ-ṣulaḥāʾ.* 3 vols. Fes, 1316/1898.

al-Khaṭṭābī, Muḥammad al-ʿArabī. "Mushāhadāt diblūmāsī maghribī fī Fransā fī ʿahd al-Mawlay ʿAbd ar-Raḥmān b. Hishām." *Daʿwat al-ḥaqq* 263 (March 1987): 19–29; 264 (April–May 1987): 36–48.

al-Manūnī, Muḥammad. *Maẓāhir yaqẓat al-Maghrib al-ḥadīth*, part 1. Rabat, 1973; 2nd ed., 2 vols., Casablanca, 1985.

Masʿūdī (Maçoudi). *Les prairies d'or.* Translated by C. Barbier de Meynard and Pavet de Courteille. 3 vols. Paris, 1864.

Mehmed Efendi. *Le paradis des infidèles: Un ambassadeur ottoman en France sous la Régence.* Translated by Julien-Claude Galland. Edited by Gilles Veinstein. Paris, 1981.

*al-Miknāsī, Muḥammad b. ʿUthmān. *Al-iksīr fī fikāk al-asīr.* Edited by Muḥammad al-Fāsī. Rabat, 1965.

al-Murrākushī, al-ʿAbbās b. Ibrāhīm. *Al-iʿlām bi-man ḥalla Murrākush wa-Aghmāt min al-aʿlām.* Edited by ʿAbd al-Wahāb Bin Manṣūr. 10 vols. Rabat, 1974–83.

an-Nāṣirī, Aḥmad b. Khālid. "Chronique de la dynastie alaouite au Maroc." Translated by E. Fumey. *AM* 9 (1906): 1–399; 10 (1907): 1–424.

———. *Kitāb al-istiqṣā li-akhbār duwal al-Maghrib al-aqṣā.* 9 vols. Casablanca, 1956.

Muhammad al-Qadiri's 'Nashr al Mathani': The Chronicles. Edited and translated by Norman Cigar. London, 1981.

al-Qazwīnī, Zakariya b. Muḥammad b. Maḥmūd. *Āthār al-bilād wa-akhbār al-iʿbād.* Beirut, n.d.

*Sauvaire, Henri. *Voyage en Espagne d'un ambassadeur marocain, 1690–1691.* Paris, 1884.

aṭ-Ṭahṭāwī, Rifāʿa Rāfiʿ. "Kitāb takhlīṣ al-ibrīz fī talkhīṣ Bārīz." In *Al-aʿmāl al-kāmila li-Rifāʿa Rāfiʿ aṭ-Ṭahṭāwī.* Edited by Muḥammad ʿAmāra. Part 2: *As-siyāsa . . . wal-waṭaniya . . . wat-tarbiya.* Beirut, 1973.

———. *L'or de Paris: Relation de voyage, 1826–1831.* Edited and translated by Anouar Louca. Paris, 1988.

*at-Tamgrūtī (Tamgrouti), Abū al-Ḥasan ʿAlī. *En-nafkhat el-miskiya fi-s-sifarat et-tourkiya: Relation d'une ambassade marocaine en Turquie, 1589–1591.* Translated by Henry de Castries. Paris, 1929.

The Travels of Ibn Baṭṭūṭa. Edited by H. A. R. Gibb. 3 vols. The Hakluyt Society. Cambridge, 1958.

at-Tūnisī, Khayr ad-Dīn. *The Surest Path: The Political Treatise of a Nineteenth-century Muslim Statesman*. Translated and edited by Leon Carl Brown. Harvard Middle Eastern Monograph 16. Cambridge, Mass., 1967.

al-Wathā'iq: Majmūʿāt wathā'iqiya dawriya tuṣaddiruha mudīriya al-wathā'iq al-malakiya. Edited by ʿAbd al-Wahāb Bin Manṣūr. 7 vols. Rabat, 1976–89.

III. PUBLISHED SOURCES IN OTHER LANGUAGES

Abu-Lughod, Ibrahim. *The Arab Rediscovery of Europe: A Study in Cultural Encounters*. Princeton, 1963.

Aubin, Eugène (pseud. Léon Descos). *Morocco of To-day*. London, 1906.

Ayache, Germain. "L'apparition de l'imprimerie au Maroc." *Hespéris-Tamuda* 5 (1964): 143–61.

———. "Aspects de la crise financière au Maroc après l'expédition espagnole de 1860." In *Etudes d'histoire marocaine*, pp. 97–138. 2nd edition. Rabat, 1983.

Azan, Paul. *L'émir Abd el Kader (1808–1883)*. Paris, 1925.

Barthes, Roland. *Empire of Signs*. Translated by Richard Howard. New York, 1982.

Beeston, A. F. L., et al., eds. *Arabic Literature to the End of the Umayyad Period*. Cambridge, 1983.

Berque, Jacques. "L'emir Abdel Kader demande à Fes une consultation sur le jihad." In *Maghreb, Histoire et Sociétés*, pp. 65–81. Algiers, 1974.

Bookin-Weiner, J. "The 'Sallee Rovers': Morocco and Its Corsairs in the Seventeenth Century." In *The Middle East and North Africa: Essays in Honor of J. C. Hurewitz*, edited by Reeva S. Simon, pp. 307–31. New York, 1990.

Braudel, F., and E. Labrousse, eds. *Histoire économique et sociale de la France*. Vol. 3: *L'avènement de l'ère industrielle (1789–1880)*, part 1. Paris, 1976.

Brignon, J., et al. *Histoire du Maroc*. Paris, 1967.

Brooke, Sir Arthur de Capell. *Sketches in Spain and Morocco*. 2 vols. London, 1831.

Brooks, L. A. E. *A Memoir of Sir John Drummond Hay*. London, 1896.

Brown, Leon Carl. *The Tunisia of Ahmad Bey, 1837–1855*. Princeton, 1974.

Brunot, Louis. *La mer dans les traditions et les industries indigènes à Rabat et Salé*. Paris, 1921.

Brunot, Louis. *Textes arabes de Rabat.* 2 vols. Rabat, 1952.

Burnaby, S. B. *Elements of the Jewish and Muhammadan Calendars.* London, 1901.

Caillé, Jacques. "Ambassades et missions marocaines en France." *Hespéris-Tamuda* 1, 1 (1960): 39–83.

———. "Un ambassadeur marocain à Paris (1845–1846)." *Le monde français* 16, 49 (October 1949): 74–86.

———. *Charles Jagerschmidt: Chargé d'affaires de France au Maroc (1820–1894).* Paris, 1951.

———. "Un document marocain: L'ambassadeur el-Haj Abd el-Qader à la cour de Louis-Philippe." *Le magazine de l'Afrique du Nord* (January 1951): 20–21.

———. "La France et le Maroc en 1849." *Hespéris* 33 (1946): 123–55.

———. *Une mission de Léon Roches à Rabat en 1845.* Casablanca, 1947.

———. *La petite histoire du Maroc, 2e serie (1727–1850).* Rabat, 1952.

Chenier, Louis. *The Present State of the Empire of Morocco.* 2 vols. London, 1788.

Cigar, N. "Socio-economic Structures and the Development of an Urban Bourgeoisie in Pre-colonial Morocco." *Maghreb Review* 6, 3–4 (May–August 1981): 55–67.

Colin, G. S. "La noria marocaine et les machines hydrauliques dans le monde arabe." *Hespéris* 14, 1 (1932): 22–49.

Collins, Irene. *The Government and the Newspaper Press in France, 1814–1881.* London, 1959.

de Cossé-Brissac, Philippe. *Les rapports de la France et du Maroc pendant la conquête de l'Algérie (1830–1847).* Paris, 1931.

Dakhlia, Jocelyne. "Dans la mouvance du Prince: La symbolique du pouvoir itinérant au Maghreb." *Annales: Économies, Sociétés, Civilisations* 43, 3 (May–June 1988): 735–60.

Davidson, John. *Notes Taken during Travels in Africa.* London, 1839.

Dehérain, Henri. *Orientalistes et antiquaires: Silvestre de Sacy, ses contemporains et ses disciples.* Paris, 1938.

Deverdun, Gaston. *Marrakech: Des origines à 1912.* 2 vols. Rabat, 1959–66.

Dunn, Ross E. *The Adventures of Ibn Battuta: A Muslim Traveler of the 14th Century.* Berkeley and Los Angeles, 1989.

Durrieu, Xavier. "Le Maroc en 1844: La situation, les moeurs, les ressources de l'empire." *Revue des deux mondes* 8 (1844): 5–63.

———. *The Present State of Morocco: A Chapter of Mussulman Civilisation.* London, 1854.

Eickelman, Dale F. "The Art of Memory: Islamic Education and Its Social

Reproduction." *Comparative Studies in Society and History* 20, 4 (1978): 485–516.

Eickelman, Dale F., and James Piscatori, eds. *Muslim Travellers: Pilgrimage, Migration, and the Religious Imagination*. Berkeley and Los Angeles, 1990.

El-Mansour, Mohamed. "Moroccan Perceptions of European Civilisation in the Nineteenth Century." In *Morocco and Europe*, edited by George Joffé, pp. 37–45. Center of Near and Middle Eastern Studies, School of Oriental and African Studies, University of London, Occasional Paper 7. London, 1989.

Emerit, Marcel. *L'Algérie à l'époque d'Abdel Kader*. Paris, 1951.

———. "Le conflit franco-marocain de 1844 d'après les notes de Warnier." *Revue africaine* 94, 424–25 (1950): 399–425.

———. "La légende de Léon Roches." *Revue africaine* 91, 410–11 (1947): 81–105.

Flournoy, F. R. *British Policy toward Morocco in the Age of Palmerston*. Baltimore, 1935.

Fussell, Paul. *Abroad: British Literary Traveling between the Wars*. New York, 1980.

Gallissot, René. "La guerre d'Abd el Kader ou la ruine de la nationalité algérienne (1839–1847)." *Hespéris-Tamuda* 5 (1964): 119–41.

Gibb, H. A. R. "An Interpretation of Islamic History." In *Studies on the Civilization of Islam*, edited by Stanford J. Shaw and William R. Polk, pp. 3–33. Boston, 1962.

Gilsenan, Michael. *Recognizing Islam: Religion and Society in the Modern Arab World*. New York, 1982.

Glick, Thomas F. *Islamic and Christian Spain in the Early Middle Ages: Comparative Perspectives on Social and Cultural Formations*. Princeton, 1979.

Goitein, S. D. *A Mediterranean Society*. 5 vols. Berkeley and Los Angeles, 1967–88.

Graburn, Nelson H. H. "Tourism: The Sacred Journey." In *Hosts and Guests: The Anthropology of Tourism*, edited by Valene Smith, pp. 21–36. 2nd edition. Philadelphia, 1989.

Grandchamp, P., and Béchir Mokaddem. "Une mission tunisienne à Paris (février–mai 1853)." *Revue africaine* 90, 406–9 (1946): 58–98.

Guizot, F. P. G. *France under Louis-Philippe (1841–1847)*. London, 1865.

———. *Mémoires pour servir à l'histoire de mon temps*. 8 vols. Paris, 1858–67.

Hadj-Sadok, Mahammed. "Le genre 'Rihla.' " *Bulletin des études arabes* 8, 40 (1948): 195–206.

Hay, J. H. D. *Journal of an Expedition to the Court of Marocco in the Year 1846*. Cambridge, 1848.

Hay, J. H. D. *Western Barbary: Its Wild Tribes and Savàge Animals*. London, 1861.

Heyworth-Dunne, J. "Rifā'ah Badawī Rāfi' aṭ-Ṭahṭāwī: The Egyptian Revivalist." *Bulletin of the School of Oriental and African Studies* 9 (1937–39): 961–67; 10 (1940–42): 399–415.

Hitti, Philip. *The History of the Arabs*. New York, 1967.

Hourani, Albert. *Arabic Thought in the Liberal Age, 1798–1939*. London, 1967.

Howard, Donald R. *Writers and Pilgrims: Medieval Pilgrimage Narratives and Their Posterity*. Berkeley, 1980.

Jackson, James Grey. *An Account of the Empire of Marocco and the District of Suse*. Philadelphia, 1810.

Johnson, Douglas. *Guizot: Aspects of French History, 1787–1874*. London, 1963.

Joly, A. "Un calendrier agricole marocain." *Archives marocaines* 3 (1905): 301–19.

———. "Tétouan." Part 2, "Historique." *Archives marocaines* 5 (1905): 161–264, 311–430.

Julien, C.-A. *Histoire de l'Algérie contemporaine*. Paris, 1964.

———. *History of North Africa: Tunisia, Algeria, Morocco*. Translated by John Petrie. Edited by C. C. Stewart. London, 1970.

Lahbabi, Mohamed. *Le gouvernement marocain à l'aube du XXe siècle*. Rabat, 1958.

Lakhdar, Mohammed. *La vie littéraire au Maroc sous la dynastie 'Alawide (1075–1311 = 1664–1894)*. Rabat, 1971.

de La Martinière, H. M. P., and N. Lacroix. *Documents pour servir à l'étude du nord-ouest africain*. 4 vols. Algiers, 1894–97.

Laroui, Abdallah. *L'histoire du Maghreb: Un essai de synthèse*. Paris, 1970. English edition: *History of the Maghrib: An Interpretive Essay*. Translated by Ralph Mannheim. Princeton, 1977.

———. *Les origines sociales et culturelles du nationalisme marocain (1830–1912)*. Paris, 1977.

Latham, J. D. "The Reconstruction and Expansion of Tetuan: The Period of Andalusian Immigration." In *Arabic and Islamic Studies in Honor of Hamilton A. R. Gibb*, edited by George Makdisi, pp. 387–408. Leiden, 1965.

———. "Towns and Cities of Barbary: The Andalusian Influence." *Islamic Quarterly* 16 (1972): 189–204.

Lavedan, P. *Histoire de Paris*. "Que sais-je?" no. 34. Paris, 1960.

Le Tourneau, Roger. *Fès avant le Protectorat*. Casablanca, 1949.

———. *La vie quotidienne à Fès en 1900*. Paris, 1965.

Lévi-Provençal, E. *Les historiens des Chorfa*. Paris, 1922.

Lévi-Strauss, Claude. *Tristes Tropiques*. Translated by J. Russell. New York, 1970.

Lewis, Bernard. *The Muslim Discovery of Europe*. New York, 1982.

Louca, Anouar. *Voyageurs et écrivains égyptiens en France au XIXe siècle*. Paris, 1970.

Marçais, William. *Textes arabes de Tanger*. Paris, 1911.

Mekouar, Hassan. *Washington Irving and the Arabesque Tradition*. Ph.D. dissertation. Brown University, 1977.

Ménétra, Jacques-Louis. *Journal of My Life*. Translated by Arthur Goldhammer. Edited by Daniel Roche. New York, 1986.

Michaux-Bellaire, E. "Au palais du Sultan marocain." *Revue du monde musulman* 5 (1908): 647–62.

———. "Le droit de propriété au Maroc." *Revue du monde musulman* 7 (1909): 365–78.

———. "El-Qçar Eç-Çeghir." *Revue du monde musulman* 16 (1911): 329–76.

———. "L'impôt de la naïba et la loi musulmane au Maroc." *Revue du monde musulman* 11 (1910): 396–404.

———. "Les impôts marocains." *Archives marocaines* 1 (1904): 56–96.

———. "L'organisation des finances au Maroc." *Archives marocaines* 11 (1907): 171–251.

———. "Un rouage du gouvernement marocain: La beniqat ech chikaïat de Moulay Abd el Hafid." *Revue du monde musulman* 5 (1908): 242–74.

Miège, J.-L. *Le Maroc et l'Europe (1830–1894)*. 4 vols. Rabat, 1989.

Miller, Michael B. *The Bon Marche: Bourgeois Culture and the Department Store, 1869–1920*. Princeton, 1981.

Miquel, André. "L'Europe occidentale dans la relation arabe d'Ibrāhīm b. Ya'qūb (Xe s.)." *Annales: Économies, Sociétés, Civilisations* 21, 5 (September–October 1966): 1048–64.

———. *La géographie humaine du monde musulman jusqu'au milieu du 11e siècle*. 4 vols. Paris, 1967–88.

Mitchell, Timothy. *Colonizing Egypt*. Cambridge, 1988.

Naff, Thomas, and Roger Owen, eds. *Studies in Eighteenth Century Islamic History*. Carbondale, 1977.

Park, Thomas. "Inflation and Economic Policy in 19th Century Morocco: The Compromise Solution." *Maghreb Review* 10, 2–3 (1985): 51–56.

Pellat, Charles. "La France dans la géographie d'al-Idrīsī." *Studi maghrebini* 10 (1978): 33–72.

Penz, Charles. *Les émerveillements parisiens d'un ambassadeur de Moulay Ismail, janvier–février 1682*. Casablanca, 1949.

Pérès, Henri. *L'Espagne vue par les voyageurs musulmans de 1610 à 1930.* Paris, 1937.

Peyssonnel, Jean André. *Voyage dans les régences de Tunis et d'Alger.* Edited by Lucette Valensi. Paris, 1987.

Pinkney, David. *Decisive Years in France, 1840–47.* Princeton, 1986.

Rackow, Ernst. *Beiträge zur Kenntnis der materiellen Kultur Nordwest-Marokkos: Wohnraum, Hausrat, Kostüm.* Wiesbaden, 1958.

Renaud, H. P. J. "L'enseignement des sciences exactes et l'édition d'ouvrages scientifiques au Maroc avant l'occupation européenne." *Hespéris* 14, 1 (1932): 78–89.

———. "Un essai de classification botanique dans l'oeuvre d'un médecin marocain du XVIe siècle." *Mémorial Henri Basset: Nouvelles études nord-africaines et orientales* (2 vols.), 2:197–206. Paris, 1928.

Rey, A. "Le Maroc et la question d'Alger." *Revue des deux mondes* 24 (1840): 617–62.

Roches, Léon. *Trente-deux ans à travers l'Islam.* 2 vols. Paris, 1884–87.

Rosenthal, E. I. J. *Political Thought in Medieval Islam.* Cambridge, 1968.

Rosenthal, Franz. *The Technique and Approach of Muslim Scholarship. Analecta Orientalia* 24. Rome, 1947.

Rouard de Card, E. *Les traités entre la France et le Maroc.* Paris, 1898.

Said, Edward. *Orientalism.* New York, 1979.

Schivelbusch, Wolfgang. *The Railway Journey: The Industrialization of Time and Space in the 19th Century.* Berkeley, 1986.

Schroeter, Daniel. *Merchants of Essaouira: Urban Society and Imperialism in Southwestern Morocco, 1844–1886.* Cambridge, 1988.

Scott, Col. *A Journal of a Residence in the Esmailla of Abd-el-Kader and of Travels in Morocco and Algiers.* London, 1842.

Sternberger, Dolf. *Panorama of the Nineteenth Century.* Translated by Joachim Neugroschel. New York, 1977.

Turner, Victor, and Edith Turner. *Image and Pilgrimage in Christian Culture: Anthropological Perspectives.* New York, 1978.

Valensi, Lucette. *Le Maghreb avant la prise d'Alger (1790–1830).* Paris, 1969.

Warnier, A.-H. *Campagne du Maroc, 1844.* Paris, 1899.

IV. REFERENCE WORKS

Bosworth, C. E. *The Islamic Dynasties.* Edinburgh, 1967.

Brockelmann, Carl. *Geschichte der arabischen Litteratur* (GAL). 2 vols. Leiden, 1943–49. *Supplementbände* (S). 3 vols. Leiden, 1937–42.

Dictionnaire d'histoire de France Perrin. Paris, 1981.

Dozy, R. P. A. *Dictionnaire détaillé des noms des vêtements chez les Arabes.* Beirut, n.d. (reprint of Amsterdam, 1845).

———. *Supplément aux dictionnaires arabes.* 3rd ed. 2 vols. Paris, 1967.

Encyclopaedia Britannica. 1911 ed., 1990 ed.

The Encyclopaedia of Islam. New edition, 1960–.

Fahāris al-khizāna al-malakiya (Rabat, 1980–). Vol. 1, *Fihris qism at-tārīkh wa-kutub ar-riḥlāt,* edited by Muḥammad ʿAbd Allāh ʿInān. Rabat, 1980.

Flügel, G. *Concordantiae Corani Arabicae.* Leipzig, 1842.

Gibb, H. A. R., and J. H. Kramers. *Shorter Encyclopaedia of Islam* (SEI). Leiden, 1961.

La grande encyclopédie Larousse. 1882 ed., 1971–76 ed.

Harrell, Richard, et al. *A Dictionary of Moroccan Arabic: Arabic-English.* Institute of Languages and Linguistics, The Richard Slade Harrell Series, no. 9. Washington, D.C., 1966.

Lane, Edward W. *Arabic-English Lexicon.* 1st ed. 8 vols. London, 1863.

al-Manūnī, Muḥammad. *Al-maṣādir al-ʿarabiya li-tārīkh al-Maghrib.* Publications of the Faculty of Letters and Human Sciences, Rabat. Part 1. Casablanca, 1983; Part 2. Mohamedia, 1989.

Mayr, J., and B. Spuler. *Wüstenfeld-Mahler'sche Vergleichungs-Tabellen.* Wiesbaden, 1961.

National Geographic Atlas of the World. 1981 edition.

Playfair, R. L., and Robert Brown. *A Bibliography of Morocco, from the Earliest Times to the End of 1891.* Royal Geographical Society, Supplementary Papers, Vol. 3, Part 3. London, 1893.

Wehr, Hans. *A Dictionary of Modern Written Arabic.* Edited by J. Milton Cowan. Ithaca, 1961.

INDEX OF NAMES AND SUBJECTS

INDEX OF ARABIC TERMS